News Media Translation

As digital convergence marks the transition from print to screen culture, translation plays an increasingly important role in the production and dissemination of the news. The translation of information in the news media is a pervasive set of practices that affects the daily consumption of the news and a topic of relevance to scholars in several areas of the humanities and the social sciences. This book provides a wide-ranging and accessible introduction to research in news media translation practices, products, and processes, illustrating and discussing historical, theoretical, and descriptive perspectives. Inter- and multidisciplinary research spans fields such as translation studies, linguistics, journalism, and media studies and includes approaches from critical discourse analysis and narrative theory to systemic functional linguistics and corpus linguistics. The book also offers firsthand analyses of news texts in English and Italian, approaching news translation from an ethnomethodological perspective.

FEDERICO ZANETTIN is Associate Professor of English Language and Translation at University of Perugia. His research interests include corpus-based translation studies, and the study of the translation of graphic narratives. He has published extensively in peer-reviewed journals, is the author of *Translation-Driven Corpora* (2012) and the editor of *Comics in Translation* (2008).

News Media Translation

Federico Zanettin

University of Perugia

CAMBRIDGE
UNIVERSITY PRESS

CAMBRIDGE
UNIVERSITY PRESS

University Printing House, Cambridge CB2 8BS, United Kingdom

One Liberty Plaza, 20th Floor, New York, NY 10006, USA

477 Williamstown Road, Port Melbourne, VIC 3207, Australia

314–321, 3rd Floor, Plot 3, Splendor Forum, Jasola District Centre, New Delhi – 110025, India

103 Penang Road, #05–06/07, Visioncrest Commercial, Singapore 238467

Cambridge University Press is part of the University of Cambridge.

It furthers the University's mission by disseminating knowledge in the pursuit of education, learning, and research at the highest international levels of excellence.

www.cambridge.org
Information on this title: www.cambridge.org/9781108470704
DOI: 10.1017/9781108568364

First published 2021

A catalogue record for this publication is available from the British Library.

Library of Congress Cataloging-in-Publication Data
Names: Zanettin, Federico, author.
Title: News media translation / Federico Zanettin.
Description: Cambridge ; New York : Cambridge University Press, 2021. | Includes bibliographical references and index.
Identifiers: LCCN 2021019849 (print) | LCCN 2021019850 (ebook) | ISBN 9781108470704 (hardback) | ISBN 9781108456401 (paperback) | ISBN 9781108568364 (epub)
Subjects: LCSH: Journalism—Translating. | Journalism—Translating—Case studies. | Translating and interpreting. | Mass media and language. | BISAC: LANGUAGE ARTS & DISCIPLINES / Linguistics / General
Classification: LCC PN4784.T72 Z35 2021 (print) | LCC PN4784.T72 (ebook) | DDC 418/.0307—dc23
LC record available at https://lccn.loc.gov/2021019849
LC ebook record available at https://lccn.loc.gov/2021019850

ISBN 978-1-108-47070-4 Hardback
ISBN 978-1-108-45640-1 Paperback

Contents

Figures and Table

Figures

Table

Acknowledgments

I would like to thank Enrico Caniglia, Patrick Leech, Chris Rundle, and Dominic Stewart who, at various stages, read parts or all of the manuscript and who provided valuable feedback. I also wish to thank Marco Ficarra for drawing the cover image.

Introduction

The book aims to offer an accessible introduction to news media translation as an important area of translation studies, a relatively new discipline that has witnessed an exponential growth since it first became established some fifty years ago. While initial research dedicated to translation was produced by scholars from the fields of linguistics and literary studies, as translation studies began to emerge as a discipline in its own right, it was also influenced by ideas and conceptualizations from other disciplinary areas. The scope of translation studies has increasingly widened to include not only all types of written texts but also audiovisual and multimedia products, as well as all types of interpreted communication.

Translation in the news media was included in the remit of translation research only around the beginning of the twenty-first century, and it was even later that scholars in communication and journalism studies started to pay attention to the pervading relevance of translation practices in the field. News media translation went mostly unnoticed, not least because it obeys norms and configures practices that are different from those traditionally associated with translation, where there is – by and large – the expectation of a linear correspondence between a source and a target text. The concept of "translation proper" held by the lay population and sometimes even unquestioningly adopted by scholars is challenged by news media translation – whose practices and products have often been conceptualized as something different from "translation" and that have, in fact, sometimes been referred to with different terms. Conversely, translation activities have been largely overlooked by news producers and have remained invisible to readers of newspapers, who are mostly unaware of what goes on during the news translation process.

This volume focuses on news media translation as a range of practices that play a central role in the way news is produced and disseminated in the current technological context. News media translation is an area that overlaps with news or journalistic translation, but it also intersects other areas – such as audiovisual translation (AVT) and research on translation and politics, conflict, and war. It addresses not only professional journalistic practices by news workers and media institutions and conglomerates, but also translation by other communities of practice such as interest groups and active citizens, in the context of digital media convergence. It includes news produced in the current information economy by actors such as bloggers, activists, lobbies, and so on. It is related to public discourse in politics and in social life; that is, it concerns the role of translation and interpreting in both "hard news" and "soft news."

While the volume takes stock of current literature concerning the study of news translation, it also contains original research. In the last part of the book, I offer examples of research in news media translation based on the ethnomethodological approach. After an introduction to ethnomethodology and two of its main research strands, conversation analysis (CA) and membership categorization analysis (MCA), I carry out a close examination of some translated news texts, looking at how they represent descriptions of reality that are different from those of the source texts in another language. In particular, I apply membership categorization analysis to the analysis of newspaper texts in English and Italian. I also show how the use of corpus linguistics tools and resources can be brought to bear on the analysis of translated news texts.

The translation of information in the media is "arguably one of the most consequential forms of translation in our time" (Bielsa 2020, p. 366). It is through newspapers, TV news shows, websites, and social media that we get to know what happens in the world, and this knowledge is intrinsically tied to translation activities, practices, and processes. It is to a large extent through translation that we learn about people and events in distant locations, and any attempt to understand how foreign news is produced and received must take into account the extent to which interlingual translation is constitutive of it. However, translation also informs the production of local information in our increasingly multilingual and multicultural virtual and physical shared space. As digital communication has multiplied the occasions for translation in the news media, the study of how translation affects the way information is produced, disseminated, and interpreted has become of primary importance not only for academic research but also for practitioners, whether they be professional journalists or active citizens reading and producing the news in translation.

The book is organized into four chapters. Chapter 1 provides a discussion of some of the historical and social contexts in which metaphorical conceptualizations and terminology related to translation have evolved. As an introduction to the different meanings and practices associated with the concept of (and the words for) translation, I consider "translation" practices before the term *traducere* and its Latinate cognates (including "translation") came into use in Europe, as compared to the modern concept of translation that became current as its practices became associated with the technology of the printing press and, more specifically, with the printed book. The technology of print was key to the standardization of vernaculars, which were shaped by translation and which provided the foundations for the establishment of national languages. These, in turn, provided the ground for national identities, while the prototypical concept of translation was defined by the translation of those texts that were fundamental for the establishment of national identities – that is, religious and literary texts.

In order to illustrate the evolving conceptualizations of the discipline and of the object of study, I then consider the conventional definition of translation currently codified in dictionaries and engage in a discussion of the so-called turns of translation studies. I discuss the concept of "translation proper," as used with reference to interlingual translation, and then look at how, since the early 1990s, the cultural dimension of translation has increasingly grown in importance as the discipline has been enriched by new areas of interest and methodological approaches. The concept of translation has broadened to refer primarily to the translation of cultures, and it has also been suggested that the humanities are in the midst of a translational turn, as languages and other features of cultural identity are negotiated through translation. While the modern meaning of translation is based on the premise of equal and homogeneous national languages and cultures, the study of translation practices and flows has shown that translation is rather a locus of power differential, taking place between one more and one less prestigious variety of human language. In the contemporary communication environment, English, which is for the most part the product of speakers who do not identify with an "English" national culture, has replaced Latin in the role of lingua franca and is the main language of translation – i.e., the main language into and out of which translation is carried out.

Translation practices are shaped by the material culture in which they take place, and in the last part of the chapter, I consider how the "medial turn" of translation has been facilitated by digital information technologies. The current context of globalization marks the transition between print culture and screen culture, a multimedia environment modeled by convergence technologies. The changed social and technological environment has led to a redefinition of translation practices as the meaning of translation "proper" is expanded to include senses that were previously seen only as metaphorical. At the same time, competing terms have surfaced to dispute the ground of the conventional conceptualization of translation. Thus, the terminology of localization, originally used to refer to the "translation" of software products, has been used to refer to translation practices and products in areas such as AVT and news translation.

The central chapters sketch the landscape of the research area of news media translation and provide an overview of this burgeoning field. Chapter 2 is divided into three parts. The first part provides an historical account of news translation since the first newsletters were printed in the Low Countries at the beginning of the seventeenth century, and which exclusively contained translated text. In the nineteenth century, the practices and the overall production context of news translation were shaped by developments in communication and travel technology and by the rise of global news agencies, while first French and then English acquired a prominent role as lingua franca. The twentieth century saw a shift to screen culture and mass media, and by the twenty-first century, the digital revolution had altered communication practices and processes in the news media, including translation.

The second part discusses the role of translation during the news production process. Translation may occur at any point between news gathering and news dissemination, from the moment a correspondent reads a text in a foreign language or has a fixer interpret the statement of a witness to the moment a report is published in the news media. News is produced not only by global news agencies or local media organizations but also by professional and nonprofessional interest groups and citizens, and it is spread through multimedia channels and social networks. In this section, I consider the role of English as a global lingua franca and, in particular, the way translated news affects issues of politics, conflict, and power. The production of translated news, which is inextricably linked to digital technologies and the new(s) media, is discussed with particular reference to translation from and into Spanish and Chinese. News translation is seen as taking place in the technological scenario of media convergence, where the cooperation or synergy between different media makes it possible for information to be translated and disseminated through and by a variety of agents and media sources.

The third part examines some key issues and concepts in news media translation. It offers a discussion of the concept of text (in)stability, showing how in the case of interlingual news translation – like in intralingual news translation – the presence of a specific, single source text cannot be assumed as the norm. Translation is often an invisible process that is taken for granted in news production and consumption. Both readers and news professionals tend to think of translation in terms of a transparent and straightforward operation, while news organizations in different political and social contexts all present translation as "faithful." Research in news translation has, however, shown that considerable transformations take place at a textual level, and several terms have been used to refer to translation practices in the news media – including domestication, transediting, gatekeeping, and localization. These concepts, which inform and are often proposed as superordinate or synonymous concepts with news translation, are illustrated and discussed.

The rest of the book discusses various approaches that can be brought to bear on the analysis of translated news. Chapter 3 provides a general overview of current research in news media translation, distinguishing between three main research perspectives in the study of news media translation, namely process-, product-, and culture-oriented research. Process-oriented research looks at work and organizational routines, guidelines, and procedures that govern the production of foreign news in news organizations. Studies have been carried out in a variety of contexts, from large private and state -owned translation agencies (including global news agencies such as Reuters and AFP and the Chinese Reference News) to local, national newspapers. *Process-oriented research* is usually carried out using an ethnographic approach to the collection of the data, as well as tools and methods from cognitive process research. Data collection methods include interviews and observation, as well as think-aloud protocols and eye tracking.

The linguistic dimension is paramount in research on news media translation, and *product-oriented research* looks at the results of translation processes, in the form of translated news texts, sometimes comparing translations and source texts. The main approach used for the analysis of translated news is critical discourse analysis (CDA), in the attempt to connect linguistic analysis with social theories. Textual and linguistic analyses carried out within the framework of CDA typically rely on the analytical model of systemic functional linguistics (SFL). Several studies also draw on narrative theory and framing theory, sometimes used in combination with and sometimes as an alternative framework to CDA, and the concepts of selective appropriation, recontextualization, and reframing are often invoked to explain the types of textual transformations that news undergoes in translation. Corpus linguistics tools and methods are also used in the analysis of collections of news texts, sometimes in conjunction with SFL. *Culture-oriented research* looks at the production of foreign news as a translation phenomenon and focuses on the role of translators and interpreters in shaping perceptions and interpretations of cultural and social identities. This includes research carried out from the perspective of imagology, which studies the representation of nations and nationalities by in- and out-groups with the aim of describing national prejudices and stereotypes.

The second part of this chapter contains a literature overview, grouping studies according to the language investigated in combination with English (or, less often, with another language) that adopt one of, or a combination of, the models and methodological approaches previously introduced. The studies reviewed focus primarily on translation between English and Spanish, Italian, Arabic, Russian, Chinese, and Korean, although studies involving Greek, Farsi, Ukrainian, Hungarian, German, and French are also reviewed. Overall, this chapter shows the range of approaches being used to study the complex phenomenon of news media translation.

Finally, Chapter 4 illustrates an approach to the analysis of news media translation based on ethnomethodology, a sociological approach that allows for the meticulous analysis of text in order to find how meanings are reflexively and indexically constituted through social interaction. First, I offer an introduction to the main concepts and analytical tools developed within the ethnomethodological research tradition and discuss the similarities and differences of this approach to the study of social life with other approaches used in news translation research – namely CDA, narrative theory, and symbolic interactionism. I then look in more detail at two research strands that seem to be relevant for news media translation research – i.e., conversation analysis (CA) and membership categorization analysis (MCA), both developed following the lead of Harvey Sacks in the 1960s. First, I provide a summary introduction to the methodological tenets of CA, which allow a detailed analysis of verbal interaction. Then I discuss some examples of the application of CA to research in dialogue interpreting, including dialogue interpreting for the news media, showing how research has emphasized the active role of interpreters as participants in the interaction. The examples discussed refer, in particular, to the role of the simultaneous interpreters during political talk shows, which are characterized by a systematic confrontational attitude by participants. It is shown that even while the setup of simultaneous interpreting seems geared to minimize the presence and role of interpreters, the latter may play a decisive role in furthering or restraining a participant's discursive strategy and thus in the outcome of a debate.

While CA has had a considerable impact in the area of dialogue interpreting, MCA has not yet been used extensively in translation studies. After a summary introduction to the main conceptual tools of MCA as elaborated by Sacks and later research, I provide an overview of studies that have applied these tools to the analysis of the news media, and to newspaper headlines and articles more in particular. Such studies have shown how fine-grained textual analysis can uncover the methods that are used to refer to people and describe their activities and the implications that are conventionally attached to how categorization is accomplished

The application of MCA to research in news media translation is illustrated through two case studies. The first study examines an English article published in *The Observer* and its Italian translation published in the weekly *Internazionale*. The analysis focuses on the respective headlines and blurbs, showing that the way they categorize people and describe what they do orients their respective readers to divergent interpretations of the story. The patterns of omission found in the translated story seem to confirm the interpretation toward which the Italian headline seems to lead the reader.

While the first case study deals with the translation of a feature story, the second is about the translation of international political news. This case study considers a corpus of news articles related to the "same" news event, an "incident" taking place at the border between Israel and the Gaza Strip in the

Occupied Palestinian Territories. More in particular, I focus on two pairs of articles published on two consecutive days in *The Guardian* and *La Repubblica*, one of the latter being a translation of one of the former. An analysis of the categorization procedures carried out in the texts reveals not only that the "incident" can be reported as being part of different narratives (Israeli politics or Palestinian occupation) but also that a video of the incident can be described as supporting both of these narratives. The analysis is supplemented with the use of corpus data. I argue that corpus linguistics tools and resources can offer a methodology for investigating common sense categorizations of people and activities, offering a backdrop of shared knowledge to the analysis of the categorization devices employed by newspaper translators and writers.

The survey and analysis presented emerge primarily from concerns within translation studies but necessarily affect other areas of research across the humanities and the social sciences – including media, communication, and globalization studies – and should be of interest to scholars who recognize the importance of considering questions of language and translation/interpreting in the news media but may not be familiar with the methods for studying those questions that have been developed in the field of translation studies. The case studies presented may also offer a contribution to research in ethnomethodology and hopefully stimulate further research in news media translation from this perspective.

1 Putting News Media Translation into Perspective

1.1 Introduction

This book is based on the premise that the term translation does not refer to a stable concept but, rather, to one which is undergoing a shift of meaning that allows for the inclusion of something called news media translation into the scope of translation research. In order to understand how the term translation is used in this book in relation to news media but also more in general as a practice and as an object of study, this chapter illustrates how the meanings of translation, as well as the practices associated with it, have changed through time and space.

I first provide an overview of the metaphorical conceptualizations and terms used to refer to "translation" in various languages and look at how the current meanings of translation in Europe are ascribed to past practices that, while considerably different, are assimilated to present ones. I consider how the shift in the terminology for "translation," which was accomplished after the invention of movable print in Europe, happened in parallel with the emergence of European vernacular languages. Translation practices have contributed extensively to the shaping of national languages, and the standard concept of translation has been framed by conceptions of national identity that obscure power differentials by presuming equality between languages. This idea of translation is now being scrutinized and problematized by non-Eurocentric perspectives in a globalized context.

I then offer a brief overview of theoretical thinking on translation since the 1950s, starting with Roman Jakobson's (1959) definition of "translation proper," which forms the basis of the received meaning of the word. I discuss the rise and developments of the new disciplinary field through the lens of so-called turns of translation studies, which respond to developments in its contemporary intellectual environment. While the study of translation underwent a "cultural turn" in the 1980s, the study of culture is now experiencing a "translational turn," as the humanities and the social sciences are increasingly using translation as an analytical notion rather than merely a metaphor that designates shifting disciplinary boundaries and cultural identities. The concept of translation proper has been expanding beyond that of translation between national languages to that of translation between cultural signs, while the notion of natural languages and national identities is being reexamined in light of globalization phenomena.

In the last section, I consider how the current revolution in information technology marks a shift in translation practices and conceptualizations that may be seen as paralleling the one brought about by the print revolution, as the term translation itself is undergoing a redefinition. Translation studies research is increasingly concerned with nonliterary or nonreligious texts in which the digital format has realized the convergence of visual and aural information.

Research in news media translation will be summarized in Chapters 2 and 3. Beforehand, however, it seems important to discuss the term translation itself and look at the meaning and concepts behind this word, as well as at theoretical discussions and approaches to translation in the field of translation studies.

1.2 Geography and History of Translation

The word translation has been used to refer to a variety of products and processes, practices and activities. Translation scholars insist that translation is an open concept and that its meaning is subject to change depending on cultural, historical, and geographical variation. According to Gideon Toury, for instance, a translation can be anything that is "regarded as such within the target culture, on no matter what grounds" (Toury 2012, p. 35), while in the words of Michael Cronin "[t]ranslation is a scalar concept which covers a wide variety of practices" (Cronin 2013, p. 129). The "etymologies, cognates, image-schemas or metaphoric meanings, lexical fields" (Tymoczko 2007, p. 68) of the words that are used around the world to conceptualize translation are highly diverse, as are the specific practices to which these words refer. In India, for instance, common words for "translation" are *rupantar* and *anuvad*, both deriving from Sanskrit, the first meaning "change in form" and the second meaning "speaking after, following." In Arabic, the word *tarjama* relates to the meanings "biography" and "definition." In Japan, the term *honyaku* is represented using the characters for *hon* – "turn, turn over, flutter" – and *yaku*, meaning "substitute word." In China, the term *fanyi* is composed by the characters for *fan*, "turning [a leaf of a book], somersault, flip," and *yi*, "interpretation" and "exchange," and is related to the images of embroidery and trade. In Nigeria, the Igbo word *tapia* has the overall sense of "deconstruct it and tell it (in a different form)" (Tymoczko 2007, p. 72). In some South Asian languages, the words for translation – for instance, the Tagalog *pagsalin* and the Malay *tersalin* – are associated with giving birth and pouring a fluid substance into a new container that will give it a new shape, and one of the most widespread metaphors of translation in history is, in fact, that of translation as a container, into which ideas can be put and transported. However, the concepts these words refer to do not translate flawlessly into each other; they refer to a range of sometimes very distinct practices. For instance, while readers of Modern English require some form of intralingual translation in order to understand texts written in Old and Middle English, in a nonalphabetic language like Chinese, where there is no necessary link between visual signs and phonetic realization, synchronic and diachronic differences are obscured, and the need for written translation between geographical and historical varieties is circumvented (Chesterman 2006; Tymoczko 2007, pp. 68–77).

1.2.1 Metaphors of Translation

The words that convey the concept of translation in different languages contribute to an understanding of its meaning in terms of the etymological and metaphorical meaning of the term used, as "the root metaphor which one uses to think about translation can influence how translation is viewed in terms of process, status of the translator, and status of the translation" (St. André 2010). Furthermore, not only is the word translation in itself a metaphor for semantic sameness, but descriptions and explanations of translation are often made using metaphorical language, both in general language and in academic literature. For example, the metaphor of translation as a portrait was widely used in seventeenth-century France, where the metaphor of the *belle infidèle*[1] also originated. More recently, the metaphor theorized by Brazilian translation scholars of translation as an act of cannibalistic devouring points to a rethinking of the relationship between colonized and colonizers (Bassnett 1998, p. 129).

Drawing on Wittengstein, Tymoczko (2007, pp. 83–90) argues that translation, as an international, universal notion is a cluster concept, membership to which is not determined by theoretical criteria but by cultural practice, based on empirical description and observation of features. Thus, members of the cluster concept "translation" are related by "family resemblance" and are recognized a posteriori and not on the basis of predetermined descriptions. The characterization as a cluster concept implies no hierarchical arrangement of features and thus avoids ethnocentrism. However, in different historical and social contexts, some features are perceived as more central than others, and while "translation" remains a fuzzy concept, dominant conceptualizations

[1] This metaphor was first used by Gille Ménage to describe (literary) translations and publicized by Mounin in 1955 (quoted in Mouning 1955, p. 6). It should be noted, however, that very literal, formally faithful translations, and not only for sacred texts, were also carried out and theorized at the time.

become prototypical and may be proposed as points of reference (Halverson 1999a). "Western" conceptualizations of translation and translation theory, as expressed in European languages and most specifically in English, currently enjoy a more central, prototypical position.

In most European languages, translation is conceptualized as transfer, a metaphor that derives from the Latinate origin of most words for it. The Latin word family *traducere*, *traductio*, *traductor*, from *trans* and *ducere*, "to lead" or "to bring", won acceptance over competing terms such as *transferre* and *interpretari* and became the basis for all its corresponding terms in Romance languages. In Spanish, for instance, the terms *traductor* and *traducción* prevailed over *translador* and *trasladation* (Pym 2000). While the *Oxford English Dictionary* also includes the words *traduce* (first attested in 1535), *traduction* (1533), and *traduci* ("translated," 1534),[2] the etymology of the current English words "translation" (first attested in 1340) and "translate" (1300), which eventually emerged as standard terms, can be traced to the alternative Latin root *translatio*, from *trans*, "across," and *latus*, the past participle of *ferre*, "to carry, bear, bring," resulting in the meaning of translate as "bear across" or "bring over." Likewise, some Slavic languages derive from a Latin word, while other European languages have calqued their words from Latin using similar roots, such as the German *Übersetzen*, "to put across," and the Russian *perevesti* (перевести) "to lead across."

It would be tempting to argue, with Bellos (2011), that all Western translation theory would have been different had a different metaphor of translation prevailed in European languages – e.g., the metaphor of embroidery rather than that of transfer. However, while any discussion about the concept of translation in the Western world is bound to be influenced by the metaphor of translation as a carrying, a bringing across a text from one language to another, with an implication of semantic sameness (Chesterman 2006), the terms and the concepts of translation, as well as the practices to which they referred, varied considerably before the Latin *traducere* and its Latinate counterparts in European vernaculars began to be used during Renaissance Humanism, and were crystallized in dictionaries after the invention of the printing press.

1.2.2 Translation before Translation

While translation practices and activities have been documented in written and visual history since Egyptian hieroglyphics, histories of Western translation thinking (e.g., Robinson 1997) usually start from the pronouncements of Roman authors such as Cicero and Horace and proceed to St. Jerome,

[2] Based on *traductio*. See Halverson (1999b) for a discussion of other terms used in Old English for translation.

Florentine Renaissance authors, and German Romantics, to arrive at current theorizations. Seeing passages from Roman authors together with the writings on translation by Schleiermacher and contemporary authors may lead us to imagine a lineage from earlier texts and practices to what we now refer to as translation. McElduff (2009, p. 134), for example, states that "Cicero ... is often seen as an originating figure, whose ideas are read back through later studies of translation or comments by later translators and assimilated with them," and in this way, these earlier texts are incorporated into later discourse about different translation practices, objects, and activities. However, "translation" practices in the Classical world, relying primarily on orality, may perhaps be seen as more akin to those of the non-Western world in more recent, even contemporary times (Kothari 2014).

Before the emergence of the Roman Empire, translation in Europe was mostly translation from Greek, the lingua franca of the civilized world, into other languages. The Greek word for translation, μετάφραση (*metaphrasi*, "speaking across") relates to intralingual rather than interlingual translation (Connolly & Bacopoulou-Halls 2009), a meaning that is not central in Latinate terms like translation, *traduzione*, and *traducción* and refers primarily to the translation between Classical and Modern Greek. Greek continued to be the language from which, rather than into which, most translation activities took place throughout the Middle Ages and beyond, as most translations were of great Greek Classical works and authors, and from the Greek translation of the Bible.

The comments left by Horace and Cicero concern the oral transmission of dramatic poetry and oratory rather than written translation. Roman literature, to which statements on translation of the time refer, was a social and oral activity, which was "released" rather than published (McElduff 2015, p. 134). When Cicero elucidates that, when translating the Greek orators into Latin, "nec converti ut interpres, sed ut orator, sententiis isdem et earum formis tamquam figuris, verbis ad nostram consuetudinem aptis. In quibus non verbum pro verbo necesse habui reddere, sed genus omne verborum vimque servavi,"[3] he does not refer to translation between written texts or "books" (which did not exist at the time) but, rather, to a Greek text learned by heart, translated and performed orally in Latin in front of an audience, and used a form of the verb *convertere*. In other texts, Cicero used the verb *interpretari* with reference to his own close rendering of short passages, whereas verbs such as *vertere*,

[3] "I did not translate them as an interpreter, but as an orator, keeping the same ideas and the forms, or as one might say, the 'figures' of thought, but in language which conforms to our usage. And in doing so, I did not hold it necessary to render word for word but I preserved the general style and force of the language." Cicero, M.T. (46 BCE) *De optimo genere oratorum*, English translation by H. M. Hubbell, in Robinson (1997, p. 9).

convertere, *exprimere*, and *transferre* are used for the translation of larger texts (McElduff 2009, p. 137). According to McElduff (2009, p. 138), the distinction Cicero draws between *interpretari* and *convertere* as an orator is related to education and social status. While being centered on the notion of information transfer, though not necessarily between different languages, the word *interpres* was used more generally to refer to "anyone who stood inter pretium, residing between whatever prize two parties wanted, whether that was meaning, information, or goods" (McElduff 2009, p. 136). The Latin word *interpres* (as well as the Greek *ermeneus*) has the more general meaning of mediator or middleman – that is, verbal interpreting is included but is not necessarily the main focus of what an *interpres* does. Whereas the interpreter and interpretation were for Cicero linked with limited education, "'proper' translation was something reserved for the rhetorical school or for keeping an orator's skills sharp throughout his life ... Cicero's problems with the figure of the interpreter is, I believe, his anxiety about the social level of those who should be entrusted with translation" (McElduff 2009, p. 143).

When, about 350 years later, St. Jerome (348–420) theorized about translation, he suggested that a literal, word-for-word translation is required for the scriptures, while for nonsacred texts he was in favor of translating sense for sense, basing his preference on the authority of Cicero's pronouncement: "Ego enim non solum fateor, sed libera voce profiteor me in interpretatione Graecorum absque scripturis sanctis, ubi et verborum ordine mysterium est, non verbum e verbo, sed sensum exprimere de sensu."[4] However, unlike Cicero, Jerome was not talking about the oral performance of Greek oratory, but about the translation and collation of Hebrew, Greek, Aramaic, and older Latin source manuscripts into the Vulgar Latin of the time – rather than into the Classical Latin used by Cicero and Horace – and was pointing to a model of translation that saw the word of God as the ultimate authority. Jerome's version of the Bible in demotic Latin (the adjective Vulgate comes from the verb *vulgare*, meaning "to make common," "to disseminate") was the basis for the crystallized written variant – which, replacing Greek, was to remain the cultural and diplomatic lingua franca in Europe until it was replaced first by French and eventually by English as the global lingua franca in the twentieth century.

During the Middle Ages in Europe, various terms were used in relation to translation activities. Beside Classical Latin terms such as *interpretari* and *exprimere* (interpret, explain) – which referred to oral reformulation and which

[4] "Now I not only admit but freely announce that in translating from the Greek – except of course in the case of Holy Scripture, where even the syntax contains a mystery – I render, not word for word but sense for sense." Gerolamo, *Liber de optimo genere interpretandi* (*Epistula* 57, 5), English translation by Paul Carroll, in Robinson (1997, p. 25).

included interlingual as well as nonverbal translation - and *verto*, *converto*, *transverto*, and *imitari* – which referred to oratory and philosophy/poetry – later additions included *mutare*, *transferre*, and *translatare* (Delisle & Woodsworth 2012, p. 31; Folena 1991, pp. 8–9; Renzi 1997, p. 15). None of these terms were specific to what we see as translation activities in the conventional sense the word has acquired now. For instance, the "Latin translatio is closer to the current meaning, but is a more general term as well, referring to the various forms of transfer, including the transfer of power, as in *translatio imperii*" (Heilbron 1999, p. 431). Certainly, interpreting activities, well documented since the Roman Empire and held in Latin throughout the Middle Ages, were always viewed as different from translation. Interpreters – who, from the thirteenth century, became generally known as dragomans (and cognate words in European vernaculars originating from the Arabic term) – were especially important in diplomatic and military transactions as well as commercial and juridical dealings between European courts and the Ottoman Empire, and embassy dragomans sometimes developed into very powerful families (Rothman 2015). It was only with the rise of national languages that European courts began to train interpreters in European languages, while the word dragoman ended up being used exclusively for those interpreting between European and Oriental languages.

As regards written translation, there is evidence in the European Middle Ages of a set of multiple practices that could fall under some description of it, and "close literal translations coexisted with very free translations" (Tymoczko 2007, p. 62). However, contemporary distinctions among writing practices such as translation, imitation, and creation would not have made sense at the time, since such practices "were inextricably bound" (Delisle & Woodsworth 2012, p. 32). Since scholarship in the Middle Ages consisted of commentary much more than creation, translators could "omit passages and insert commentaries to an extent never again equalled in the history of translation in the West" (Delisle & Woodsworth 2012, p. 133), and there was no conceptualization of translation as an activity independent from other forms of cultural transmission such as imitation and appropriation (Laurenti 2015, p. 37). No clear-cut distinction between translation and original writing could be posited – on the one hand because, as argued by Mortier (1982), the concept of originality is a theoretical construct of the eighteenth century[5] and, on the other, because, at the time, there was no mechanism "to distinguish between composing a poem and reciting one, or writing a book and copying one" (Eisenstein 2005, p. 95). Rather than distinguishing between "translation" and

[5] According to Byung-Chul Han, the concept of originality is also specific to European culture and alien, for instance, to Chinese thought, which "does not accept the idea of the original" as "a kind of creation that occurred at one absolute, unique point" (Han 2017, p. 3).

other writing activities, the medieval vocabulary for "rewriting" (Lefevere 1992)[6] related to the function and type of texts involved, differentiating sacred, didactic, legal, historical, and poetic texts (Simon 2007, p. 109) – which were compiled, adapted, and commentated for different audiences, often combining unspecified passages from different sources. As stated by Delisle and Woodsworth (2012, pp. 164–165):

> The role of the translator depended not only on the new audience and possible new use of the translated work, but also on its genre. There were three principal types of work: liturgical hymns and religious poetry in general, narrative texts (lives of Christ and the saints) and texts used for religious instruction. . . . [T]he particular content and structure of religious texts made them relatively easy to adapt to different uses, and they were frequently and liberally "abridged, expanded, and rearranged." (Barratt 1984, p. 427)

Translation was mostly carried out from Greek into Latin, with the notable exception of the translations from Arabic produced in Spain in the twelfth and thirteenth centuries, at a time and place when paper also first appeared in Europe, introduced by the Islamic civilization. The mostly philosophical and scientific texts translated were based in their turn on, and often outlived, the Greek and Syriac manuscripts translated into Arabic in Baghdad in the ninth century. In the twelfth century, these Arabic translations were translated into Latin and later retranslated into vernacular languages throughout Europe, while in the thirteenth century, the Spanish king Alfonso X commissioned a large number of translations directly into the vernacular (Delisle & Woodsworth 2012, pp. 96–97).

Translation was interlingual translation only in the case of translation into the more prestigious variety of language – i.e., from Greek into Latin – whereas translation between Latin and vernaculars can be considered a case of intralingual translation (Cornish 2011, pp. 3–4). Vernaculars were not languages in the same sense in which Greek and Latin, which could count on a prestigious written heritage, were languages, and the diachronic distinction between Latin and vernaculars during the Middle Ages was rather a synchronic distinction of sociocultural dialects. Latin and the Italian vernacular(s), for instance, can be seen not as different languages but as different registers, Latin being the frozen variety that had become the language of culture and the evolutions of Latin into vernaculars being "lower," local, and mostly spoken registers of the same language. Translation from vernacular languages into the learned variant of Latin based on St. Jerome's Vulgate did not appear until the fourteenth century when vernacular literatures emerged,

[6] A term that, according to Lefevere (1992, p. 9), refers to the basic process that is at work not only in translation as its most recognizable form but also in "historiography, anthologization, criticism, and editing."

and Latin was also used as a lingua franca for translating between vernaculars, a most famous example being Petrarch's translation into Latin of Boccaccio's *Griselda* (the last novella from *Il Decamerone*), which was then used as the source of translations into various European vernaculars (Laurenti 2015).

1.2.3 Modern Translation

The more specific sense of the word "translation" as translation of texts from one's local "native" language into another emerged only in the Renaissance. The Latin word *traducere* was first introduced as a technical term by the Florentine humanist Leonardo Bruni in a letter of September 5, 1400, in reference to a passage from Gellio where there is mention of a "vocabulum graecum traductum in lingua romana" (a Greek word translated into Roman language). The role played by Bruni – who, according to Folena (1991), was also responsible for introducing the terms *tradurre*, *traduzione*, and *traduttore*, which would later become standard Italian[7] – in the introduction of the new word is somewhat controversial. Some scholars, like Sabbadini (1916, quoted in Cornish 2011, p. 227), assume that particular usage might be the result of a misunderstanding, a semantic "translation error." Rener (1989, p. 274) argues that there is no clear proof that Bruni attributed a particular importance to the introduction of the new term, since he entitled his treatise on translation *De interpretatione recta* and continued to use the word *traductione* (and its derivatives) as synonymous with other terms in his writings, as did his fellow humanists. Folena instead contends that Bruni's choice was deliberate, an intentional semantic innovation that was part of a program of the Italian humanists to introduce a new method of translation and that hinted at an understanding of translation that was different from that of the Middle Ages. Folena argues that Bruni needed a new term and found it in *traducere* – which, being related to *ducere* and to *dux*, comprises, behind the semantic features of "transfer," also those of individuality and subjective causality, underlining the originality, the personal involvement, and the "literary properties" of this operation, which was becoming less and less anonymous (Folena 1991, pp. 67–68). According to Folena, the change in terminology that occurred at that time represents a watershed moment between the medieval and the modern history of translation in Italy and in Europe and was a clear indication of an ideological and cultural break with the past.

Whether or not one agrees with Folena that the Latin term *traducere* was introduced by Bruni intentionally and that the standard terms for and meaning

[7] Although this attribution is only recoverable by reading an anti-humanistic pamphlet by Domenico da Prato, which makes reference to Bruni's translations from Greek to Latin (Folena 1991, p. 71).

of translation in European languages have a common origin in Florentine humanism, the conceptualization of translation as linguistic transfer (primarily of religious and literary texts) did not emerge fully until the following century, after the revolution of knowledge brought about by the new intellectual technology of the printing press. During the Renaissance, a renewed interest in Classical languages was coupled with an increasing use of vernacular languages. Translating from Classical languages into vernacular languages, which did not have an established written tradition, meant that translators created many neologisms in order to introduce concepts and popularize knowledge that did not exist in the spoken vernaculars, contributing in this way to the creation of a standard for scholarly writing. Translators into vernaculars before the introduction of print helped the development and evolution of national languages by creating a learned register and establishing their status, which was later strengthened by formal grammars (Delisle & Woodsworth 2012).

Translations and linguistic creation in the vernacular paved the way for compilations that took the form of bi- or multilingual glossaries and then dictionaries (Delisle & Woodsworth 2012, p. 230), which predate monolingual vernacular works. The first bilingual glossaries from Vulgar Latin to vernaculars, to be used mostly for biblical exegesis, were produced in the Early Middle Ages, while the first bilingual dictionary between vernacular languages, a French–English vocabulary for travelers, was produced in 1480 by the merchant, diplomat, writer, and printer William Caxton (1473–1474), who had also printed the first book in English, a translation from French (Armstrong 2015, p. 85). The first formal grammars were produced as printed books (Spain 1492, Italy 1495, France 1527, and Germany 1535), as were the first completely monolingual dictionaries, which only appeared as European languages were codified in the following century. The first monolingual dictionary in a national language was the Italian *Vocabolario* published by the Accademia della Crusca in 1612, while the first English dictionary was printed in 1623 by Henry Cockeram,[8] and the first French dictionary, the *Dictionnaire françois*, was published in 1680 by César-Pierre Richelet (Delisle & Woodsworth 2012, pp. 227–230). Until the fifteenth century, translating from Greek into Latin (what Folena calls vertical translation) was not the same type of activity as translating from Latin, the official language of Christianity, into the vernaculars, which were corrupted forms of Latin (what Folena calls horizontal translation). Translation into European vernacular languages happened when these vernaculars were endowed, like Greek and Latin, with a symbolic capital, so that it became possible to "translate" into them as well as between them. In

[8] Based on previous word lists, see https://web.archive.org/web/20080309181613/http://angli02.kgw.tu-berlin.de/lexicography/b_history.html (last accessed on October 16, 2020).

other words, people began to *traducere* when they also began to *tradurre, translate, traduir, traducere* printed books, and these words were recorded first in bilingual dictionaries, then in monolingual dictionaries and grammars.

***

The standardization of the vernaculars – which evolved into the dialects that eventually became crystallized by novels, newspapers, and dictionaries and turned into national languages – was made possible only by the invention of modern movable-type printing in the mid-fifteenth century. Writing and translating were, before the printing revolution (Eisenstein 2005), still the province of a very restricted group of people. During Renaissance Humanism, translation was still mostly from Greek into Latin, and it was only in the sixteenth century, at the time when printing was replacing handwriting as a means of publication, that translation from Latin into the vernaculars multiplied and that the practice of translating between vernaculars, including indirect translations[9] became widespread, as "staffs of translators were employed to turn out vernacular versions of the more popular works by ancient Romans and contemporary Latin-writing humanists" (Eisenstein 2005, p. 96). Printing had a strategic role in fixing literary vernaculars, and printers, who contributed to a new definition of literary property rights and new concepts of authorship, were largely responsible for the new impetus given to the "vernacular-translation movement" (Eisenstein 2005, p. 36) in various countries. This happened very quickly: for instance, in Venice between 1515 and 1528, the share of translations into vernacular with respect to those into Latin increased from one into vernacular for every thirty into Latin to one for every three, and in Florence from one for every three to three for every one (Ballard 2007, p. 96, quoting Larwill 1934, p. 36). While Latin remained the official European lingua franca of culture and diplomacy until the eighteenth century, thanks to printing technologies, translations into vernaculars started to be the majority, and vernaculars, first Italian and later French, began to compete with Latin as lingua francas (Bates 1911, pp. 47–52) – i.e., as "languages" rather than corrupted variants of it.

The mass circulation and dissemination of the Lutheran Bible (1534) in Germany would have been impossible without modern printing techniques (Kittel & Poltermann 2009, p. 414).

> Between 1517 and 1520, Luther's thirty publications probably sold well over 300,000 copies … Altogether in relation to the spread of religious ideas it seems difficult to exaggerate the significance of the Press, without which a revolution of this magnitude could scarcely have been consummated. (Dickens 1968, p. 51, quoted in Eisenstein 2005, p. 164)

[9] e.g., Thucydides was translated into English from French, in its turn translated from the Latin translations of the Greek texts (Laurenti 2015, p. 121).

Though Luther's was not the first translation of the Bible into High German, the first German grammars were directly based on his translations, which continued to exert a lasting influence, as did his ideas favoring German, which was the everyday language, over Latin, which were still dominant in the seventeenth century. While during the Middle Ages the Bible was vulgarized from Jerome's Latin version, Luther translated from the former Greek and Hebrew sources. Similarly, around 80 percent of the King James's Bible of 1611, which was "the culmination of efforts to shape the English language" (Delisle & Woodsworth 2012, p. 31), was derived from William Tyndale's early 1500s translations, which – like Luther's – had been carried out from Greek and Hebrew rather than from Latin. The first Swedish version of the Bible, the Vasa Bible of 1541, which remained in use until 1917 and is widely considered the most important document in the history of the language, is instead based on Luther's German translation (Delisle & Woodsworth 2012, pp. 39–42). While, in Protestant areas, translations of the scriptures were largely responsible for the development of standard national languages, in Catholic areas, where Latin remained the language of the Church, national languages were modeled in the same years as a literary canon, whose formation was, to a large extent, based on translated literary works.

As Heilbron (1999, p. 431) suggests, "[t]ranslations into the vernacular had existed well before the Renaissance, but the printing press gave the vernaculars, and translations in the vernacular, an entirely new social significance." Translation was the main medium through which the lower variety of language, the vernacular, climbed to the same level of the higher variant, Latin, the language of religion and culture. Before then, vernaculars were essentially spoken varieties of the language, versions of which first became recognized as main variants when adopted for official, institutional purposes. However, it was only when a written version was standardized through translations of religious and literary texts – first from Classical languages and then from other written, standardized vernaculars – that vernaculars began to replace Classical languages as the languages of culture (and, in Protestant countries, of religion) and later offered a foundation for the construction of national identities. As vernacular literatures were created out of translation (Laurenti 2015), translation turned the vernaculars from a continuous chain of infinitesimally separated neighboring variants into national languages. Intralingual translation between Classical Latin and (local variants of) a vernacular register became interlingual translation when French, Italian, English, German, and Spanish were recognized as languages in the same way that Greek and Latin were, establishing clear borders between geographical varieties. This happened when European languages could count on a body of linguistic knowledge, which was created largely through translation and standardized and disseminated through print.

Even when vernacular languages became officially established in the following centuries – for instance, in 1539, King Francis I made French the official language in the kingdom instead of Latin or regional languages like Occitan – Latin remained the lingua franca of culture in Europe. In Elizabethan England (1558–1603), most publications were written or translated into Latin, while translations into English, both from Latin and from other European vernaculars (especially literature in Italian vernaculars) accounted for about 20 percent of all works published (Delisle & Woodsworth 2012, p. 196). Until around the mid-seventeenth century in Europe, "more books were printed in Latin than in any vernacular language, and Latin was generally understood by European intellectuals. Hobbes and Newton wrote and published in Latin and thus could extend their influence over large parts of Europe" (Anderson 2016, p. 138). In 1691, Thomas Power translated Milton's *Paradise Lost* into Latin "in order to reveal Milton to the world as a great poet" (Beeby Lonsdale 2009, p. 86), while in Germany translations from Latin still accounted for 70 percent in 1650 (Laurenti 2015, p. 186), with French and – to a lesser extent – English becoming more important toward the end of the century. It was only during the eighteenth century or even, in the case of Scandinavia, in the nineteenth century (Delisle & Woodsworth 2012, p. 116) that people stopped writing and translating into Latin, and European languages replaced it as the languages of culture, having already effected a change in the reading public that included, by then, not only the learned elite but also merchants, travelers, and women.

1.2.4 Translation and Nation

The combination of print technology and cultural and religious factors promoted the creation of vernacular literary traditions, which eventually led to the identification of languages as national properties. A sense of national identity developed together with mass literacy, after vernacular translation reinforced linguistic barriers and Europeans "ceased to speak the same language when citing their Scriptures or saying their prayers" (Eisenstein 2005, p. 185). Anderson (1991), according to whom "nation-ness is the most universally legitimate value in the political life of our time" (p. 3), argues that nations are "artifacts" that were created toward the end of the eighteenth century, imagined communities built around a notion of national identity based on a single unitary language and a shared national body of texts that all individuals in the nation have in common. According to Anderson, the idea of nation was born in "Creole" American colonies in the course of the eighteenth century, when the territorially rooted colonial communities acquired, through administrative unity and local newspapers, a sense of shared identity that successfully fueled national liberation movements. Nations were born with the independence of colonies, and it was only later that languages became the basis on which to found a nationalistic ideal in European states, which were – until the eighteenth century – not nations but reigns.

According to Gellner (1983, p. 35), nationalism – "the organization of human groups into large, centrally educated, culturally homogeneous units" – relies on the ability to communicate with a large number of people through written, impersonal messages whose mutual understanding requires a shared and standardized linguistic medium. Modern translation is a tool for the construction of nationalism (of a sense of national identity), and at the same time, it is defined by national identities. The notion of "nationhood inevitably depends upon cultural – and specifically linguistic – means for its creation" (Bermann 2005, p. 2). Nationalisms find nurture in national languages and literatures, which are grounded in translation, as the concept of a national language rests on the idea that one can translate from and into them, since in a national framework the act of translation is conceptualized by constituting languages as equivalent self-contained entities. National languages and literatures, whose founding texts are often themselves translations (e.g., the Bible), are the result of a process that led to the formation of national vernaculars through a body of written material whose standardization was made possible by print technology. The creation of discrete linguistic systems through translation practices and their widespread dissemination, thanks to print, provided a basis for shared cultural identities that made national identification possible. European languages evolved from Latin (and other languages) to become national languages whose boundaries were defined by dictionaries and grammars, as a result of a historical process established through translation and the printing press.

> [T]he nineteenth century was, in Europe and its immediate peripheries, a golden age of vernacularizing lexicographers, grammarians, philologists, and litterateurs. The energetic activities of these professional intellectuals were central to the shaping of nineteenth-century European nationalisms in complete contrast to the situation in the Americas between 1770 and 1830. Monolingual dictionaries were vast compendia of each language's print-treasury, portable (if sometimes barely so) from shop to school, office to residence. Bilingual dictionaries made visible an approaching egalitarianism among languages – whatever the political realities outside, within the covers of the Czech-German/German-Czech dictionary the paired languages had a common status. (Anderson 1991, p. 71)

Contemporary Western ideas about translation are largely based on theories dating from German Romanticism (Lefevere 1977) – a time when, in many theoretical discussions on (literary) translation, leading writers and philosophers such as Schlegel (1772–1829), Goethe (1749–1832), Schleiermacher (1768–1834) and von Humboldt (1767–1835) promoted the notion of national languages as each having its own "genius." As much as each individual Author (with a capital A) had his or her own peculiarities, translation started to be considered a creative act rather than merely as an act of "repetition" or "imitation" like in previous theorizations. The metaphor of translation as "in-between" can also be seen as connected with "the Romantic notion of the translator as poet genius alienated from allegiances to any culture, and the view that cultures are homogeneous and fixed" (Brownlie 2007, p. 137). During the nineteenth century, translation prototypically became that between national literatures that were posited as having equal status, while various International Copyright Acts were passed to grant protection to the authors of works published abroad and changed the legal status of translators (Bassnett & France 2006).

Schleiermacher famously articulated a view of translation as a way of enriching a language by appropriation, positing a binary opposition between a method of translation consisting in either "taking the author to the reader" or in "taking the reader to the author," which has been extremely influential in contemporary Western thinking on translation. Schleiermacher's dichotomy is echoed in Berman's (1984) distinction between ethical and ethnocentric translation, Meschonnic's (1973) decentring vs. annexationist translation and Venuti's (1995) foreignizing vs. domesticating translation. Though they are by no means inspired by the nationalistic project behind Schleiermacher's theorizations, the concept of translation of these contemporary theorizations is informed by the nationalist framework of Western languages and literatures.

While the idea of translation fostered by nationalist thinking posits an equal relationship between languages, as can be seen from this very cursory overview, translation is rarely a matter of equality and cooperation. Rather, it is based on an unequal distribution of power and can be a site where the distribution of power is negotiated. Translation has always been a matter of one language (Greek, Latin, French, now English) being the dominant language from which, rather than into which, translation is mostly carried out. During Roman civilization, Greek texts were "translated" into Latin oral performance and later into Medieval codexes handwritten in vulgar Latin; later still, printed books were translated into European national languages from Greek, Latin, and other European languages. However, the flow of translation has never been a reciprocal exchange but a site of power differential. Translation has always been primarily from a more prestigious to a less prestigious language, and the same strategies may have different effects when translating "up" or "down" (Bellos 2011, p. 160). French was the European language of translation in Modern Europe, but it lost some centrality in the eighteenth century, especially in favor of German, and declined rapidly between the end of the eighteenth century and the beginning of the nineteenth century, until it was finally replaced by English, which became the dominant language after WWII. Currently, translation is mostly from English, which has reached the status of global lingua franca, and translation from or into English do not necessarily entail the same set of practices.

Translation flows and languages are difficult to gauge, but UNESCO data on translated books, which have been available since the1930s, combined with other data, provide a general picture of the field of transnational publishing – i.e., the translation of books considered as an international system. In around 1980, more than 40 percent (about 50 to 70 percent in Europe) of all translated books worldwide were translated from English, a percentage that increased to 59 percent in the 1990s. After the decline of Russian, two languages (French and German) maintained a proportion somewhere between 10 percent and 12 percent, together with English accounting for three-quarters of the total number of translated books worldwide. A few other languages (Italian, Spanish, Danish, Swedish, Polish, Czech, Chinese, Japanese, Arabic, Portuguese, and Korean)[10] had percentages between 1 and 3 percent. From 1960 to about 1987, English increased its dominant position despite the decreasing share of English in the total proportion of books published worldwide (Heilbron 1999, p. 434; Sapiro 2012, p. 34). Furthermore, while translations from English represent the main share of all translations worldwide, translations make up a small percentage of publications in English in the UK and the USA: less than 5 percent of all published books since the mid-twentieth century (Heilbron 1999, p. 439).

Any form of knowledge/theory, including the conceptualization of translation, is affected by the specific circumstances in which it is enunciated, the time, place, social and material context, and subject position. Translation has not meant the same thing at all times, as each temporal, geographical, and linguistic context has its own prototypical conceptualization of translation. The prototypical meaning of translation and the practices, processes, and products commonly associated with this type of activity within a given cultural community may sometimes be attributed universal validity, and the definition of a "core" type of translation can be presented as all-encompassing while, in fact, being based on a specific type of practice. The contemporary Western concept of translation, which is based on the twentieth-century geopolitical order defined by nation-states in which Western nations have an advantage in the balance of power, foregrounds national languages and literatures as constitutive of translation. As concisely put by Tymoczko (2007, p. 57),

> Western European words for "translation" and the history of translation practices in Western Europe indicate that dominant Eurocentric conceptions of translation are deeply rooted in literacy practices (as opposed to oral translation practices still

[10] It should be noted that several of these languages have a supranational character and do not coincide with a nation-state.

predominant in most of the world). They also suggest that Eurocentric ideas about translation are shaped by the practices of Bible translation. Western European conceptions of translation are heavily influenced by the close connection between language and nation, and the history of Eurocentric translation is also closely associated with imperialism and its ancillary belief in a hierarchical relationship of languages and cultures.

1.3 Translation in the Twentieth Century

During WWII, translation became central to wartime activities involving intercultural communication (not necessarily to build bridges) and propaganda (Tymoczko 2007, p. 26). The war's outcome was a world divided into spheres of influence, with many new national boundaries determined. Nation-states that did not exist before were created as a result of the decolonization process, and geopolitical borders were redesigned within the Eastern Bloc after the fall of the Soviet Union. With the start of the Cold War, the rise of machine translation provided a new impetus to apply linguistics to translation. The linguistic approach of the time is perhaps best exemplified by a quotation from a provocative statement by MT researcher Warren Weaver in his well-known 1949 memorandum: "When I look at an article in Russian, I say, 'This is really written in English, but it has been coded in some strange symbols. I will now proceed to decode'" (Weaver 1955, p. 4). Translation was understood as transfer of meaning taking place between self-contained linguistic and largely equivalent sign systems, or codes.

1.3.1 Translation Proper

The prototypical meaning of translation that emerged in the postwar period, and is still current in the lay population, is neatly exemplified in semiotic terminology by Jakobson's (1959) tripartite distinction between intralingual, interlingual, and intersemiotic translation. Jakobson famously defined "translation proper" as "an interpretation of verbal signs by means of some other language" (Jakobson 1959, p. 233) and then metaphorically extended the meaning of the word "translation" to two other types of practices and products – that is to say, ""translation within the same language" involving reformulation, paraphrasing (intralingual translation), and translation between a language and a different semiotic system (intersemiotic translation or transmutation). While the latter are presented as instances of translation in a figurative sense rather than in the proper sense, in both cases, they are seen as taking place out of "a natural language." Jakobson clearly has in mind a definition of translation as a purely linguistic activity (even in intersemiotic translation, a source language must be involved), with "language" as the main subject of the act/process/product of translation. The definitions of "translation" that can be currently found in most English dictionaries are often rather straightforward, nontechnical reformulations of Jakobson's definition of "translation proper" as "interlingual translation." Thus, for instance, the *Random House Unabridged Dictionary of American English* defines translation as "the rendering of something into another language or into one's own from another language," the online *Cambridge Dictionary of English* defines it as "something that is translated, or the process of translating something, from one language to another," and the online *Oxford Dictionary* defines it as "the process of translating words or text from one language into another."

Behind the standard, received, nonspecialist meaning of the word translation lies a conceptualization of translation as interlingual transfer between "equal" languages, as embodied in national European literatures and codified in written texts and a textual practice based on printed texts. Until the twentieth century, translation was the province of the relatively small number of intellectuals who had access to more than one written language, and translation was discussed almost exclusively in terms of the translation of books – most prominently sacred scriptures, literature, and other written works endowed with cultural and symbolic capital. During the last century, translation entered the realm of everyday life, with information being translated over a wider spectrum of media than just books, through the radio, cinema, and the press. After WWII, "translation" began to be used consistently to refer also to "pragmatic" texts, and the remit of translation studies was increasingly expanded to include film translation, machine translation, and oral interpreting. Research on translation was subsumed under the academic scope of linguistics. The work of earliest translation studies scholars such as J. C. Catford (1965), Eugene Nida (1964), and George Mounin (1963) was informed by linguistic thinking of their time – namely British functional linguistics, American transformational linguistics, and French and Russian structuralism. In the USA and in Europe, translation was also the object of attention in some comparative literature departments, and from the end of the 1970s, a network of scholars began to elaborate a nucleus of disciplinary thinking.

1.3.2 Turns of Translation Studies

Translation studies is a relatively new field that has witnessed an exponential growth since its beginning about fifty years ago and is now firmly established as a vibrant research area – thriving with journals, monographs, textbooks, handbooks, and encyclopedias covering almost every aspect of translation; and with departments in many, if not most, academic institutions around the world. Since the 1980s, translation studies has seen books published, conferences held, and programs founded all over the world. In its rather short history, this relatively new discipline has gone through a number of different stages. While the first studies dedicated to translation were produced by scholars working in the fields of linguistics and literary studies, as translation studies began to emerge as a discipline in its own right, it has been influenced by new ideas coming from adjacent fields. The metaphor of turns often has been used as a conceptual tool to interpret and periodize different theoretical and methodological approaches; a brief survey of the literature produced in the field shows more than twenty in translation studies.

Linguistics is, of course, central to a conception of translation that focuses on languages, but references to a "linguistic turn" (e.g., Chang, 2011, p. 413; Cronin, 2010, p. 1) postdate Jakobson's famous definition. When translation was first made an object of study by the scientific community and academic publications on translation started to appear, research on translation was simply conceived of as an application of the science of linguistics; however, before de Saussure laid the foundation of the discipline of linguistics, language itself was something that was the exclusive concern of literature, philosophy, and philology. Torop (2002) argues that, following Jakobson's work, a semiotic turn took place "on the borderline between translation studies and cultural semiotics" (Torop 2002, p. 595), exerting a continuing influence on later developments. However, Gentzler (n.d.) suggests that a failure to properly value and continue the theoretical contributions of Eastern European scholars like Jiri Levy, František Miko, and Anton Popovič in the 1970s resulted in a "semiotic turn not taken."[11]

The first mention of a turn in relation to translation studies is possibly the pragmatic turn, made (in a German publication) by Mary Snell-Hornby (1986, quoted in Hermans, 2009, 86). "Pragmatic" here is to be understood in the sense of linguistics pragmatics, or the direction taken by linguistics from the 1970s – which includes text linguistics, speech act theory, and M.A. K. Halliday's systemic functional linguistics – away from transformational generative grammar models that had informed previous work in translation – such as Eugene Nida's (1964) work in Bible translation – or away from Vinay and Darbelnet's (1995) contrastive linguistics approach. The pragmatic turn refers to the shift of emphasis from a view of translation as involving a transfer between texts embodying abstract systems of codes to one that sees translation as something happening between texts understood as meaningful events, the definition of which is not inclusive only of verbal texts.

However, the most celebrated turn of translation studies is the cultural turn, first articulated in a landmark 1990 thematic collection of papers edited by

[11] More recently, a call for a "humble semiotic turn" has been invoked by Luc van Doorslaer in connection with Douglas Robinson's (Robinson 2016a) *Semiotranslating Peirce* (see www.tyk.ee/semiotics/00000011943, last accessed on October 16, 2020).

Susan Bassnett and Andrè Lefevere (1990b). According to Bassnett (1998, p. 130), who later described the cultural turn as the meeting of translation studies and cultural studies, the two followed a similar trajectory in the establishment of a subject as an academic discipline, having in common an "interdisciplinary" or "adisciplinary" approach that called into question disciplinary boundaries. Rather than prioritizing discussions about linguistic equivalence or literary value, researchers shifted the emphasis to the study of text production across linguistic borders, integrating concerns and methods from sociology, anthropology, and historical research in the study of (literary) translation as part of culture. The cultural turn in translation studies could thus be seen largely as a "cultural studies" turn. Bassnett and Lefevere's publication marked the culmination of a decade, whose beginning could be traced to Bassnett's own programmatically labeled *Translation Studies* (Bassnett-McGuire 1980). In their introduction to the 1990 volume, entitled "Proust's Grandmother and the Thousand and One Nights: The 'Cultural Turn' in Translation Studies," Bassnett and Levefere described what they saw not merely as a new direction, but as a founding moment of the discipline, stating that "[t]he growth of Translation Studies as a separate discipline is a success story of the 1980s" (Bassnett & Lefevere 1990a, p. ix). Since then, the success story has continued to grow, while more and more turns have been claimed to have happened, be happening, or be about to happen. The cultural turn of translation studies also opened the way to a translation turn in cultural studies, as cultural studies moved toward increased internationalization and discovered the comparative dimension of intercultural analysis (Bassnett 1998; Snell-Hornby 2006, 2009).

In her 2006 monograph entitled "The Turns of Translation Studies," Snell-Hornby describes the driving forces behind the cultural turn as being the descriptive, empirical, and target-oriented approach originating from the so-called Manipulation School (Hermans 1985; Toury 2012) and functionalist approaches such as Vermeer and Reiss's *Skopostheorie* (Reiss & Vermeer 1984; Vermeer 1978) and Justa Holz-Mänttäri's (1984) theory of translational action. These two influential lines of thinking highlighted the contexts in which translations were produced and received, rather than focusing on earlier preoccupations with the source text and linguistic equivalence.[12] While the Manipulation School was primarily concerned with literary texts, research focusing on "pragmatic" texts – i.e., scientific, technical, and legal documents, whose output has doubled since the last century (Zanettin et al. 2015) – has been conducted mainly within the framework of *skopos* theory, which will be

[12] Morini (2008) refers to the general reorientation of translation studies in the 1990s, when descriptive translation studies and the so-called manipulation approach questioned linguistic-informed concepts of equivalence, as a skeptical turn.

discussed in more detail in the subsequent chapters in connection with news translation. The cultural turn was also influenced by theoretical thinking coming from outside the Anglo-European area, like the Brazilian "anthropophagic" or "cannibalistic" approach, which anticipated a later postcolonial turn (Trivedi & Bassnett 1999).

According to Snell-Hornby, the pragmatic turn of the 1970s marked a convergence between linguistics and literary studies, which led to the cultural turn of the 1980s, and then to the empirical turn of the 1990s. The empirical, or "methodical," turn, as Snell-Hornby also calls it, consisted in a growing number of empirical studies concerned with both translation and interpreting, and which included descriptive research on literary case studies and research on the translation process in the form of "think-aloud protocols" (TAPs), as well as case studies based on actual interpreted events (Pöchhacker 2015, p. 204; Snell-Hornby 2006, p. 115; 2010, p. 368). Similarly driven by empirical and methodological preoccupations is the corpus linguistics turn that took place in the second half of the 1990s, when corpus linguistics resources and tools began to be consistently used to test descriptive and theoretical hypothesis as well as being applied to translator training (Laviosa 2004).

The social (Wolf 2007), or sociological, turn (Angelelli 2014; Merkle 2008), already prefigured by the cultural and empirical/methodical turns of the previous decades, refers on the one hand to the attention paid to human agents – that is, translators and interpreters – and on the other to the social and institutional agencies – that is, to the actual contexts in which translation and interpreting activities take place. Wolf calls for the establishment of a sociology of translation as well as for a sociology of translation studies, which is able to explore the role played by translation in the construction of the concepts of society and culture and deal with "the issues that arise when viewing translation and interpreting as social practice as well as symbolically transferred interaction" (Wolf 2007, p. 4). Much research following this approach incorporates insights and methodologies from sociological research, notably Bourdieu's notions of *habitus*, *field*, and *capital*. Also informed by Bourdieusian sociology is what has been called the reflexive or self-reflexive turn (Inghilleri 2005), which emphasizes the recognition of the interdependence of theory and method and draws attention to the need for the researcher to exercise critical self-analysis and examine his or her positioning in relation to the object of study – in this case, translation and interpreting practices, processes, and products.

In interpreting studies, which by this time was being reclaimed as a distinct field of research with its own specific interpreting turn (Pöchhacker 2013, p. 70), the term social or sociological turn was used to point to the expanding area of dialogue, service, or community interpreting, informed by research in conversation analysis and other approaches to social interaction (Pöchhacker 2006; Straniero Sergio & Falbo 2012, p. 28). Pöchhacker also argues that another turn, a qualitative turn, took place in interpreting studies as researchers started to resort to social science techniques such as interviews and questionnaire-based surveys, and interpreting research started to engage with qualitative data (Pöchhacker 2015).

The first years of the twenty-first century were extremely productive concerning the proposition of further turns. An ethical turn was invoked, among others, by Anthony Pym, who – in his introduction to a special issue of the journal *The Translator* entitled "The Return to Ethics" (Pym 2001) – argues that translators, who operate in an intercultural space, should enable effective interlingual communication by fostering cooperation and aim at achieving mutual benefit and trust between all parties engaged in intercultural communication. This potential ethical turn – which, according to Snell-Hornby (2006, p. 78), had "yet to be taken" in 2006 – is discussed in a number of publications by Pym and others, often drawing on Antoine Berman's (1984) discussion of "ethnocentric" and Venuti's (2000, p. 219) "foreignizing" translation. Other issues often raised in connection with the ethical turn include professional deontology (Chesterman 2001), subjectivity and reciprocity, translator and interpreter agency, activist and interventionist agendas, ethical and political responsibility and accountability, and so on (Baker & Maier 2011; Inghilleri & Maier 2009). However, no consensus has ever been reached on what exactly an ethical and responsible attitude or action would be on the part of translators and interpreters, and – as the ethical turn in the ultimate analysis is concerned with issues of power, self-reflexivity, and politics – its contours tend to blur with those foregrounded by the proposers of other turns – including the power turn, the postcolonial turn, and the ideological turn.

With the term power turn, Tymoczko and Gentzler (2002) wanted to highlight a growing focus in translation research on issues such as agency, cultural change, dominance, cultural assertion, cultural resistance, and activism. Regarding in particular literary translation, Pettersson (1999) argued that – as translation studies had become increasingly interested in questions of power and discourse and, more specifically, in postcolonial literature and criticism – the cultural turn in translation studies had evolved into a postcolonial turn. While most postcolonial approaches refer to translation in a more "metaphorical" sense – which includes the relations of power between cultures at large and, for some scholars, may not even imply a textual exchange – postcolonial theories have highlighted the asymmetrical relations between languages. Bhabha's (1994) influential *The Location of Culture* theorized postcolonial translation as a "third space" in between cultures, so that the writings of migrant and diasporic writers like Salman Rushdie contain a new language created out of a layering of the colonizers' and the colonized's language and belong to a hybrid zone in which culture and nation do not overlap.

Other scholars have posited the emergence of further turns in the wake of the cultural turn. Kaindl (2014), for instance, writes of a fictional turn with reference to the integration into translation theory of reflections on translation found in works of fiction. The translational dimension in works of fiction as a source for theorizing about translation was first highlighted by scholars such as Vieira (1995, p. 50) and Pagano (2000, p. 81) with reference to South American literature, and has been articulated in different ways. Some researchers – like Kurz (1987) for instance – have focused on contrasting real and fictional translators and interpreters or real and fictional translation and interpreting contexts. Others have focused on the use of translation in literary works – for instance, in stories describing cosmopolitan fictional realities – and as a metaphor of social processes such as exile, migration, nomadism (Polezzi 2012), and identity (Cronin 2006). Gentzler (n.d.) draws a connection between the theme of translation in literature and the formation of national identities in Latin America. Italiano (2012) uses the term spatial turn to refer to the growing body of research on what he calls the ''translation of geographies,'' referring to both travel writing and writing originating in multicultural urban zones. Italiano defines such literature as a rewriting of spaces, "a performative negotiation of cultural differences across constructions of worlds and identities" (2012, p. 2).

While the postcolonial turn is informed by poststructuralist theory, the ideological turn (Fortea Gil & Santana Lopez 2012; Leung 2006) – which Leung (2006, p. 129) defines as stemming from "a new/renewed focus on the ideological significance of the act of translation . . . a changed perspective of seeing translation as a means of ideological resistance" – is related to the critical discourse framework of analysis and incorporates tools and concepts from critical and systemic functional linguistics. While the postcolonial turn has addressed primarily the concerns of literary translation, the ideological turn is usually related to conflicts of power and interests in the translation of texts such as academic writing, legal and scientific documents, political interviews, and advertisements (Cunico & Munday 2007). It is within this framework that a number of studies of news translation have been conducted, as will be seen in Chapter 3.

Turns of translation studies are the result of a changing "intellectual climate" and have happened under the influence of theories from neighboring disciplines and in relation to more general turns in the humanities and social sciences. Snell-Hornby (2009, p. 42) defines a turn as "a clearly visible change of direction, even amounting to a redefinition." However, while sometimes overlapping with "approach" and "school of thought," the term "turn" seems to have become somewhat of a buzzword. The announcement of a turn may, to some extent, amount to a claim for the relevance of one's research interests and stakes, and it may certainly have to do with advancing one's research agenda, and with academic funding and recognition. Turns may thus be thought of as intellectual fashions emerging from competition between theories – which, however, function both as "drivers of innovation" and as "signposts that appear to point to the consensual pressures of research" (Bachmann-Medick 2016, p. 8).

Metaphors like that of a "turn," which implies abandoning a previous course, concern not only translation studies as a(n) (inter)discipline, but also the concept of translation itself. However, while the extent to which a discipline such as translation studies can be "turned" can vary from a minor twist to a major change of emphasis, according to Bachmann-Medick (2016, pp. 9–12), it cannot be equated to a new paradigm that completely replaces a previous one, since the research premises in the humanities and social sciences are already built on competing theoretical positions so that turns can only be experimental, gradual, and fragmented. Rather than as major changes of direction, turns of translation studies may thus been seen as conversational turns, in the interdisciplinary dialogue between translation studies and other disciplines.[13]

1.3.3 The Translational Turn

Bachmann-Medick (2009) argues that we are in the midst of a "translational turn," a major reorientation in the humanities as translational approaches pervade its various disciplines, while translation is becoming a key term and is being used as an analytical tool and not simply as a metaphorical concept. The concept of translation has broadened to designate the translation of cultures, where culture is not defined in terms of national languages and literatures, and translation activities are carried out in a globalized world not only across but also within state borders. According to Bachmann-Medick (2016, p. 26), "the category of translation has been developed as one of the basic concepts in the social sciences and the study of culture." This new translational concept of culture, of "culture as translation," consists of "an ongoing effort to explore new methodological approaches to the 'in-between spaces' that transcend dichotomous demarcations and binary epistemological attitudes" in relation to cross-cultural phenomena such as identity, migration,

[13] I am indebted for this suggestion to a colleague who pointed it out following a presentation at the VI conference of Greek-speaking translation studies scholars in Thessaloniki, May 25, 2017.

and exile – which "need to be viewed as concrete scenarios of interaction shaped by translation processes and the necessity for self-translation."

As culture has become more central in the conceptualization of translation and vice versa, Jakobson's characterization of translation proper as interlingual translation has been expanded and revised. The representation of translation "proper" as something happening between "natural" (national) languages has been challenged by the provision that the term may also properly apply to translation not involving natural language (or not only natural language). Thus, revised versions of Jakobson's translation typology have taken into account the possibility of translation taking place between other "semiotic systems" that do not necessarily involve verbal communication – e.g., music and visual art. In 1986. Toury posited a first-level distinction between inter- and intrasemiotic translation and a second-level distinction within the latter between inter- and intralinguistic translation. Eco (2001, 2003), highlighting that translation is a type of interpretation, proposed a more articulated classification of various types of intersystemic translation – including not only "translation proper" but also adaptation, ekphrasis (using words to describe an image), and parasynonymity (showing an object in order to interpret a verbal expression) – and intrasystemic translation – including paraphrasing and summary (intralingual translation) as well as musical performance.

While Eco's classification maintains Jakobson's distinction between linguistic systems as the basis of translation "proper," the conceptualization of translation as cultural translation has led to questioning Jakobson's distinction between intra- and interlingual translation. Derrida (1992, p. 225) argues that a distinction between inter- and intralingual translation "presupposes that one can know in the final analysis how to determine rigorously the unity and identity of a language, the decidable form of its limits." However, the criteria that are often invoked to define boundaries between languages are not applied consistently, and it is difficult to decide where one language ends and another begins. Tymoczko (2007, p. 55), for example, illustrates how criteria based on historical development are not applied consistently to a Romance language like French, for which we distinguish between Modern French, Old French, and Vulgar Lati, and Chinese, which has remained the "same" language during the past two thousand years. Criteria based on mutual intelligibility fail instead to account for why Swedish, Norwegian, Danish, and Icelandic, or Spanish and Portuguese, are regarded as different languages, as opposed to Mandarin and Cantonese, which are seen as variants of Chinese, and many so-called dialects of English, which are not mutually comprehensible to most speakers.

Central to the understanding of translation proper as interlingual translation is the definition of "a" natural language as a system that is itself defined by translation. Jakobson's definition is grounded on a historically determined conceptualization of languages as distinct national entities, which was "[m]ost conspicuously manifest in eighteenth-century movements such as Romanticism in Western Europe and *Kokugaku* (National Studies) in Japan" (Sakai 2009, p. 76). Sakai calls the "modern" way of conceiving of translation a "cofigurative regime of translation" defined as "an ideology that makes translators imagine their relationship to what they do in translation as the symmetrical exchange between two languages" (1997, p. 51). The cofigurative schema makes it possible to imagine a nation as a homogeneous sphere and implement what Sakai has called a regime of "homolingual address" – i.e., one based on the assumption of "two separate language-communities modelled as 'national' in identity … and treated as homogeneous" (Morris 2006, p. 178). Regimes of national monolingualism can be taken for granted and make it difficult to imagine other regimes of translation. As argued by Sakai (1997, p. 2), however, "it is not because two different language unities are given that we have to translate," but, rather, "it is because translation articulates languages so that we may postulate the two unities of the translating and the translated languages as if they were autonomous and closed entities." According to Sakai (2009), it is translation that retrospectively allows the representation of languages as units, by tracing a border between them.[14]

To posit a distinction between inter- and intralingual translation is to posit the existence of distinct and autonomous linguistic systems, a representation of translation that is based on the idea of natural languages and cultures primarily as manifested through national written literatures. The assumption of homolingual communities behind translation between national languages is becoming undone by the reality of heterolingualism, multilingual and multicultural contexts in which individuals interact by switching to and from different languages and registers. This happens both in the physical world, especially in increasingly multicultural large urban areas, and in the virtual world of mobile digital communities, whose liquid borders (Bauman 2000) are replacing social and territorial networks that previously provided people with a static national identity.

While nation-states still provide the political and linguistic regulations that define translational borders, with the redefinition of cultural communities across geographical space brought about by phenomena of migration and cosmopolitanism, colonial languages have evolved into supranational varieties. Languages like English, Spanish, and French no longer belong uniquely to the countries with which they were historically associated, but have become transnational languages, often spoken alongside others by communities whose geographical extension does not coincide with national borders. Migration

[14] With reference to Sakai's theoretical thinking, Robinson (2016b) posits the emergence of an intercivilization turn based on relationships and *co*figurations between, rather than on "centers" of, civilizations.

movements have created bilingual and plurilingual states, dissolving the illusion of homogeneous, monolingual nations. For new virtual communities of speakers that are not geographically located, translation is increasingly being seen as cultural translation, as languages and other features of cultural identity are negotiated through translation rather than overlapping with nationality.

1.3.4 English in and out of Translation

English is one of the main postcolonial languages– that is, one of the main languages of people who do not identify this language with national affiliation, claiming a right to a non-English identity in English. It has also acquired the role of a global, dynamic, and hybrid lingua franca, "whose complexity cannot be fully grasped without taking into account its interaction with other languages and cultures" (Taviano 2013, p. 156). Most English is the product of speakers of other languages (Crystal 2003), and much of it is the result of translation activities. English is currently used primarily by speakers for whom English is not a native or first language, and native varieties of English (British, American, Australian, etc.) are less spoken than functional varieties, used both internationally and intranationally by speakers who do not share either of their first languages and for whom English is a means of intercultural communication not tied to particular countries or ethnicities (Jenkins 2007). The spread of ELF has been paralleled by an increase in the demand for translation (House 2003, 2013). Thus, English is the language of power and the language of translation, not only in the sense that more is translated out of English than out of any other language, but also considering that English is the language into which most translation is carried out, though mostly as a functional variety, to be used in an international context and possibly as an intermediate version for translation into other languages. Most translation into English takes place not in countries in which English is the national language, where translation plays a minor role in text production, but in countries where English is not the only national language, and in which translation is a major text production activity. International varieties of English predominate in source texts as well as in terms of the international readership of translation, and translation into English as a second or foreign language – and English as a lingua franca (ELF) more in particular – is becoming increasingly important (Stewart 2008).

English has overtaken all other languages in international communication, but most texts written both in translated and nontranslated English, such as EU and UN documents, are the hybrid "product of negotiations between different cultures and languages, resulting from overlapping rhetorical and discourse norms, created by and addressed to a supranational community, in which the traditional distinction between source text/culture and target text/culture is no longer applicable" (Taviano 2010, p. 8). The pluricentric nature of global Englishes and ELF challenges the "biological" notion of native speakers as "owning" a clearly identified core language originating in a specific linguistic and cultural context and addressed to a specific, nationally defined target audience. Traditional concepts of language variety and speech community are being replaced by the notion of community of practice, with reference to a repertoire of linguistic resources jointly built up over time through mutual engagement by people who share interests and practices (Marra 2015).

1.4 Translation and Technology

Turns of translation studies can generally be related to changes taking place in the social sciences. Conceptual and terminological shifts, however, have also been prompted by the changed physical environment and material conditions in which translation practices take place and which necessarily affect the way in which these practices are conceptualized in the first instance.

Snell-Hornby (2010, p. 638) has suggested that, concurrently with the empirical/methodical turn of the 1990s, a globalization turn took place due to "breath-taking developments in information technology and hence world-wide communication, which have revolutionized many aspects of modern life and brought radical changes for the language industries." Michael Cronin has argued that translation studies is undergoing a technological turn which is not "driven ... by theoretical developments in cognate areas of inquiry, though it can be informed by them, but is an emergent property from new forms of translation practice" (Cronin 2010). These practices are so pervading, in fact, that Cronin (2013, p. 103) contends that "our present age, which is often referred to as the information age ... should more properly be termed the translation age" (compare with Bachman-Medick's "translational turn" mentioned previously). While Cronin describes the technological turn with specific reference to the context of digital media and globalization, Littau (2011) sees this technological development as a stage of a more general medial turn, which she relates to the material history of translation.

Littau highlights the importance of considering material culture in shaping conceptualizations of translation, in that it is the physical support of inscription instruments and surfaces and recording machines that shape translation practice and theory: "media make history, transmission, culture, communication and translation possible" (Littau 2016b, p. 87). She argues that since "medial forms – handwritten, printed, electronic – bring about changes in the ways in which we write, read and translate... media technologies have arguably shaped practices of translation" (Littau 2016b, p. 90). The globalization turn, the medial turn, and the technological turn are terms that describe closely interrelated phenomena, or different aspects of the same basic phenomenon – that is, how current technologies/digital (multi)media have impacted on the way we think of translators and translation practices, processes, and products.

1.4.1 Translation and Screen Culture

Since conceptualizations of translation are related to the media contexts and its technologies, the study of translations cannot be separated from their physical history (Burkette 2016). Thus, translation in the digital age is different from what Cicero, St. Jerome, and Schleiermacher understood as translation and based their theorizations upon, since they relied on different technologies. The main technology of information transmission in Classical Greek and Latin times was mnemotechnics, whereas during the Middle Ages, knowledge was disseminated through handwritten manuscripts. In scribal times, codices and volumen were usually "read aloud in a kind of murmur to oneself, in order to hear sense emerge from the continuous stream of words" (Littau 2011, p. 274), and silent reading only became an established practice with printed books. The new technology of the printing press – which introduced and systematized reading aids such as interword spacing, punctuation, consistent layout, standardized spelling, and clear typeface – was instrumental as a medium for disseminating reading, writing, and translating practices to an audience larger than the narrow monastic or scholastic readership of manuscripts. The technology of print cannot in its turn be separated from vernacular translation, as the corpora of printed literatures created largely through translation laid the foundations for the institution of national languages, on which the "modern" concept of translation, which still currently enjoys wide recognition at lay level, is based.

In the same way that the printing revolution affected translation practices, the innovations brought about first by audio and video recording technologies and then by digital media have impacted the way knowledge is currently produced, stored, and transmitted. Some striking analogies can be drawn between the "printing revolution" and the "digital revolution." Eisenstein (2005) explains how the whole system of knowledge prior to the invention of the printing press was reassessed as a consequence of the new technology, which allowed for the (re)production of written texts at a pace unheard of before. It has been estimated that the number of books published in the half-century following the invention of print equaled the total production by European scribes during the previous one thousand years (Clapham 1957, p. 37, quoted in Cronin, 2013, p. 23). The conditions under which texts were produced, distributed, and consumed were transformed by printing, and this happened not by discarding the products of scribal culture, but by reproducing them in much greater quantities. Eisenstein illustrates how the sheer availability of printed records – including written texts but also maps, tables, and charts created the basis for a whole new understanding and method of knowledge production:

> systems of charting the planets, mapping the earth, synchronizing chronologies, codifying laws, and compiling bibliographies were all revolutionized before the end of the sixteenth century. In each instance . . . Hellenistic achievements were first reduplicated and then, in a remarkably short time, surpassed. In each instance, the new schemes, once published, remained available for correction, development, and refinement. Successive generations could build on the work left by sixteenth-century polymaths instead of trying to retrieve scattered fragments of it. (Eisenstein 2005, p. 87)

The "reduplication" of previous scientific achievements and the progressive refinement of feedback that followed the invention of the movable-type printing press as opposed to scribal culture is analogous to even larger changes triggered by current technological developments. As printed books had allowed the establishment of a system of knowledge sharing that was previously technologically unavailable, computers and the global digital infrastructure have exponentially multiplied the ease of access to information with respect to the analogical world. In 2010, Google's CEO Erich Schmidt reportedly estimated that, by 2003, the amount of information (written, visual, oral) published/released on the Internet every two days would equal the amount of the information produced since that year (Lobe 2018). Computers, mobile phones, and other devices that characterize the digital world have allowed the simultaneous sharing of ideas, data, and resources, and more than ever before, knowledge is miniaturized, multiplied, and made portable and publicly accessible.

The medial turn in translation (studies) can, in fact, be seen as having been brought about by a technological paradigmatic shift, between print culture and what Littau calls the media context of "screen culture." The late nineteenth and early twentieth century saw the proliferation of new communication media allowing for the reproduction and distribution of images and sound. McLuhan (1962), who famously argued (with reference to the then-new medium of television) that what mattered most was not the content carried but the medium itself, "belonged to the first generation to be shaped by a world in which a print-biased media ecology had been altered by new ways of recording, storing, and transmitting sounds and voices" (Winthrop-Young & Wutz, 1999, p. xii) and "grew up in an era when the dominance of the printed paper as a medium of communication was first challenged by new media such as broadcasting and oral recording." Just as print culture "remediated" (Bolter & Grusin 1999, p. 45) or "transmediated" (Coldiron 2016, p. 99) – that is, represented in another medium – the products of scribal culture, screen culture remediates previous cultural products. As argued by Coldiron (2016.

pp. 97–98), translation and remediation/transmediation are "allied transformative processes," as each process of translation involves a remediation, and new meaning is created through new media as "re-languaging cooperates with ... re-mediation." Past knowledge first reproduced, recorded, and stored in analogical media (books, magnetic tapes, records, films, microfilms, etc.), is now being converted into digital code, as new media systems flank and interact with, rather than replace, existing ones, as cultural and technological innovations always have done.

The computer is a convergence technology, as it provides for the (re) production of texts, sounds, and images, formerly associated with different media, in a single format and interface. Littau (2016b), in fact, suggests that, in order to better understand how new forms of translation emerge, we may profitably look at studies of media convergence culture (Jenkins 2006). Convergence is a process of coexistence, cooperation, and intersection between different media systems, which "alters the relationship between existing technologies, industries, markets, genres and audiences [as well as] the logic by which media industries operate and by which media consumers process news and entertainment" (Jenkins 2006, pp. 15–16). While the smooth flow of content across media systems relies on the convergence of visual and aural reproduction technologies into digital format, media convergence is defined by a new type of participatory culture that sees a redefinition of the roles of producers and consumers in the circulation of media content. Convergence is a complex process of transition whose often competing and contradictory terms are still being negotiated between different corporate, collective, and individual actors, who do not have equal power in determining the circulation of media content. Corporate processes of convergence are driven by the economic opportunities offered by synergically remediating content across different delivery media and have resulted in the concentration of large sectors of the entertainment and information industries in the hands of a few large multinational media conglomerates. Grassroots processes of convergence are driven by engaged communities of consumers/fans and associations, pressure groups and citizens empowered by access to the new technologies.

As noted by Coldiron (2016, p. 100), "times of media change and technological innovation are also phases of increased translation activity." In the same way in which "print created conditions in which demand for translation rose" (Littau 2016b, p. 917), the exponential increase of textual (re)production and information flows produced by the "information-immersive environment" (Cronin 2010, p. 3) of mobile/distributed/cloud computer technology has generated a growing need for translation and has led to the emergence of new translation practices and products. The demand for translated texts is met partly by human and partly by machine translation, with different degrees of interaction. Currently, the vast majority of "translation proper" is carried out by machine translation systems (Och 2012), the quality of whose output is accepted as part of evolving reading practices and literacy norms (Cronin 2010, p. 5). On the other hand, the individuality of translators, who "can no longer be conceived of independently of the technologies with which they interact" (Cronin 2003), is being eroded by collaborative endeavors such as crowdsourcing initiatives, which can be seen as part of the new participatory culture afforded by convergence media.

Collaborative translation practices, which are now expanding and becoming as widespread as in the European Middle Ages, have been generated to meet the needs of the rapid dissemination of online social networking practices. These new translation needs have been partly met by "wiki-translation" practices, whereby "translation consumers are increasingly becoming translation producers" (Cronin 2010, p. 4), and crowdsourcing translation and interactive, user-generated content can be seen as "a reinvestment of translation technology by the human, a strategic use of technical resources to further human concerns or agendas" (Cronin 2013, p. 102). New practices of collaborative translation are advanced both by commercial enterprises, since "it became more economic to meet this demand by employing not an individual but a team of translators" (Littau 2016a, p. 917), and by nonprofessional, grassroots forms of community translation such as fansubbing (O'Hagan 2009, 2011, 2016) and politically engaged "volunteer translation" (Pérez-González 2012a, 2014b).

Changes in the technological environment have led to "changes in working practices . . . and to a rethinking of the relationship between source and target texts" (Baker & Maier 2011, p. 1). The result has been an increase in new translation practices, particularly into and out of ELF, whose most distinctive characteristics are user-generated content and social networking (Desjardins 2017).

1.4.2 Translation and Localization

In Western cultures, translation has been traditionally identified with written translation of primarily religious and literary texts. Literary translation still represents the largest area of interest in translation research in the twenty-first century, and research on Bible and religious translation, though in seemingly relative decline, still attracts much attention (Zanettin et al. 2015).[15] However,

[15] The paramount role played by literary texts can also be inferred by considering that the two most cited works in translation studies literature (Franco Aixelá 2013) – that is, Toury's (1995) *Descriptive Translation Studies and Beyond*, and Venuti's (1995) *The Translator's Invisibility* – are both primarily concerned with literary translation.

while still looming large in the interest of translation studies scholars, literary and religious texts are only a minor part of the amount of translation carried out today. As the field of translation studies has increasingly widened to be more inclusive of the kind of phenomena and activities in its remit, it has come to include not only all types of written texts, but also audiovisual and multimedia products, from films and TV series to videogames and live performance, as well as all types of interpreted communication. Growing areas of research increasingly relate to the role played by audiovisual, multimedia and multimodal translation, news translation, the translation of advertising, and localization (Zanettin et al. 2015).

According to Gambier (2009) subfields of translation studies that have developed separately such as audiovisual translation (AVT), news media translation (referred to as "transediting global news"), and localization (referred to as "multimedia translation") "could very soon be integrated because of the convergence between e-tools, since most of the future documents to be translated will be not only increasingly multisemiotic, but will also include more and more different media" (Gambier 2009, p. 24). O'Hagan and Mangiron (2013, p. 106) suggest that "the emergence of new media resulting from the convergence of technologies is seeing the previously separate domains of localization and AVT come together to cater for the new type of products needing to be prepared to go global. Whether AVT subsumes localization or vice versa remains to be seen."

Localization specifically seems to have become one of the most important areas of growth in translation studies. It has been proposed that the term localization, defined by Schäler (2009, p. 157) as "the linguistic and cultural adaptation of digital content to the requirements and locale of a foreign market, and the provision of services and technologies for the management of multilingualism across the digital global information flow," could, in fact, properly account for all "translated" digital objects and for the new practices of "translation" that surround them. The term was first introduced by the computer industry to refer to the production of multilingual software, computer manuals, and websites for foreign markets, which are often designed and engineered in such a way that they may function as international versions, which are then localized according to diverse cultural and linguistic needs. Interlingual translation is seen as only a part of the whole process of localization, which begins with internationalization and is followed by linguistic and cultural adaptation, and provides for the marketing requirements of (quasi) simultaneous release and constant update.

In the scenario of digital translation/remediation/convergence, the terminology of localization can also be used to describe other types of text transformation processes. For instance, Pym (2014, pp. 121–125) discusses how, in film translation/localization, translators of local dubbed and subtitled versions rely on an intermediate script, which is internationalized by including instructions about culture specific elements and cross-references. Similarly, in global news production, the initial report of an event is first internationalized by news services like AFP, Reuters, and Associated Press (AP) , and then localized by local news outlets, with different degrees of adaptation, so that "the process of adapting a text from a news agency release for a newspaper story corresponds to its passage from a global product to a localised version in the local press" (Orengo 2005, p. 175). (See Section 2.5.4 for a more detailed discussion.) Elsewhere (Zanettin 2008, 2014), I have argued that the production of comics in translation can be considered a kind of localization in that the translation of the verbal content is seen as only one component in a larger process that involves various actors, from publishers and editors to letterers, possibly altering also the publication format, page layout, the drawings, etc. Pym argues that "even within literary translation, the terms of localization are not completely lost" (Pym 2014, p. 123), offering as an example the case of the Canadian-based publisher Harlequin, which "can put out the same novel in some 24 languages and about 100 locales, in each case not just translating but also editing the text to suit local expectations about length, and styles of storytelling." Geographical rather than national localization of linguistic features includes lexical and syntactical changes according to varieties of English, as in the American and British editions of *Harry Potter* (Hatim & Munday 2004, pp. 4–5). Another analogy with respect to literary translation is the process of "simshipping" – which, introduced by software companies with reference to localization, can also be observed with respect to international best sellers such as Salman Rushdie's novels, which are translated even while the source (English) texts are being written and are then simultaneously published in many languages (Zanettin 2001). While the vast majority of studies in literary translation focus on interlingual translation, considering the written text independently of the medium, others have begun to look at paratextual (Poldsaar 2010) and even nonlinguistic features of translated books, including book cover design (Sonzogni 2011) and the material form of the book (Baule 2016; Emmerich 2014).

Translation studies is increasingly dealing with the diverse points of contact between cultural groups, as patterns of language(s) and conceptualizations of translation are in fluctuation in the wake of globalization phenomena. Not only is the meaning of translation "proper" being expanded to include senses that were previously seen as metaphorical, but competing terms have surfaced to dispute the ground of its conventional conceptualization. The changed social and technological environment points to a redefinition of writing practices. For instance, the term "transediting" has been used as an alternative to "translation" – both in the field of popular fiction (Hemmungs Wirtén 1998, 2004) and news translation (Chen 2011a; Stetting 1989; Zhang 2013). (See Section 2.5.2

for a more detailed discussion.) Whether the word "translation" becomes inclusive of concepts such as localization or transediting or, vice versa, whether translation can be seen as part of a wider range of activities and practices referred to by these latter terms, in the digital and global information age, translation can be seen, in the words of Emily Apter (2006, p. 11), as "the name for the ways in which the humanities negotiates past and future technologies of communication, while shifting the parameters by which language itself is culturally and politically transformed."

2 Translation as News

2.1 Introduction

This chapter examines news translation from a diachronic and synchronic perspective and provides an introduction to key terms and concepts in news media translation research. I first offer an historical overview of the role of translation in journalism, "a word that did not itself appear until the early nineteenth century" (Woolf 2001, p. 80), looking at translation during the early stages of printed news production and dissemination in sixteenth-century Europe. I examine the role of news agencies and foreign correspondents since the mid-nineteenth century and consider the current scenario of globalized information flows. I then discuss the role of translation in the different stages of the production and dissemination of foreign news and look at translation practices and strategies in the workflows of different types of media outlets – from global news agencies, which provide multilingual coverage and produce in-house translations, to smaller organizations such as national newspapers and activist sites, which often rely on distributed models of translation.

Translation in the news media calls either for a redefinition of the meaning of translation to include other practices in addition to those of translation "proper" or for the adoption of alternative terms. In the rest of the chapter, I examine issues related to the relationship between translations and source texts in news media and the visibility of translation, and I discuss some of the main terms and concepts used in news media translation research – namely domestication, transediting, gatekeeping, and localization. These terms refer to related aspects of the news media translation process, and while they are sometimes used in combination, their meaning may vary depending on the theoretical and methodological framework adopted.

2.2 Translation and the News

From the seventeenth to the twentieth century, newspapers were the most widespread written texts, "an 'extreme form' of the book, a book sold on a colossal scale," as Anderson (1991, p. 34) puts it. The newspaper, whose "very conception … implies the refraction of even 'world events' into a specific imagined world of vernacular readers" (Anderson 1991, p. 63), together with the novel provided "the technical means for 're-presenting' the kind of imagined community that is the nation" (Anderson 1991, p. 25). Translation, which has been associated with news production since its very beginning (Valdeón 2015b, p. 638), has always played a paramount role in news gathering and dissemination and thus in the establishment of national languages and identities.

2.2.1 The News, Translated and Printed

Factual information began to be printed in Europe with the invention of the printing press, under the name of *news pamphlets* in England, *Neue Zeitungen* in Germany, *occasionnels* in France and *relaciones* in Spain, Italy, and Portugal (Espejo 2011, p. 190). By the second half of the sixteenth century, European countries had developed a network of printed newsletters, mostly devoted to single events (Ettinghausen 2016) but also containing "political handbills, political poetry, commentary and engravings" (Dooley 2001, p. 8). Translated news from abroad was a considerable part of what was printed, and, in fact, early news translation practices should be seen, according to Barker (2013, p. 241), as having a bearing on the push to periodicity in the journalistic press. The first publication containing a variety of news items "appearing at regular short intervals of at least once a week, produced in relatively large print runs, sold to the public at a moderate price and providing information to a sizeable number of readers" (Weber 2006, p. 387) was the *Relation aller Fürnemmen und gedenckwürdigen Historien* – printed in Strasbourg in 1605 by Johann Carolus, who had previously earned his living by collating reports from abroad and producing handwritten newssheets for wealthy subscribers (Pettegree 2014, pp. 182–184). The Thirty Years' War – the religious conflict that raged in Central Europe between 1618 and 1648, during which countries often changed sides for economic and political reasons, and which is considered to be at the origins of journalism (Dooley & Baron 2001; Pettegree 2014; Valdeón 2012a, p. 853) – sparkled a spate of news publications, mostly containing "dry, purely informative reporting of the foreign news concerning mostly military and political fluctuations" (Brownlees 2005, p. 273). The main center of production of this new type of news pamphlets, printed in quarto-size book format, were the rich merchant towns of the Dutch Republic (1581–1795), and Amsterdam in particular (Brownlees 2019). It was there that the first folio-size single-sheet news pamphlets were published in Dutch (or Low German), as well as the first newspapers translated from German and Dutch into English and French and exported to the English and French markets (Pettegree 2014, pp. 195, 201; Simeček 1972). The first Dutch newssheet, or coranto, *Courante uyt Italien, Duytslandt, &c.*, was published in 1618. England initially received news from continental Europe in the form of pamphlets written in Dutch, until the first English-language coranto, *Corrant out of Italy, Germany, etc.*, was printed in Amsterdam in 1620. This was followed, a year later, by the *Corante, of Newes from Italy, Germany &c.*, which was printed in London and described itself as "a translation from the German copy printed at Frankfurt" (Hutt 1973, p. 9).

Most of these first newspapers, like the first English officially licensed, dated, and numbered weekly news pamphlet – the *Weekely Newes – from Italy, Germany, Hungary Bohemia, the Palatinate, France and the Low Countries: Translated out of the Dutch copie* (1622, later changing its main heading to *A Coranto*) – and the first French news pamphlet, the *Gazette de France* (1631), which was backed by Cardinal Richelieu and functioned as a semiofficial organ (Weber 2006, p. 398), were typically heavily censored and dealt almost exclusively with translated foreign news (Pettegree 2014, p. 201). The news items contained there were, in fact, mostly presented as translations from Latin, German, or French. Similarly, the first newspapers in other cities across Europe were almost exclusively based on translations of news published abroad (Valdeón 2012a, p. 855). The sources of the first periodical publications in Northern Europe – in Stockholm, the *Ordinari Post-Tijdender* (1645), and in Copenhagen, the *Berlingske Tidende* (1649) – were news pamphlets in German (H⊘yer 2003; Ries 2001), whereas in the Iberian peninsula – including in Barcelona (the *Gazeta*, 1641), Lisbon (the *Gazeta*, 1641), and Madrid (the *Gazeta Nueva*, 1661) – the main sources were mostly French news pamphlets (Arblaster et al. 2016, p. 88; Espejo 2016, pp. 15–17; Ettinghausen 2001, p. 202). In Italy, Venice, and Rome were two of the main European hubs for the dissemination of news, often translated from documents and newsletters in other languages (Lomal 2016), though they remained at "the centre of the most intense network of commercial manuscript *avvisi*" (Pettegree 2014, p. 168) and did not produce periodical printed newssheets. The first newspapers were instead established in the 1640s in much smaller cities like Genoa, Naples, Bologna, and Florence (Pettegree 2014, pp. 205–206).

Attributed sources for the news printed in newssheets were mostly foreign newspapers, though manuscript and printed newsletters and information from travelers are also referenced. Typically, "the entire elaborate publishing process" consisted in a number of stages, namely "selection, translation, censorship, and printing" (Ries 2001, p. 242).[1] Translators, who were often also the printers themselves, "played a crucial role in establishing and maintaining the

[1] Translators manipulated information to comply with censorship expectations, and "[i]f the translated versions did not meet the expectations of the governments the publication was

news networks of early modern Europe" (Arblaster et al. 2016, p. 100). They congregated in the hubs and nodes of the postal networks, where they mediated between merchants, diplomats, travelers, and soldiers and formed relationships with scribes and printers, translating between vernaculars both from word-of-mouth and from various manuscript and print sources. Printed news was "structurally transnational" (Dosquet 2016, p. 654) and largely based on translation. Foreign newspapers were also the primary sources of newspapers printed in the overseas colonies. The North American colonies received news from newspapers brought in ships from Europe, often originally in French and Spanish, while the first newspapers in vernacular languages printed in the Indian subcontinent were translated from newspapers in English (Valdeón 2015b, pp. 638–639). Since the early eighteenth century in the South American and North American colonies, newspapers played a decisive role in creating a new consciousness of imagined national communities (Anderson 1991pp. 61–65), predating the formation of a national consciousness in most of Europe (Anderson 1991, p. 50).

While in the second part of the seventeenth century newspapers started to include local news also, translation remained the main news production practice. The first issue of the first English daily newspaper, *The Daily Courant* (1702), consisted entirely of items translated from Dutch and French newspapers (Valdeón 2015b, p. 638). The term newspaper did not appear until 1667 (Oxford English Dictionary n.d.), and while in the first half of the seventeenth century most news pamphlets had four quarto-size pages set book style, it was only in the second part of the century that the folio-size page became the standard (Brownlees 2009, p. 57), as did the inclusion of advertising. However, while the news business evolved to include editorial figures and functions besides those of translators, journalism's growth is still mostly linked to the thirst for news of wars and accounts of disasters taking place abroad. In the late seventeenth and early eighteenth century, Huguenot translators played an important role in British journalism (Leech 2020). Many Huguenots, an important group of well-educated and ideologically motivated migrant Protestants expelled from France after the revocation of the Edict of Nantes in 1685, were responsible not only for translating scientific and philosophical books between English and French but also for translating literary reviews into French. This cosmopolitan diaspora of "cultural intermediaries" (Leech 2020, p. 32) was, in fact, "also responsible for translating into English for English newspapers the vast amount of foreign news" (Leech 2020, p. 32), which "made up the bulk of news in all contemporary newspapers" (Gibbs 1987, p. 23). During the same years, Daniel Defoe's *A Review of the Affairs of*

cancelled altogether" (Valdeón 2012a, p. 853). News publications were closely monitored by the state, and in England under Charles I, from 1632 to 1638, all licenses were withdrawn.

France (1704–1713) and Jonathan Swift's *The Examiner* (1710–1714) contained translations as well as commentary, and Defoe also worked as a governmental agent disguised as a translator for a different newspaper (Valdeón 2012a, p. 852). In the Americas, translation practices continued to play an important role in the development of journalism, as shown, for instance, by Navarro and Hart (2019), who investigate the role of translation in the *Gaceta de Guatemala* between 1797 and 1807, and by Gasca Jiménez et al. (2019), who analyze an extensive corpus of Spanish-language newspapers published in the USA between 1808 and 1980.

As noted by Hernández Guerrero (2009, p. 9), the news publication formula established in the eighteenth century, consisting of either translations from foreign newspapers or translations alongside editorial newswriting, still continues to the present day. However, as "the journalistic profession evolved from a linguistic transformation of foreign texts to a fully independent activity, translation was relegated to a secondary position" (Valdeón 2012a, p. 859), and the trajectory of translation in the news from being featured in the headline of newssheets to invisibility was completed in the course of the nineteenth century. For journalists increasingly required to fill newspapers with original writing regarding domestic matters and advertising material, translation became part of the practice of newswriting rather than the job itself.

Translators have played a large role in the development of professional journalism not only in Europe and the Americas but also in countries like China, where modern journalism was introduced in the nineteenth century by Protestant missionaries as a tool for evangelism and scientific education (Zhang 2007); Japan, where the first modern Japanese language newspapers in the 1860s contained mostly translated content (Matsushita 2019b, pp. 45–46); and Afghanistan, where independent journalism developed after the new constitution of 1964 (Bezhan 2014).

2.2.2 *Translation and News Agencies*

The emergence of newspapers had rested on the creation of a "new postal infrastructure of relays of couriers . . . and a ramified system of political correspondence across Europe" (Weber 2006, pp. 389–390), and since in the late 1700s newspapers "still lacked a corps of news reporters and relied on correspondents to send in items" (H⊘yer 2003, p. 455), the physical transfer of foreign newspapers and their translation for the new readers "would remain a common practice until the early nineteenth century" (Valdeón 2015b, p. 638). The main change that took place in the way foreign news reporting reached readers happened in connection with technological innovations, primarily following the invention of the telegraph in 1833, which – together with "the widespread use of steam shipping and the expansion of the railway network" – "led to increased spatial integration" (Bielsa & Bassnett 2009, p. 21). By using the telegraph, information could be instantly made available from where the events reported were taking place without the need to rely on imported foreign newspapers. The global infrastructure for communication created by the telegraph allowed an experience of global simultaneity since newspapers could select events "according to their significance and no longer to where they took place and the newspaper became a palimpsest where different events from the most diverse places coexisted" (Bielsa & Bassnett 2009, p. 40).

With the advent of the telegraph, a new type of news broker came to the fore: international news agencies. The first news agency, Agence Havas (later to become Agence France Press), which translated foreign newspapers for the French media, was opened in 1835 by Charles Havas, who since 1832 had run Bureau Havas, primarily offering news translation services to businesses such as banks and government agencies, rather than to local newspapers (Valdeón 2015b, p. 638). Agence Havas, which became the main client of the state-owned French telegraphic network (Bielsa & Bassnett 2009, p. 40), was followed in 1848 by the Associated Press in New York and in 1849 by the German Wolf. In 1851 Julius Reuter, who had previously worked in Agence Havas as a subeditor, founded his own news agency in London. In the 1850s, the European cable and telegraphic networks quickly developed; this linked the main European cities, and soon, following "the geography of empire" (Bielsa & Bassnett 2009, p. 42), the most distant parts of the world were connected to the metropolitan centers. During the 1860s and 1870s, India, Australia, Hong Kong, Shanghai, Tokyo, and Aden were connected to London by overland and submarine cables. By the end of the nineteenth century, "the British owned 72 per cent of the approximately 190,000 miles of submarine cable in the world" (Bielsa & Bassnett 2009, p. 42), establishing an hegemony in the global network of communications that was not successfully challenged until the development of new communication technologies in the 1950s (Bielsa & Bassnett 2009, p. 42).

European and North American news agencies at first specialized in providing foreign news for national markets, and later, "through alliances with other news organizations worldwide" (Bielsa & Bassnett 2009, p. 56), in covering information and distributing it on a global scale. In 1862, the Associated Press and Reuters reached a news exchange agreement, and Reuters became the major supplier of American news in Europe. Havas, Wolff, and Reuters signed an agreement in 1859, and later agreements also included the Associated Press. International news agencies soon became the largest providers of foreign news for national newspapers. In France, Havas became the almost unique provider of information to other media organizations, the large majority of which could not count on foreign correspondents. In Britain, instead, *The Times*, which already had its own network of foreign correspondents, did not subscribe to

Reuters until 1859. International news agencies could obtain fast information from their agents in strategic places, and newspapers in general could not compete with the international infrastructures for news production supported by the news agencies in their respective zones of influence. These included France, the French colonies, and Southern Europe (and later South America) for Havas; Britain, the British colonies, and Holland for Reuters; Germany, Scandinavia, and Eastern Europe for Wolff; and Northern America for Associated Press. Within these territories, the agencies "collected news either by developing their own networks or by establishing links with other national agencies" (Bielsa & Bassnett 2009, p. 43). This arrangement lasted until the first decade of the twentieth century, when the newly created United Press International (1907) entered into competition with Associated Press, leading to the abandonment, after WWI, of news exchange agreements and of the principle that granted exclusivity of news distribution according to zones of territorial influence.

While "[t]he history of journalism may have begun as accounts of people and events in foreign lands [which] involved translating and editing foreign texts rather than sending reporters to the foreign land itself" (Valdeón 2012a, p. 856), the system of international news production that came into being as a result of the telegraph in international news agencies was based on the figure of the foreign correspondent. Journalists working abroad were usually required to know foreign languages, though this was restricted to the main European languages (and Asian languages for Japanese reporters [Matsushita 2019b, p. 56]), and seniority was often a criterion taking precedence over language proficiency. When foreign correspondents had no working knowledge of a language, they relied on local permanent or temporary staff to carry out translation tasks. However, while reporters usually wired news items from the place where the reported events took place, some foreign correspondents did not leave the news agency's home country but rather wrote their reports by collating, translating, and editing information gathered from various sources (Valdeón 2012a, pp. 856–858). News agencies' headquarters in European capitals and the USA became the centers to which information, in some cases already translated and in others not, was sent, and in which it was further processed, translated, and transmitted both to local news media and to the peripheries (Delisle & Woodsworth 2012, p. 192).

In the aftermath of WWII, five major news agencies – Associated Press (AP), United Press International (UPI), Reuters, Agence France-Press (AFP, formerly Agence Havas), and Telegrafnoe Agentstvo Sovetskovo Soyuza (TASS, which distributed news in the Soviet bloc) – "were the source of 80% of the information received by national news agencies and media throughout the world" (Valdeón 2012a, p. 860). The German Wolff disappeared, while China relied on Western agencies, translating and rewriting foreign-language publications appearing in Hong Kong, Shanghai, and Tientsin. In the twenty-first century, news agencies still supply the bulk of information to all news media, whether as written news or as audiovisual information. Most countries have one or more national agencies – either private, such as the UK's Press Association (PA), or governmental, such as state-owned China's Xinhua News Agency. While some of these agencies – like the Italian ANSA, the Spanish EFE, and the German Deutsche-Presse Agentur – use foreign correspondents and cover news from abroad to some degree, they all rely to some extent on the few largest global news agencies, currently Reuters (which in the meantime has specialized in and derives most of its profits from financial information), AP, and AFP. News agencies have established a network of relationships between them and other media, so global agencies that provide worldwide coverage supply their services to regional or local agencies and to individual news media, while regional and local agencies supplement the news gathered by the international news agencies' representatives, who maintain offices in major news centers. The major international news agencies produce newswire in English as well as in other languages. AP produces news in English, Spanish, and Arabic;[2] AFP produces news in English, French, Spanish, Portuguese, German, and Arabic; while Reuters produces news in English, Arabic, Chinese, French, German, Italian, Japanese, Portuguese, Russian, and Spanish. Translation into these languages is undertaken by the news agencies themselves, whereas subscribing news organizations translate the information received in any of these languages into other languages (Bielsa 2007, p. 36; Valdeón 2012a, p. 861). Thus, the news agencies "can be viewed as vast translation agencies, structurally designed to achieve fast and reliable translations of large amounts of information" (Bielsa & Bassnett 2009, p. 56). The four major world news agencies use English as their vehicular language (Bielsa & Bassnett 2009, pp. 33–35). Most international and national agencies provide information in local languages but also in English translation, as well as sometimes in other languages.

News agencies play a key role in the dissemination of translated texts, as they distribute their content to subscribing national media that use them for their international reporting. Hernández Guerrero (2009), for instance, investigated the processes of selection, translation, and distribution of translated news in the Spanish journalistic sector and found that, in the international news section of the newspapers, a large percentage of the articles published was based on agency sources, followed by articles sent in by foreign correspondents and by articles based on other news sources. Hernández Guerrero notes that, in Spain, between 60 and 80 percent of the news items

[2] www.ap.org/about/annual-report/2017/ap-by-the-numbers.html (last accessed on October 16, 2020).

published by regional newspapers comes from news agencies, whereas in the case of the larger companies the percentage goes down to 5–10 percent (2009, p. 51). International agencies are also the major suppliers of international news photos. Park (2016, pp. 504–505), for instance, observes that Korean and Japanese news agencies and newspapers receive photos primarily from AP and Reuters.

Global agencies are organized differently, and translation work also varies according to areas of interests. At AFP, for instance, a considerable amount of translation is carried out at the Paris headquarters, typically in the news desks of the various regions. Thus, "the Latin American desk in Paris is responsible for translations into Spanish of news relating to Europe, the Middle East and Africa, while Spanish translations of news relating to the Americas are done in the regional desk in Montevideo" (Bielsa & Bassnett 2009, p. 59), whereas AFP journalists translate reports from the French and English wire for the Spanish wire and produce a French-language version of Spanish-language news about Latin America. On the other hand, the Reuters headquarters in London "receives only news items in English from their international journalists for the English newswire" (Bielsa & Bassnett 2009, p. 59), while all translation activities are carried out at agency bureaus or regional offices. The Reuters bureau in Madrid thus employs both international journalists, who produce English-language reports about Spain for the English newswire, and local journalists, who translate reports written in English and write original reports for the Spanish market (Bielsa & Bassnett 2009, pp. 78–79). Reuters is almost absent in the South American market, which is dominated by AFP, together with AP, the Italian ANSA, the Spanish EFE, and IPS (Inter Press Service), which is "the largest supplier of information about the less developed nations" (Bielsa & Bassnett 2009, p. 50). Global news agencies also play a paramount role in the Arabic-speaking world as "massive amounts of Arab media productions count to a great extent on translation work from foreign media agencies into Arabic" (Bazzi 2009, p. 185).

2.2.3 Translation and New(s) Media

News agencies are not, however, the only players in the circulation and translation of information that "operate globally and multilingually [and] rely heavily on translations of messages to be translated into many different languages" (House 2013, p. 284). Since the 1960s, the incremental multiplication of information brought about by technological developments such as TV and satellite communication and, from the late 1900s, by the Internet have radically changed the global scenario of information exchange, together with the translation practices related to it. The commercial satellite channel CNN (Cable News Network) was launched in the USA in 1980, and by 1992, the network had a global dimension, its live coverage of events and breaking news being watched in more than 140 countries by hundreds of millions of people. The BBC – which provides radio news, current affairs programs, and updated website newsfeeds in forty languages (as of 2017) through its World Service network, and whose government-funded Monitoring Service compiles news in English from worldwide printed, broadcast, and social media sources translated from more than one hundred languages (BBC Monitoring 2019) – acts "as both public-access news media and as news agency" (Holland 2013, p. 337).

Since the 1990s, all major news media – including newspapers, TV networks, and cable channels – have launched information portals on the Internet, often creating multinational conglomerates with entertainment and technology companies. In the USA, the number of online newspapers increased from seven in 1990 to sixty-nine in 1994, while all the main UK news organizations had a website by 1995. By 2002, there were 3,400 online newspapers in the USA and two thousand outside, and the audience of online news as a proportion of total readership grew from 2 percent in 1996 to 31 percent in 2006, complementing offline news consumption, which declined during the same period (Stanyer 2009, pp. 201–202). With the transition to the so-called Web 2.0, news websites evolved, both in terms of content presentation and its reception and production. Thanks to broadband connectivity and increased speed of access, they began to include – besides text and graphics – video and audio streaming (a common feature on US news websites by 2005), and user-generated content has been increasingly incorporated into journalistic practice, either through interactive features or from social networks such as YouTube, Twitter, and Facebook (see, e.g., Creech 2015). Internet news sites and social networks have offered the opportunity to customize news reception through personal communications packages but have also offered opportunities to contribute to news production and shape news content through what is known as citizen journalism – by "witness reporters" including freelancers, compilers, and members of the public. Together with the increase in mobility brought about by Wi-Fi technology and portable devices, these changes have taken place as different media sectors such as TV networks, cable channels, and newspapers have converged into similarly conceived outlets vying for the same online audience (Stanyer 2009), while online news consumption, especially on mobile devices and through social media, has increased dramatically in the second decade of the 2000s (Bialik & Matsa 2017; Goggin et al. 2015).[3]

Thus, through media convergence, the digital extensions of so-called legacy media companies such as the BBC, CNN, *The New York Times,* and *The*

[3] In Asian countries such as China, this has happened even more rapidly than in Western countries (Sparks et al. 2016).

Guardian compete in the digital space for the largest share of the market with the most popular news websites owned by the largest US media corporations, including Time Warner and Microsoft/NBC, and news aggregators such as Yahoo! and Google News. The websites of the main news organizations and news aggregators are the main providers of online information in the USA and in the Western world in general because they have brand strength and credibility, and the financial resources to pay for exclusive content that attracts large numbers of visitors and subscribers with premium content and services.

The global news media environment is no longer exclusively dominated by European and North American outlets, and information has started to flow following multidirectional currents. The pan-Arab channel Al-Jazeera was founded in 1996 in Qatar, also reaching out to global and diasporic audiences and launching an English-language channel in 2006 (Bielsa & Bassnett 2009, pp. 52–54). While "many Western television networks are closing their foreign bureaus, and international radio broadcasting, offering ever-diminishing numbers of language services, is shifting to the internet" (Rawnsley 2015, p. 275), news broadcasted by networks such as Japan's NHK, Russia Today (RT), China's CCTV-N, India's NDTV, and Singapore's Channel News Asia is freely and globally available and is used as source of news by other news outlets.

Translation is of paramount importance in news broadcasting and is one of the key components of public diplomacy, or "soft power." While this concept, which is "increasingly linked to the notion of nation branding" (Cronin 2013, p. 111), was originally developed with regard to the USA (Nye, Jr. 1990, 2004), other players more recently have begun to invest heavily in the expansion of their international broadcasting capacity, where "international broadcasting" is used as "the elegant term for a complex combination of state sponsored news, information, and entertainment directed at a population outside the sponsoring state's boundaries" (Price et al. 2008, pp. 152–153).[4] In the rapidly evolving media landscape, the global open Internet model initially promoted by Tim Berners-Lee's World Wide Web is thus being challenged not only by corporate interests in democratic countries but also by state control and censorship in authoritarian ones, while "the Chinese model of state-dominated Internet governance . . . is being internationalized through

[4] China's growing sensitivity to the perception of its image by international audiences is notably demonstrated by its phasing out the use of the word "propaganda," replaced by terms such as "communication" or "information" as a translation of *xuanchuan*. For instance, since 2004, the English translation of *xuanchuanbu*, formerly "Propaganda Department," has been changed into "Publicity Department."

the Shanghai Pact" (Hartley et al. 2017, p. 9).[5] Hartley et al. (2017), in fact, argue that the Internet is now used in international relations as a weapon of "information warfare" and that "the *militarisation of the Internet* – both across and within national borders – is official policy in countries that represent more than three billion people, well over a third of the world's population" (Hartley et al. 2017, p. 10).[6]

Central China TV (CCTV) and other Chinese news outlets such as China Radio International (CRI) and the Xinhua News Agency, whose routine practice also includes "promoting the party's policies and ideologies via social and digital media" (Xin 2018, p. 15), have been both developing foreign language services and investing in their international expansion (Flew 2016, p. 284). In 2000, CCTV International (rebranded in 2010 as CCTV News or CCTV-N) began broadcasting in English across China. The channel has been available in the USA since 2002,[7] and CCTV-N has been broadcasting worldwide in English, French, Spanish, Russian and Arabic since 2009. In 2010, Xinhua's own English-language television channel, China News Network News Corporation (CNC), was launched, while "the *People's Daily*, *China Daily* and *Global Times* newspapers all have a strong web presence too, including Twitter feeds" (Rawnsley 2015, p. 277). Furthermore, Chinese media have developed cooperation with international news media groups and invested extensively in infrastructural developments across the world.

Similarly, Russia has invested heavily in international broadcasting (Rawnsley 2015, p. 278). The state-funded Russia Today (RT) television network was launched in 2005 "with content directed to audiences outside the Russian Federation" (Flew 2016, p. 286), developing news services in English but also in Arabic, Spanish, and other languages, and building a strong social media presence. By 2014, the channel had twenty-one bureaus in sixteen nations and had acquired a small but distinctive audience in international news broadcasting. In 2014, a new multimedia news agency, Sputnik, was also launched, with "hubs in major cities across the world and producing broadcasting and web material in 30 languages" (Rawnsley 2015, p. 278), while state-sponsored Russia beyond the Headlines operates a website and, like Chinese newspapers, contributes paid inserts to major Western newspapers.

These huge media efforts are carried out in order to "break the monopoly of the Anglo-Saxon mass media," in the (translated) words of Russian president Vladimir Putin (Bidder 2013), and in the hope of presenting a credible

[5] The Shanghai Cooperation Organisation (SCO), sometimes nicknamed the "Eastern NATO," as of 2018 comprises China, India, Kazakhstan, Kyrgyzstan, Pakistan, Russia, Tajikistan, and Uzbekistan.

[6] Italics in the source text.

[7] In exchange for access to the Chinese market of Rupert Murdoch's News Corporation (Rawnsley 2015, p. 274).

alternative to Western news outlets. Russian outlets focus on critical reporting of Anglophone media rather than on creating a "positive perception" of Russia. RT, for instance, is particularly significant "as an outlet where various alleged Western conspiracies can reliably receive a hearing" (Flew 2016, p. 289). Chinese international broadcasting instead mostly focuses on promoting the image of China abroad (Ke et al. 2004; Zhang 2011), and "foreign-language broadcasts intended for audiences outside China are often allowed to be more critical and liberal in tone and content than their Chinese-language counterparts" (Rawnsley 2015, p. 282). According to Rawnsley (2015, p. 274), however, Russian and Chinese news providers face a "credibility gap" problem, since they are effectively perceived as structurally tied to their governments, and because of the difficulties in moving from older propaganda models to the new dialogical, interactive, and collaborative model of public diplomacy based on social media. Thus, the potential audience size of Chinese and Russian international media is not currently matched by real international viewership (see, e.g., X. Zhang, 2011, p. 63).

Translation into the languages of authoritarian states is carried out by state-controlled media in states where these languages are spoken (e.g., Qin & Zhang 2018), or by institutional and commercial outlets in foreign countries. For instance, *The New York Times* publishes translations of its own articles into Russian (Conway & Vaskivska 2010).

2.3 News Gathering and Dissemination

Translation occurs whenever events deemed worth reporting involve people speaking a language different from that in which these events are reported or commented upon. While in the past such events would take place mostly in "foreign" countries, different languages and cultures increasingly coexist in the same geographical space, especially in large urban areas. News translation does not occur through a "clearly established, unified process" (Holland 2013, p. 336), but rather it may take place at any stage of news production in the overall process of news gathering and dissemination, "depending upon the particular type of news 'event' and where this takes place, the particular news-gathering organization(s) covering it, the languages involved, the human, financial and technological resources available in source and/or target locations, and so on" (Holland 2013, p. 336). It may occur during the reporting or initial-news gathering stage; during the editing stage, where reports are transformed into output text – which may derive from more than one original report; and during the dissemination process, where reports are transferred between different news organizations. In fact, translated news texts might follow different routes, as "[a]ny given item of reported information may be translated at any of these points, or indeed at more than one of them, which may lead to divergent translations of the same original text circulating simultaneously" (Palmer 2009, p. 187). This may happen as regards news stories, feature articles, and editorials across all sections of newspapers, in TV news programs, and in a vast array of Internet-based media formats.

2.3.1 *Translation and News Gathering*

Since the mid-nineteenth century, the main centers of production of international news have been news agencies relying on a staff of foreign correspondents working either in the agency's headquarters located mostly in major European and US cities such as New York, London, and Madrid or sent to gather news in the locations where the events worth reporting were taking place – for instance, Jerusalem, the international city with the third-largest number of foreign correspondents after Washington and Brussels (Bourdon 2016). During the initial news-gathering stage, reporters in "the field" may get their news in the local source language, both through direct experience and by relying on locally produced information. The news, however, may also be produced by journalists located in the country of news dissemination who translate from global news agency bulletins, interviews, social media, and other sources. In fact, the foreign correspondents of some media are what have been called "home-based foreign correspondents" – that is, "journalists who do not leave the country and whose main task is to translate and to edit the information gathered from various sources such as agencies or others news media" (Valdeón 2012a, p. 858). Thus, Valdeón argues, foreign correspondents of newspapers that no longer have permanent reporters outside their country of origin rely on translation in a more invisible way than foreign correspondents abroad.

Print and broadcast reporters are traditionally stratified in a professional hierarchy, the "elite" being "tenured" journalists working for big, often US or European news agencies, television networks, and newspapers; followed by correspondents of less prestigious media outlets; then by freelancers; and finally by photographers, cameramen, and local fixers – who may be referred to as "producers" if recruited as assistants. The borders between these categories, however, are blurred, and their fuzziness is accrued by the growth of the Internet, so that, for instance, depending on the country and medium, some reporters may be "fixers in one medium and actual journalists in another" (Bourdon 2016, p. 764). The term "foreign correspondent" can be used to refer to any journalist working for a media outlet producing news (both hard news and features) for a foreign-language audience, regardless of whether this audience is located abroad or in the same country where the news is gathered – as may be the case, for instance, for reporters writing for minority-language communities in the UK (Archetti 2012, p. 848). Major media outlets may have their own foreign correspondents who write the news on the basis of their personal experience and translating from oral or written sources. Newspapers like *The New York Times*, for instance, have the greatest number of reporters abroad. Smaller media outlets, rather than permanently stationing reporters in a number of outposts, may dispatch a so-called parachute foreign correspondent (Hamilton & Jenner 2004, p. 306) to cover a major story, resort to local or international freelancers (or "stringers," in journalistic parlance), or rely on global news agencies. Local agencies may also be used as news sources, and they will often not only provide their own news but also translate it themselves into English or another main lingua franca to facilitate international circulation. Increasingly, English translations of political statements and commentary – issued by official and nonofficial sources such as news agencies, English language channels, newspapers, and websites in the countries in which the events take place – may be made use of, or compete with global news agencies and other global media (Holland 2013, p. 340).

The main difference between reporters working for news agencies and other foreign correspondents is that the former write primarily for other journalists rather than for the general public. Furthermore, while foreign correspondents write directly in the target language, news agency's reports are likely to be written in one of the main languages and then translated for the target market either at a news agency's regional desk (for major languages like English, French, Spanish, etc.) or by target news producers. Global news agencies and other major outlets produce a stream of news that is translated into local languages, and these texts then are used as sources for most foreign news published in local papers. At international agencies, news stories are translated either at the place of production or elsewhere – for instance, at the European headquarters – to be transformed into target local news stories by local media outlets and incorporated into local news production for the target audience and readership.

Foreign correspondents located in the field, either working for international news agencies or outsourcing media, may read and speak the language of the people involved in the news, or may resort to translation to gather information from media in the local language, and incorporate the translation in their story, both by "literally" translating from one or more source texts and by summarizing or extracting data from them. When reporters do not speak the local language, they may resort to local translators and interpreters, who translate out of the source language, to provide translations of written texts as well as textual renditions of what they hear from local informants. Foreign correspondents usually rely on a network of more or less trusted local contacts and "fixers" who provide translation and interpreting services (Holland 2013,

p. 338).[8] Their work "consists of advising journalists about the content of local media and interpreting interviews with relevant sources of information; such translation commonly consists of summary rather than in extenso translation" (Palmer 2009, p. 187). Translation in this context may be indirect and go through multiple languages and stages – for example, "from a local language into a more commonly spoken national language and on into the target language or a transnational language" (Palmer 2009, p. 187), as when a local language in Darfur is typically translated into Arabic and then into the final target language by a second interpreter. Palmer and Fontan (2007, p. 11) report that, on the whole, fixers are more likely to stress the importance of word-for-word translation than journalists, who often find it time-consuming and unnecessary, with the exception of interviews with politicians, where they are more interested in the exact nuances of statements.

According to Hamilton and Jenner (2004, p. 302), "transformations of the media environment have led to systemic changes in how we receive news and information from other countries . . . [and] changed the way in which foreign news is reported and consumed." Since a laptop computer and a camera or even a mobile phone may be all that is needed for a journalist, larger news organizations have been able to cut costs by relying on a lighter organizational structure, and at the same time, new media technologies have lowered the economic barriers of entry to publishing and broadcasting, allowing smaller news organizations, including from poorer countries, to have their own foreign correspondents. Recourse to foreign correspondents may vary depending on a number of issues, including pressure of time and linguistic resources available – i.e., languages known by journalists in the newsroom and the availability of quick recourse to external resources, such as the possibility of outsourcing "exotic" languages to individual translators and translation agencies (Holland 2013).

Since the beginning of the twenty-first century, the number of foreign correspondents per news organization has been declining, and a number of them have closed their foreign desks. However, while the "alleged disappearance of correspondents seems supported by the figures concerning the closure of foreign bureaus" (Archetti 2012, pp. 847–848), there has also been an increase in the number of stringers/freelancers, especially in smaller locations. The average age of correspondents, often working as a "one-man-band" for several organizations, has decreased, while new work practices have taken hold also as a consequence of less stable contractual and financial

[8] The role and agency of fixers and interpreters, with particular reference to situations of war and conflict, has been discussed in a number of publications – including Inghilleri (2009), Footitt (2012), Palmer (2007), Dragovic-Drouet (2007), Bishara (2013), Footitt and Kelly (2012), Footitt and Tobia (2013), and Palmer (2019).

arrangements (Archetti 2012, p. 851).[9] Social media such as YouTube, Facebook, and Twitter are increasingly treated as news sources, particularly during breaking news coverage or crisis news events, although the monitoring of social platforms has become part of the daily journalistic routine (Paulussen & Harder 2014). Businesses, institutions, or celebrities use social media accounts as promotional platforms, and the content they produce is often translated and incorporated into news reports. For instance, Twitter accounts are used as sources of "translingual quotations,"[10] which are often reported in translation together with a screenshot of the source tweet, thus giving visibility to translation and acting as "indicators of credibility in light of the high level of uncertainty which characterizes the production and circulation of digital news" (Hernández Guerrero 2020, p. 382).

While freelancers tend to resort to different news-gathering routines, relying to a larger extent on online and social media sources, they often try to add value to their reporting by providing specific angles and tailoring news for specific home audiences. Thus, rather than producing "churnalism," the "shallow journalism" that may result from the endless recycling of online sources, they often find news stories which are not covered by the main news organizations, sometimes also producing news independently through their personal blogs and social media accounts. According to Archetti (2012, p. 853), "the very struggle for economic survival in an extremely competitive environment that is causing the shrinking of foreign desks is also leading to greater reliance on foreign journalists." The availability of online material has not resulted in the replacement of first-hand reporting, but, rather, in the offer of "more foreign news, with more varied and unique insights, across more platforms" (Archetti 2012, p. 854).

This new type of foreign correspondent includes many locally recruited journalists with multicultural profiles, such as naturalized immigrants sent as foreign correspondents to their countries or communities of origin (Baumann et al. 2011b), possibly resulting in conflicting loyalties and identities. Correspondents are also affected by the feedback of their audiences, especially networked diasporic groups interacting directly with them through digital communication technologies. Whereas the interaction with audiences was previously mediated by the editors back home, now "journalists have direct contact with audiences, at least with the more committed or critical audience members" (Bourdon 2015, p. 772), while "[a]lternative media are radicalizing

[9] Archetti's ethnographic study is based on in-depth interviews with foreign correspondents based in London.

[10] Haapanen and Perrin (2019, p. 16) use the term "translingual quoting" to refer to the "process of news-writing in which the original discourse is translated during quoting."

journalistic practices with their progressive sourcing strategies, 'native reporters', the significance of 'active witnessing' and a consideration of 'social movement news' in mainstream media culture" (Ustad Figenschou 2012 p. 358). According to Bourdon (2015, p. 773), foreign correspondents "might thus become less like reporters for a specific nation and more like multicultural mediators for citizens who are not so different from themselves."

Foreign news is often first translated into English, and then from English into a different target language, possibly together with information extracted from media both in the source and target language, both of which may not be English. Foreign correspondents in the field, or stationed in the organization headquarters, provide English texts by extracting information from text in other languages, and from there, they are disseminated to either an international or a local audience, often in languages other than English.

Sometimes it may be possible to follow upstream a news cycle and trace back a particular piece of news and the agents (e.g., local journalists, freelance translators, interpreters, foreign correspondents, fixers) involved in its production. Bellos argues that "[a] report of the latest speech by the Iranian president, for example, could perfectly well be attributed to a named journalist's adaptation of a Reuters English-language wire originating in Kuwait based on a report in Arabic from Al Jazeera that had provided the information from listening to a radio broadcast in Farsi from Teheran" (Bellos 2011, p. 129). At other times, however, it may be more difficult to trace the exact route followed by a piece of news. Thus, a news story about Brazilian elections published in an Italian newspaper may come from a news agency wire from AFP (translated from French) and other international sources, mostly in English, originating in the field, as well as from a story written by an AP correspondent in Washington (using various sources) and translated into Italian by the Italian news agency ANSA and published in various Italian outlets. Part of the text may derive from sources in the foreign locale and local language – such as foreign news agencies, newspapers and social media – some of which may provide information translated into English for an international readership. Or part of the text could have originated in a story published in Portuguese in an online newspaper in Belo Horizonte, then translated by a machine-translation system, and arrived at through a comment retweeted by a Spanish reporter followed by the Italian journalist.

2.3.2 Translation and News Dissemination

At the dissemination end, translation practices vary according to media outlet type, the languages and language directions involved, and the place of dissemination. Most news is produced in large cities, where global news agencies and international news outlets, as well as media targeting the local but multicultural urban areas, are located. Like the cities in early modern Europe postal networks, urban areas in the twenty-first century act as the nodes where networks of translators establish links and spread the news.

Hernández Guerrero (2017, p. 63) distinguishes between publications that totally or partially reproduce the content of a parent publication and media that generate their own content but use translation to produce new information based on journalistic material from external sources. "Translated," "international" versions of US and European newspapers, magazines, and news sites fall within the first group, while the second group comprises all national media insofar as they include international news in their information offer. In the following sections, I first provide an overview of these two groups; then I look at the changing nature of translation practices in the digital environment. In Section 2.3.2.1, I focus on international versions of news media outlets; in Section 2.3.2.2, I look at news translation in some national contexts; and in Section 2.3.2.3, I discuss translation practices in different types of online news media.

2.3.2.1 International News Media Newspapers such as *The New York Times* and *The Herald Tribune* publish international versions that are produced in New York in collaboration with European newspapers – for instance, with *El Mundo* in Spain and *La Repubblica* in Italy. US-based magazines such as *Elle*, *Cosmopolitan*, *National Geographic*, and *Vanity Fair* also publish international versions for European markets that are, to a large extent, based on translated content. The magazine *Newsweek* is published in several different language editions, including Japanese (Barnard 2000) and Korean (Kang 2007). The *Chinese Financial Times* (*CFT*), based on the Nikkei-owned British newspaper *Financial Times* (*FT*), has been published in China since 2003, and "[a]s of early 2018 *FT Chinese.com* claimed 2.6 million registered users" (Liu 2019, p. 2). The French monthly current affairs newspaper *Le Monde Diplomatique* publishes twenty-nine international editions in eighteen languages.

Some media propose international versions of national newspapers targeted at expatriate, migrant, and diasporic communities. For instance, *Il Globo*, a newspaper published in Melbourne since 1958, contains (mostly) translations from English to Italian and caters to first- and second-generation Italian migrants as well as to learners of Italian as a second language (Aragrande 2018). European newspapers such as *El País*, *SUR*, *Suddeutsche Zeitung*, and *Le Monde* publish English-language editions for an international readership both abroad and at home, with a selection of local and international news translated from the Spanish, German, or French editions. *Le Monde* also publishes international versions translated from French into Spanish and Italian. These editions are weeklies or monthlies rather than dailies, and are often distributed with national newspapers.

Newspapers in English in non-English-speaking countries may primarily be targeted either at an international readership or at local readers. An example of translation from a minority language into English for local purposes is *The Vietnamese News*, a government-funded, English-language newspaper whose news stories are translated from Vietnamese and whose intended readers are tourists and expatriates (van Leeuwen 2006). In Taiwan, approximately 30 percent of the readers of the *Taipei Times* are from Taiwan and other Asian nations and 70 percent are from the USA, the UK, Canada, Germany, France, and other countries, because the primary purpose of the *Taipei Times* is to promote Taiwan's international visibility, while the intended readers of the *Liberty Times* are mainly Taiwanese who support Taiwan's independence and are concerned about sovereignty (Chen 2011a, p. 699).

2.3.2.2 National News Media A fairly well-investigated scenario with reference to the role of translation in a national news media context is that of Spain, thanks in particular to a number of studies by María José Hernández Guerrero, Roberto Valdeón, and others (see, e.g., Cortés Zaborras & Hernández Guerrero 2005).

Hernández Guerrero (2009, 2012, 2016) examines translation practices in the Spanish national press, with particular reference to reports and opinion articles published in the foreign news section. Agency reports account for the largest share of text published in this section, followed by articles by foreign correspondents and, to a lesser extent, translations of stories published in foreign media. The two main Spanish newspapers, *El País* and *El Mundo*, subscribe to Reuters, AFP, and EFE (Hernández Guerrero 2009, pp. 66–67) and receive information in English (Reuters), French (*El País* subscribes to the French wire), and Spanish. Foreign correspondents often use as source text stories provided in translation by global or local news agencies, or translate them from a number of news sources, usually themselves the result of translation. Translations from foreign media – i.e., articles that are attributed to external sources – are generally taken from a range of publications connected by collaborative projects, economic links, or ideological affinity. In the case of *El País*, translated articles are mostly taken from *The New York Times* and *Le Monde*, whereas *El Mundo* includes among its sources *The Guardian* (and *The Observer*), *The Times* (and *The Sunday Times*), *Libération*, and *Il Corriere della Sera*.

Translated opinion articles are either commissioned from regular contributors (about 50 percent) or nonhabitual contributors (about 30 percent), or are taken from syndicate services like Tribune Media Services or Project

Syndicate (about 20 percent) (Hernández Guerrero 2012, p. 962).[11] According to Hernández Guerrero, while the inclusion of well-known international intellectuals of different opinions allows the publication to legitimate a claim to neutrality, the selection of translations sustains and reinforces the editorial policy of the newspaper and its position with respect to the events. The global news service Project Syndicate has been the largest independent, nonprofit distributor of opinion articles in the world since 1994, and many of its articles are reproduced throughout the world with only minor changes in publications such as *El País*. Project Syndicate commissions articles in English and then translates them into twelve languages.[12] Some articles, written by speakers of other languages, are first translated into English and then from English into the other languages. The source texts are copyrighted, and translations, which are acknowledged as such, tend to be rather literal. According to Hernández Guerrero (2016, p. 58), the aim of the organization, which is funded by international foundations and has a distinct liberal Western bias, is to retain a global hegemonic position in the selection and distribution of opinion articles through translation.

Different types of national publications that are (almost) entirely or partly based on translated text include magazines like the Italian weekly *Internazionale*, in which almost all articles are translated from English, French, German, Spanish, and Portuguese (Bani 2006; Manfredi 2018; Troqe & Marchan 2017). Bilingual newspapers and magazines are also published on a regular or occasional basis. For instance, "the German news magazine *Der Spiegel* published texts in German and English side by side in its issue devoted to the Brexit referendum (11 June 2016)" (Schäffner 2018, p. 328), whereas *El Periodico de Catalunia* features articles translated from Spanish into Catalan (Hernández Guerrero 2009, pp. 16–21). National newspapers and magazines may also include translation from a minority language spoken by a diasporic community. For instance, Hamill (1998, p. 107) reports that in the 1990s, *The Daily News* had a "weekly page of excerpts from the immigrant press," which was translated by staff members and freelancers into English in the UK.

While news producers at national newspapers and broadcast stations "work in the space between the global and the national" (Clausen 2004, p. 25), global news agencies and international news services such as the CNN, Euronews, the BBC, Al Jazeera International, Russia Today, Xinhua, Deutsche Welle, Press TV, Sky News, and others operate both as "wholesale" news providers,

[11] Based on a corpus of forty-seven translations out of total of seventy-three opinion articles published in *El País* during a two-month period of the so-called Arab Spring of 2011.

[12] However, research shows that, for some languages, translations are carried out at the target side (Davier & van Doorslaer 2018, p. 245).

typically accessed by news "retailers," and at the level of "retail," as their foreign language services are accessed directly by the public. For instance, CNN, BBC, and Reuters all feature a Spanish version of their websites. Most news reports posted on the CNN's Spanish-language website in early 2004 were literal translations of reports posted on the English-language CNN website, and the texts posted were often identified as news agency dispatches, both in their Spanish and English versions, while reports posted on the BBC Spanish website were flagged as translations and attributed to specific authors from the English website (Valdeón 2005b, 2005a, 2007b, 2007a, 2008).

Western democracies are characterized by a varied offer of international news from a range of different public and private outlets, whereas in China, the translation of foreign news is organized according to a rather different model. *Reference News* (参考消息, Cankao Xiaoxi), which presents itself as a "world digest," is the newspaper with the largest daily circulation in China and the only official and authorized source of information about news originating outside the country (Xia 2019, pp. 4–10). The Editorial Department of *Reference News* (RN) "is an internal unit of Xinhua News Agency, which has always been an official organ of the State Council and overseen by the Publicity Department of the Communist Party of China (CCPPD)" (Xia 2019, p. 156). Translations "of foreign news articles written in dozens of languages, and collected from most of the major international wire services and foreign national news media" (Pan 2014a, p. 550) make up about 90 percent of the content of the newspaper, the rest being reports in Chinese from outside mainland China. News is translated from more than thirty languages and 100 countries, though the vast majority is translated from English (more than 80 percent). Most news (almost 60 percent) is translated from reports published by the main global agencies (AFP, Reuters, AP) (Xia 2019, pp. 74–75), and news related to China represents about one-fourth of all news published (around seventy items daily [Xia 2019]). In contemporary China, news media struggle between the demands of party propaganda and market forces. Though media organizations such as *Reference News* are formally private and run for profit, they receive subsidies and concessions from the state, and must strictly follow government directives as laid out in laws, regulations and guidelines and implemented under the State Administration of Press, Publication, Radio, Film, and Television (SAPPRFT), the agency responsible for managing publishing in China. Although, according to Xia (2019, p. 109), censorship is somewhat more lenient in the case of *Reference News* than that of other government-controlled newspapers, like in all other media whose function is to be the "mouthpiece of the government," "[c]ensorship is massively exercised in [*Reference News*] news production to control the information and ideas circulated among its readers" (Xia 2019, p. 136). Translation may also serve internal political purposes. According to a senior editor at *Reference News*, for instance, on March 4, 1982, *Reference News* translated as "Origin of Political Fairy Tale – Great Director Deng Xiaoping was not Dead" a report published on February 14 in the Italian newspaper *Il Tempo*. The newspaper, which reported a conversation between Deng Xiaoping and the Italian minister Vittorino Colombo, was instructed to publish the story by President Deng Xiaoping himself, to dispel a rumor that he was seriously ill (Xia 2019, p. 141).

Reference News's website has been active since 2012, and a streaming app for mobile devices was launched a few years later (Liu 2019, p. 2). The website publishes reports from the printed version as well as from partner websites of news outlets such as Xinhua, *China News*, *China Daily*, China Radio International (CRI), and *International Herald Leader* "after rewriting, integrating, and technical elaboration to avoid copyright infringement. The whole procedure . . . is followed by a triple review and proofreading process" (Xia 2019, p. 144).

2.3.2.3 New(s) Media The radical change induced by digital media in the context of globalization has brought about a new scenario in which the Internet has become the privileged means of social communication. New forms of reporting and translation are practiced by news producers, ranging from commercial operations managed by professionals to low-budget independent news outlets run by amateur citizen media organizations. Such usually Internet-only news providers occupy a growing niche of specialist information, catering to the needs of groups with particular ideological views and minorities such as diaspora communities, who can access news outlets with which they have a cultural or linguistic affinity.

For instance, Hernández Guerrero has investigated the role of translation in the online news websites Huffington Post (Hernández Guerrero 2013) and Mediapart (Hernández Guerrero 2017), again with reference to the Spanish context. The two news websites – which mix traditional periodical journalism with a platform open to reader participation, especially through opinion blogs – represent two different models of multilingual news production in which translations are offered as a service provided to a community, which also interacts through postings in the local language.

Started in the USA in 2005, The Huffington Post (renamed HuffPost in 2017) has, since 2011, opened various international versions in different countries in collaboration with major national news publishing groups by exporting their technology and communication model based on a combination of original articles and contents from a network of blogs by an involved community of readers. Each edition is produced by independent local staff and includes both original content and translation of blog posts published in different national editions (and, in a minority of cases, in other blogs). Translation policies differ in the various language editions regarding the selection of material translated, the (lack of) acknowledgment of translators, and paratextual publishing practices.[13] Translators include both in-house and freelance commercial translators, and activist, engaged translators who participate in the selection of the material to be translated (Hernández Guerrero 2013, p. 125). According to Hernández Guerrero, the selection of translated articles in the Spanish version of The Huffington Post shows that translation is used mostly to disseminate and bring to a wider audience the opinion of writers/bloggers in line with the editorial, liberal line of the news outlet.

The French Mediapart is, instead, a paid-for, publicity-free independent newspaper that provides investigative reporting in the form of articles written by the staff as well as by subscribers or members. As part of its communication strategy, the news website offers English and Spanish editions, which are related but remain independent from the French site. The editorial staff at Mediapart English and Mediapart Español autonomously select and translate French articles while, at the same time, offering translations of their articles into French (about one article a day out of six or seven published on average in the French site). While material from the French parent site grants them the prestige of the brand name, "the bulk of the interest in the English and Spanish sites is on the participatory section, which allows readers to access content with which they feel a connection and play an active role in the creation of the site" (Hernández Guerrero 2017, p. 302).

Commercial and institutional news sources, both in democratic and authoritarian states, also face international competition from a different group of organizations and individuals involved in the process of news gathering and dissemination – that is, "monitoring organizations, such as government departments, NGOs and activist/advocacy groups, which circulate reports to clients, colleagues or supporters and potential supporters" (Palmer 2009, p. 187). Schäffner et al. (2014) show that the translation of press releases and other documents at national, supranational, and nongovernmental news-producing organizations is usually carried out in a collective, anonymous, and standardized manner. Tesseur (2017) investigates translation activities at NGOs; a significant portion is still carried out by volunteer translators, though large organizations such as Amnesty International are increasingly making recourse to professional translators.

As with institutional media, translation plays an important role in the production of information by public and private companies, organizations,

[13] Thus, for instance, the US edition publishes very few translations as compared to European editions (especially the French one), while the Italian edition mostly translates blogs "distributed" in the US version of the online news site (Hernández Guerrero 2013, pp. 121–123). Translators are never acknowledged in the US and Italian versions, and rarely in the others. Editions differ also in how they translate titles (which, in some cases, may be altered radically) and deal with hypertextual links and images.

and individuals, who disseminate information via dedicated news agencies and social networks, accessed either directly or through aggregators. Inghilleri (2017, pp. 32–33) provides an overview of a number of organizations promoted by activists that provide translation services with the aim of helping to "establish and maintain rights-respecting economic, social, cultural, and political institutions and practices." These include, among others, Tlaxcala, a "network of translators for linguistic diversity" (Talens 2010, p. 22), which focuses on "producing and circulating written translations of texts that they themselves select" (Baker 2013, p. 32), and Project Lingua, the translation division of the nonprofit news aggregator Global Voices that "amplifies Global Voices stories by translating them into dozens of languages, with the help of hundreds of volunteers".[14] Translation is among the most important activities of the citizen journalism site, and translators play a paramount role, since "by selecting texts [they] influence the configuration of the pool of themes discussed" (Tyulenev 2018, pp. 13–15).

Both governmental and nongovernmental sources in non-English-speaking areas often offer English translations of their releases to communicate with the international community. For instance, reporting of the hostage disaster in Beslan on September 1, 2004, was made available in English translation by RIA-Novosti, a major state-controlled Russian news agency, as well as by two alternative news agencies – Kavkazcenter, the website of the Chechen armed resistance, and Caucasian Knot, a news site close to a Russian human rights society (Harding 2011, 2012a, 2012b).

While research in news translation has mostly foregrounded activities and practices carried out by professional news organizations and journalists, nonprofessional/collaborative/volunteer/user-generated news translation practices (see Jiménez-Crespo [2017] for a discussion of terminology), favored by digital media through crowdsourcing in social networks, are increasingly gaining ground. In a series of pioneering studies, for instance, Pérez-González (2010, 2012b, 2012a, 2014b) examines the role played by fansubber networks of activist translators in producing and distributing subtitled videos of political interviews. As a case study, he discusses a translation project that involved the Spanish subtitling of a political interview first broadcasted by BBC News 24. The project was promoted by an activist community of engaged individuals, Ansarclub. The aim was to promote the circulation of a potentially controversial interview, which was not being aired in full in Spanish institutional news media, in order to seize the "opportunity to lambast the Spanish Prime Minister and, in so doing, reinforce their own narratives" (Pérez-González 2010, p. 276). As a fluid amateur translator network of

[14] https://globalvoices.org/lingua/ (last accessed on October 16, 2020).

nonprofessional subtitlers, Ansarclub subsequently carried out further "fansubbing" projects, thus engaging in the production and circulation of political content. Pérez-González argues that, by capitalizing on the potential of networked communication to exploit their collective intelligence, amateur translation networks play an important role in the process of media convergence, and "the proliferation of co-creational practices pertaining to the production, translation and distribution of subtitled media content blur the distinction between the roles of producer and consumer in political news interviews" (Pérez-González 2014b, p. 202).

Tsai (2015) looks at the use of YouTube downloaded videos in news programs broadcasted by commercial TV stations, in which news translators increasingly play the role of journalists. Adopting an extensive understanding of the concept of translation as remediation (Bolter & Grusin 1999) – i.e., the "repurposing" of content in one medium into another medium, in relation also to the concepts of intersemiotic, intralingual translation (cf. Section 1.3.1.) and recontextualization (cf. Section 3.3.3), Welbers and Opgenhaffen (2019) discuss how the coverage of news about immigration in national newspapers in the Netherlands differs from that on the newspapers' Facebook pages.

Social networks function as news sources when written texts, images, and videos posted by political and social actors or citizens are recirculated, commented upon, and incorporated in news discourse, including in newspapers and TV news programs. For instance, Hernández Guerrero (2020) investigates the translation of tweets that are inserted in news texts, accompanied by screenshots of the original tweets. She looks at the strategies used by journalists/translators to translate tweets by the former US President Trump that were quoted in a blog published by the Spanish digital newspaper *El País* and argues that this practice makes more visible the use of translation in the news. President Trump's direct communication through social media and the translation of his tweets in other languages has, in fact, attracted much attention. Studies include research into the ethical and linguistic challenges posed by the translation of Trump's language (Viennot 2017, 2019), a study of politeness and impoliteness strategies as regards translation into Arabic (Abudayeh & Dubbati 2020), and a "playful and enlightening" (Bloomfield & Robert-Foley 2017, p. 469) application of the model of Oulipo to the translation of a number of Trump's tweets.

In authoritarian countries such as China and Singapore, where the state exercises ample control over communication technologies and where commercial and independent websites and social media are selectively blocked, "it is not unknown for people to resort to using Virtual Private Networks (VPNs) to access banned websites" (Lim 2017, p. 44). Thus, officially sponsored news reporting can be challenged "in an instant by film and photographs taken by witnesses or 'citizen journalists' on a mobile telephone, uploaded to the internet and distributed around the world in seconds, even as the recorded event is unfolding" (Rawnsley 2015, p. 281), and digital technology can be used to mobilize dissent – for instance, to organize mass strikes and protests in China (Lim 2017, p. 44).

Institutionally multilingual countries such as Canada and Switzerland and international political bodies such as the EU promote policies of multilingualism, which are enacted in the media through translation. A policy of multilingualism may, however, be pursued or promoted by a news organization anywhere large enough communities of multilingual speakers provide an audience (see the BBC multilingual policy in the UK). In cosmopolitan cities, where large communities of multilingual speakers use English along with other languages, translation operates in a context that favors what Kelly-Holmes terms hybrid multilingualism. Kelly-Holmes defines this concept in opposition to a more traditional model of parallel multilingualism – i.e., the coexistence of internally coherent cultures and groups alongside each other. Hybrid multilingualism appeals to the concept of community of practice rather than that of speech community, in a move "from fixed locations and bounded communities to groups constituted in terms of mutual engagement for a particular purpose." The online production and distribution of information through news websites and social networks is instrumental to heteroglossic practices that involve a mixing of languages as well as of verbal and visual semiotic resources and challenge the categorization of people into national and regional groups "by having the capacity to address speech communities without regard to territory" (Kelly-Holmes 2012, p. 334). In this context, "media products leak easily across designated 'linguistic borders,' thus making the creation of homogenous speech communities more an aspiration than a reality in many cases" (Kelly-Holmes 2012, p. 343). Kelly-Holmes refers to "super-diversity" as the recognition that the focus has shifted from a view of multiculturalism conceived as parallel monolingualism to one that acknowledges a more complex situation characterized by internal diversity and hybridity.

2.4 Issues and Concepts in News Media Translation Research

While translation norms and practices in the contexts of the news media may vary considerably and be subject to different parameters and work conditions, they generally differ from those associated with literary and religious translation, and challenge traditional categories of translation. In the nineteenth century, Schleiermacher distinguished between the job of the (literary) translator (*Übersetzer*), who deals with art and science, and that of the interpreter (*Dolmetscher*), a term that includes the translator of worldly texts such as "newspaper articles and ordinary travel brochures" (Schleiermacher 1997, p. 226), and for whom translating is "a merely mechanical task" (p. 227).[15] Since it lacked the central traits of translation – i.e., those of religious or literary translation – news translation was not classified as translation "proper" by Schleiermacher, but as *Dolmetschen*, a lower practice closer to oral translation and requiring neither hermeneutics nor creativity.

Various scholars have noted that the practices of news translation blur the boundaries between written translation and interpreting (Bielsa & Bassnett 2009, p. 16; Holland 2013, p. 337; Tsai 2005, pp. 66–67). As argued by Bassnett (2005a, p. 125),

> what happens in news stories comes much closer to what happens to texts that are transmitted orally, i.e. through interpreters. An interpreter, rendering a speech into another language, reshapes, alters emphases, adds and subtracts where necessary, seeks to maintain a suitable linguistic register, in short recreates a version for the target audience. New [sic] reporters appear to operate in the same way, with the emphasis on the destination of the story.

While translation theories developed with reference to literary and religious translation have not offered many conceptual and terminological tools to news media translation research (though see the discussion of domestication in Section 2.5.1), Skopos theory has often been seen as a viable framework within which to accommodate news translation (Bazzi 2009; Bielsa & Bassnett 2009; Schäffner 2012a; Shi 2014). Bassnett (2006), for instance, holds that "skopos theory seems to be undergoing a revival among younger researchers who find it a useful way of talking about intercultural and interlingual shifts". Bazzi (2009, p. 187) argues that general concepts and terminology of Skopos theory can offer "practical explanations for the kinds of translation produced in the media world."

The Greek word *skopos* was introduced by Hans Vermeer (1978) as a technical term to foreground the purpose or aim of a translation. Translation is seen as a form of action, with an aim that leads to a result called "translatum" (Vermeer 2000, p. 221). According to Vermeer's theory, later incorporated in Reiβ and Vermeer's (1984) general theory of translation, a translation is a complex action carried out by experts to produce a functionally appropriate or "adequate" text, which has to achieve a particular communicative purpose. It is the intended purpose of the target text that determines translation methods and strategies, while the source text loses its centrality and is seen merely as information offer, which must be tailored to the expectations of receivers in the target culture in accordance with a specific translation commission. Skopos

[15] It should be noted that Dolmetschen, which did not have its current sense of "oral translation," was also the word used by Luther to refer to his translations of the Bible.

theory and Holz-Mänttäri's (1984) coeval but independently elaborated theory of translatorial action were conceived primarily with reference to technical and scientific translation and to a professional world in which the purpose of each translation is laid down by a client, and the commission is determined by a set of implicit or explicit specifications.

From a Skopos theory perspective, the function of the translation may be very similar or very different from that of the source text, since translation is considered as "a new offer of information in the target culture about some information offered in the source culture and language" (Nord 1997, p. 26). Thus, while "maximally faithful imitation" (Vermeer 2000, p. 228) of the source text may be most common in literary translation, this is not the only possible type of relationship between source and target text. The function of a target text may be very different from that of the source text, resulting in very little intertextual coherence between the two, since coherence with the source text is subordinated to coherence with the target situation. The "dethronement" (Nord 1997, p. 25) of the source text operated by Skopos theory allows for a wider concept of translation which includes translation as practiced in the news media, where the status of the source text(s) and its/their relation to the translation is often rather uncertain.

2.4.1 *Source Text's (In)Stability*

The uncertain relation of source text to translation means that, in news translation, there may be no specific source text to go to. A news agency item, for instance, can be described as "actually a patchwork of many different sources, many of which were originally in a different language" (Davier 2014, p. 58). News reports produced by the same agency in different languages are most often not direct translations of each other, since global news agencies "do not typically translate news reports produced in one language into the other languages of the agency's news-wires. Rather, different reports are produced in different languages for different markets" (Scammell 2018, p. 23). Scammell (2018, p. 43), for instance, shows that reports about French news events produced for Reuters' English-language newswire draw on French sources about the same events rather than being "direct" or "proper" translations of Reuters French reports. Possible sources for quotations would include Reuters reports published in French on the same news story on the same day, material published by other outlets, official speech transcripts, and television footage.

In some cases, it may be difficult to identify a specific source text because a piece of news may incorporate information originally released as multilingual versions by a news source as part of their communication strategy. For instance, a press release by an ONG may be released in English but also translated in other languages for circulation in non-English national news media (Tesseur 2014), while the text of a public statement may be provided by governmental sources in both a local language and in English translation, and the two texts may sometimes differ quite considerably (Holland 2006).

Similar to agency wires, a news report in a national outlet is not necessarily related to one source text alone but can be produced by combining information from various sources, by cutting and reordering paragraphs from "agency wires, correspondents' reports, and articles published by associated media or simply by other outlets" (Valdeón 2015a, p. 451). News agencies do not usually require media that subscribe to a wire service to credit them or preserve the integrity of the texts in any way. National media can either publish in part or in full reports from news agencies they subscribe to, or use them as sources in stories written by local reporters. In fact, news wires favor the selection of only some parts or paragraphs in that they are usually structured as an inverted pyramid, with paragraphs containing essential information preceding those with background and secondary information (Bielsa & Bassnett 2009, p. 69). Subscribers can use only part of, paraphrase, summarize, translate, and reorder information.

Though news agencies are sometimes credited for stories published in translation, when text from news agencies is used as source, translation may not be explicitly acknowledged even when a text is a literal rendition of a specific source. While this would amount to plagiarism in other textual genres – for example, in academic writing – it is accepted practice in news writing. The official guidelines of many news organizations require transparency in the attribution of sources in translated news – i.e., the clear identification of a source of information, including when these are other media – and warn against plagiarism. Large news media providers tend to provide an attribution when they use facts gathered by another organization. For instance, *The New York Times* provides attribution even for AP reporting, though as a subscriber, it would not be required to do so (Hong 2021, p. 793). However, not all news providers abide by their often self-imposed principles and guidelines, so, for instance, in translation from Korean into English in South Korean newspapers, attribution can sometimes be rather vague. Hong (2021) argues that a failure to acknowledge other media as sources of translated articles deletes information about the setting and weakens the authoritativeness of a source by obscuring reference to his or her hierarchical status.

Hernández Guerrero (2009) distinguishes between three main types of news items published in the international news section of Spanish dailies, depending on their relationship (or lack thereof) with a specific source text or source texts. A foreign news article in Spanish can be either an instance of "compilative" translation, a term Hernández Guerrero borrows from Toury (2012, p. 100) to refer to information collated from various source texts – or it can be the result of rewriting "strictu sensu" – whereas a source text has been used merely as a starting point to create a new text; or it can be a "fragmented" translation – i.e., a translation of only part of a source text. Translated articles in the opinion section are instead often copyrighted texts by prestigious foreign authors and are usually translated in their entirety. Based on her data, Hernández Guerrero proposes a distinction between stable and unstable sources in news translation. The former are identified in texts written by prestigious authors and protected by copyright, and translations of stable sources often feature as editorial and opinion columns. Blog entries can usually be classified as opinion articles and, therefore, as "stable" sources (Hernández Guerrero 2013, p. 125). News genres such as interviews would instead classify as unstable sources, in that they are usually selectively edited and reorganized when published in translation (Hernández Guerrero 2010). However, Valdeón (2015a) argues that a binary distinction between stable and unstable sources is unproductive; he shows that sometimes supposedly stable sources such as signed editorials are in fact heavily edited in translation, while rather literal translations with identifiable source texts include reposts found on some news translation websites or multilingual media websites (Valdeón 2009). An unequivocal identification of "stable sources" is, in fact, difficult even in the case of direct quotations. Matsushita (2019b) – who focuses on the translation of "direct quotations" in Japanese newspapers, defined as "literal representations of the original speech ... clearly identifiable because of the presence of grammatical markers such as quotation marks" (Matsushita 2019b, p. 15) – acknowledges, first, that the identification of "stable sources" does not apply to text surrounding the quotations; second, that such a definition only applies to hard news articles and not to other journalist genres, such as "opinion pieces, commentaries, and editorials" (Matsushita 2019b, p. 84), where even direct quotations are "often paraphrased versions of those already reported in previous reports" (Matsushita 2019b, p. 84); and, finally, that there may be exceptions – i.e., the example by Holland (2006) quoted previously (see also Zanettin 2016b).

The media guidelines of a large range of state and private news organizations – from those of Reuters, the BBC, and *The New York Times* to those of *Reference News* – highlight the prominence of the concept of "faithfulness," and all claim to be faithful. Translated news texts, however, "are not straightforward and faithful reproductions of their source texts, as often assumed by lay-people" (Schäffner 2008, p. 22). Matsushita (2019b) shows that even in the case of translingual direct quotations, which in newspaper guidelines are usually defined as "faithful reproductions" of what a speaker actually said, a literal, word-for-word translation is the exception rather than the rule. Both official guidelines and practitioners, in fact, also highlight the importance of fluency when translating quotes – i.e., the importance of using idiomatic language (see, e.g., Bielsa and Bassnett 2009; Matsushita 2019b; Scammell 2018). According to Haapanen and Perrin (2019, p. 23),

> Quotes perform important functions in journalistic narration: they enhance the reliability, credibility, and objectivity of an article and characterize the person quoted, to mention but a few. . . . [J]ournalists primarily aim to execute their preliminary idea of what the emerging story should and could look like, and to produce quotes that fulfil their function in the storyline accordingly. Providing faithful reproductions of original utterances and intentions is less important.

In the end "faithfulness" only amounts to a compromise with limitations of space and time – i.e., a balancing act between "speediness, accuracy, and conciseness" (Matsushita 2019b, p. 137).

Van Doorslaer (2010c) argues that the status of the source text disintegrates in this multisource situation, and that the multiplication of source texts, which makes it hardly possible to reconstruct the production of a target news text, is paralleled by the uncertain status of the author. The concept of authorship in the field of journalistic translation is rendered problematic not only by the multiplication of source texts, but also by the multiauthored nature of many journalistic target texts (Davier et al. 2018, p. 157). Multiple agents – including translators, revisers, editors, and experts – are often involved and cooperate in the production of the news, and "[i]n news agencies in particular, in the media in general, but also in news producing organizations such as NGOs, it is the rule rather than the exception that several people collaborate on the same news report" (Davier & van Doorslaer 2018, p. 242).

2.4.2 Translation (In)Visibility

Even though translation has always been part and parcel of newswriting, translation activities and practices have, over the last two centuries, increasingly become invisible (Valdeón 2012a) and are currently largely overlooked by both news producers and consumers. Thus, translation is often not acknowledged in journalistic writing, even when reporting speech that is obviously translated from another language, as in the case of official reports, interviews, press conference, and political speeches (Federici 2010, 2011; Gu 2018; Matsushita 2019b; Schäffner 2008, 2010, 2012b; Zanettin 2016b; Zheng & Ren 2018). The words used by translators and interpreters are taken as if they were the actual words spoken by political actors, and it is on the basis of these words as reported by the news media that positive or negative reactions ensue.

However, while translation is often invisible in the news, some news items in national media may be clearly presented as translations, with an identifiable source text, author, and possibly translator. International versions of newspapers such as *The New York Times* and *Le Monde Diplomatique* reproduce the formal and typographic elements of the source publication (Hernández Hernández 2017), while the title, design, and layout of *Newsweek Hankuk Pan*, "a Korean language news magazine which offers both translated and non-translated articles on domestic and international events" (Kang 2007, p. 225) is "highly suggestive of a straightforward translational chain based on identical content, meaning and style between *Newsweek* and *Newsweek Hankuk Pan*" (Kang 2007, p. 226). However, this ostensive visibility creates an illusion of transparency, as readers expect texts presented as translations to be "proper" translations, according to a conceptualization implicitly based on religious and literary translation. The typical assumption is that there is a source (written) text, to which the translated text is formally related by linear correspondence, so that each segment in the source text can be mapped onto a target text segment, and vice versa.

Journalists, reporters, and foreign correspondents do not consider themselves as translators (Bassnett 2005a; Filmer 2014), preferring to call themselves "international journalists" or "bilingual journalists" (Schäffner 2018, p. 332). Some authors have suggested labels such as "journalators" (Filmer 2014; van Doorslaer 2010a, 2013a) or "journalist-translators" (Hernández Guerrero 2011; Skorokhod 2016) to refer to these practitioners and stress the uniqueness of news translation. As noted by van Doorslaer (2013a, p. 78), while "forms of a broader concept of translation (including rewriting and adaptation) are omnipresent in everyday news production practice ... journalists usually use a more traditional and narrower concept of translation and do not want to be associated with translation work." Though they readily admit to translating being a good amount of their job, journalists often see translation as a burden (Davier 2014, pp. 61–62). Translation is described by journalists in terms of translation "proper" according to the traditional concept prevailing about literary and religious translation, and literal translation, or linear correspondence between a source and a target text segments, seems to be perceived as the expectancy norm. Among news text producers, there seems to be an understanding of translation as strictly interlingual transfer, implying linear correspondence between stretches of (written) texts in two languages. Professional journalists generally see translation as a linguistic operation involving replacement of linguistic material rather than as a practice concerned with the negotiation of cultures. Rather than seeing it as largely coinciding with foreign news reporting, as in much of translation studies research, they see it as one of the various tasks which are part of newswriting. However, in journalistic text production, "[t]raditional interlingual (and integral) translation of articles is rare" (Davier & van Doorslaer 2018, p. 245). Translating and writing are brought together in one integrated process, and since there is no clear distinction between inter- and intralingual translation, it is hardly possible to distinguish between the functions of "writing 'original' reports or journalists translating and rewriting on the basis of existing sources" (van Doorslaer 2010a, p. 181). The invisibility of translation activities in newswriting can thus arguably be seen as proving that translation "has been successfully integrated within journalism" (Bielsa 2007, p. 151) and is perceived "as an integral part of interlingual newswriting ... not as a separate activity" (Schäffner 2018, p. 332).

Whereas in global news agencies and national news outlets in Europe and North America translation is usually carried out by journalists as part of writing and editing, and professional translators are not employed unless under specific circumstances, a different model of foreign news production is operative in other contexts. According to Hong, for instance, most translations into English in newspapers published in South Korea "are produced by translators rather than journalists, whose main job is rather to write original Korean-language articles based on English-to-Korean translations of original English articles" (2021, p. 789). Kang shows that the production of translated news stories on North Korea in the magazine *Newsweek Hankuk Pan* is a systematic and institutionally controlled collaborative process involving "cultural adaptation, proofreading, revising, naturalizing, editing and other textual processes that are carried out repeatedly and cyclically" (Kang 2007, p. 238) by different agents, while "the translated article increasingly becomes divorced from the source text as it moves through the system" (p. 238). In China, at *Reference News*, the tasks of selecting, translating, and editing foreign news are kept separated and carried out by different individuals. Teams of professional translators translate selected (pieces of) reports – which are proofread and revised and then forwarded to editors, who modify the target texts according to a set of implicit and explicit guidelines and take responsibility for their publication (Pan 2014a; Xia 2019). Hojmohammadi (2005) describes work at the Islamic Republic of Iran Broadcasting (IRIB) news agency, whose subscribers include the domestic press, broadcast organizations, and government institutions. Translation is carried out by translators recruited to translate news materials into Persian from a variety of languages – including English, French, Arabic, and German – and the translated versions are then edited and possibly revised by senior translators.

2.5 Key Terms

In current translation research, four terms have often been used to refer to news media translation practices and processes: namely, domestication, transediting, gatekeeping, and localization. The use of these terms, and the concepts to which they refer, differ depending on whether the operations of textual selection and transformation they point to are subsumed under a more general understanding of translation, as is now more common in translation studies, or whether translation is interpreted in the more restricted sense of "translation proper" – i.e., as interlingual transformation, as is still common within other disciplinary traditions as well as among news professionals. These terms are sometimes used in conjunction with one another and sometimes with overlapping meaning, again depending on the scholarly traditions drawn upon.

2.5.1 Domestication

In research on news translation, the term domestication has been used with reference to two different research traditions. The first is based on the distinction introduced by Lawrence Venuti between domesticating translation and foreignizing translation, and the second has been put forward by Gurevitch et al. (1991) within the tradition of media and journalistic studies.[16]

Venuti (1995, pp. 19–23) observes that the dominant form of literary translation in the Anglo-American context is domestication or acculturation, which prioritizes the needs and expectations of the receiving culture. Texts translated into English are adapted to target norms, privileging fluency and erasing any sign of foreignness. A foreignizing translation, on the other hand, is one that adheres to source cultural conventions and foreign language syntax at the expense of fluency and, by retaining foreign elements in the translated text, allows the reader to encounter the foreign culture and language. Venuti argues that domesticating translation strategies favor "an ethnocentric reduction of the foreign text to target-language cultural values" (Venuti 1995, p. 20) and suggests that, "insofar as foreignizing translation seeks to restrain the ethnocentric violence of translation, it is highly desirable today" (Venuti 1995 p. 20). One of the first studies making reference to Venuti's concept of domestication in its discussion of news translation is Barnard (2000), in which the author compares an issue of the Asian edition of *Newsweek* sold in Japan with an issue covering the same story of the apparently very similar *Nyūzuwīku Nihonban*, whose owners are Japanese rather than American. Using a critical discourse analysis (CDA) approach (see Section 3.3.1) and tools from functional grammar (see Section 3.3.3), Barnard argues that, whereas the Asian edition of *Newsweek* offers an example of domesticating strategies, the way the news was translated in *Nyūzuwīku Nihonban* can only be explained in terms of censorship.

Based on their survey of global news agencies' translation practices, as well as on evidence from agencies' style guides, Bielsa and Bassnett (2009, p. 10)

[16] The term domestication is also used in media and communication studies to refer to the making of media and technological objects familiar and acceptable in a domestic context (Helle-Valle & Slettemeas 2008). See also Brienza (2016) for a discussion of the "domestication" of the manga comics industry in the USA.

suggest that "Venuti's foreignization hypothesis ceases to hold any value" when considering the journalistic field, since domestication appears to be the norm for the vast majority of translations in global news reporting. Holland (2013, p. 335) argues that domestication/acculturation may be "more appropriate – even necessary" in the case of news translation. A rather different approach is proposed by Scammell (2018), who reformulates Venuti's arguments surrounding the ethical value of foreignizing strategies in the context of news agency translation, with specific reference to translated text produced by the Reuters news agency. While acknowledging that domesticating translation strategies are currently the norm in global news reporting, in her case study, Scammell suggests that a "foreignized" approach to news agency translation would help readers acquire the cultural competence "necessary to living in an increasingly cosmopolitan world" (Scammell 2018, p. 34), and she argues that news agencies could benefit from "introducing a degree of foreignisation as a means to maximising the potential for translation in the news to facilitate cross-cultural engagement and understanding" (p. 93).

While Venuti's distinction between domestication and foreignization was elaborated with reference to global translation strategies in the literary field, Scammell uses the terms to refer to translation at the local textual level. After classifying culture-specific references and quotations in a corpus of Reuters reports according to a taxonomy ranging from more to less domesticating strategies, Scammell finds that by and large translators implicitly abide by the suggestions laid out in the *Reuters Handbook of Journalism*. These guidelines promote translation strategies that favor referring to people and events taking place in a foreign context primarily using domestic cultural references and terms. Scammell formulates five updates that "revise and expand guidance on the translation of culture-specific concepts and quotation" (Scammell 2018, p. 75), and suggests that these modifications could be unobtrusively incorporated into the existing Reuter's Style Guide. The updates consist in practical advice for Reuters journalists on implementing "local" translation strategies, concerning the translation of foreign-language quotations and culture-specific references, which would "increase the visibility of the translation process and foreign cultural/linguistic context, but without resulting in a non-fluent text" (Scammell 2018, p. 44).

The term domestication has also been used in research carried out in media and journalism studies to refer to the overall process of production and dissemination of foreign news. The concept, first introduced by Gurevitch et al. (1991) when discussing the changes brought about by global satellite TV channels in the 1980s, has since been taken up also in translation studies research (e.g., Hernández Guerrero 2009, p. 65). Gurevitch et al. (1991) argued that the collaboration between large TV news organizations had led to the creation of cross-national news exchange systems – for instance, the

Eurovision News Exchange, which they call the "global newsrooms" (p. 198), and that foreign news is "domesticated" by casting faraway events in frameworks that render them more familiar, compatible, and relevant to different domestic audiences, so that the accounts of news events are couched in "'stable' narratives ... that are already stored ... in the collective memory of different societies and cultures" (p. 205). According to Clausen (2004), who carried out a comparative study of Danish and Japanese newsrooms, both globalizing and domesticating strategies are at work in the production of foreign news. She argues that, while TV news formats, framing processes, and presentation styles are similar across nations, national broadcasters deliberately use domestication strategies by framing events according to particular frameworks of interpretation shared by a local audience in each nation. Thus, while local news programs rely on the system of distribution and exchange of information of global news providers, they simultaneously maintain a culturally specific orientation by "domesticating" global news – i.e., by making them "particular to each country" (Clausen 2004, p. 27).

Both Gurevitch et al. (1991) and Clausen (2004) refer to the use of visual materials, often unedited footage including only "natural sound," which are relatively more "open" than verbal texts – that is, "susceptible to a wider range of interpretations or 'stories' based upon them" (Gurevitch et al. 1991, pp. 203–204), and which are edited into news stories by different broadcasting organizations. In media studies, however, the term domestication has also been used in relation to written foreign news as found in newspapers. Cornia et al. (2016), for instance, compare news reporting of the same international event (swine flu) in Italian, Swedish, and British newspapers, finding that while publication trends in terms of number and distribution of articles published over a period of time exhibited comparable patterns, global issues were domesticated in different ways: whereas in Sweden the issue was treated more like a health emergency, in the United Kingdom and in Italy, newspapers gave more attention to how the government reacted to the crisis. According to the authors, the ways in which the event was covered in different countries correlate with Hallin and Mancini's (2004) typology of national professional models of journalism. The concept of "domestication" is revisited by Olausson (2014) (see also Olausson 2011), who looks at the reporting on climate change in Indian, Swedish, and US newspapers within a CDA framework. Olausson (2014) is interested in the constructions of the transnational beyond the genre of foreign news and identifies three discursive modes of domestication, according to whether global and local events are presented as disconnected (introverted domestication), interconnected (extroverted domestication) or deterritorialized (counter-domestication). According to Van Leuven and Berglez (2016), who examine the news output of three mainstream quality newspapers in different media systems (*The Times*, *Le Monde*, *De Standaard*),

Olausson's (2014) study shows that domestication is a complex phenomenon, pointing to the development of global journalism, a new type of journalism that is different from foreign reporting and "is rooted in an emerging media ecology initiated by processes of digitalization and globalization" (Van Leuven & Berglez 2016, p. 1). The distinction between local and foreign news is becoming more blurred as transnational events are reported and integrated both in domestic and foreign news. The permeability of the border between home and foreign news is highlighted by the increasingly diversified terminology used by different researchers, as well as different media, to describe global news reports; this terminology includes phrases such as international news, transnational news, and world news (Van Leuven & Berglez 2016, p. 4), as well as by the emergence of a new, hybrid kind of "glocalized" domestic news that focuses on how the local context is affected by global events.

In order to uncover communication strategies and decision-making processes in global news production, some of these studies are carried out using ethnographic methods such as newsroom observation and staff interviews (e.g., Gurevitch et al. 1991; Clausen 2004), but most studies are based (also) on content analysis – i.e., on the interpretation of quantitative data derived from features coded in the corpus by the analysts. Thus, for instance, Gurevitch et al. (1991), though acknowledging that a classification of news as "foreign" and "domestic" is problematic (p. 200), coded news stories according to their topic and to whether they were aired as home or foreign news; Cornia et al. (2016) coded their corpus for topic, actors, and type of framing, finding that Italian newspapers seem to align according to political faction, whereas British newspapers seem to act independently of political affiliation. Van Leuven and Berglez (2016) classified different sections of "building blocks" of the articles as belonging to local, international, or global news, based on the circumstances and location of the event, and on the outlook/mode of reporting used to present it, finding that building blocks of global journalism were extensively present in all sections of the newspapers.

While the data used in research belonging to the tradition of journalism studies are obviously based to a large extent on translated content, these analyses do not take into account the way news about international events is processed by broadcasters and newspapers or the role of translation in their transmission. Interlingual translation is seen "as a secondary process that promotes the domestication of news items for local audiences" (Valdeón 2015b, p. 644), rather than as the very process of delivering global news. These studies also point to the invisibility of translation (for instance, translation is mentioned in passing only by Clausen [2004, p. 42]) and to its widespread practice, since they show how translation has increasingly become part of everyday news and cannot be consigned to the foreign news section of newspapers and TV news programs. Bielsa (2014, p. 393) argues that "the assumption of transparency has led social scientists to ignore the fact that different translating strategies generate radically different texts, and to underplay the degree to which translation questions the whole relationship between different languages and cultures."

2.5.2 *Transediting*

In the context of newswriting, to translate usually means to "cut, edit, reformulate, clarify and then adapt to in-house style preferences" (Bassnett 2006, p. 6), and translation often implies a "change of title and lead, elimination of unnecessary information and addition on background information, change in the order of the paragraphs [and] summarizing of information" (van Doorslaer 2010c, p. 182). The translation strategies at work in the context of news production have been described as "reorganisation, deletion, addition, and substitution" (Schäffner 2012a, p. 870), and "synthesis, reorganization, omission, addition and generalization" (Tsai 2006, p. 60), among others.

Such strategies, in fact, go back to the origins of print news. As Valdeón (2012a, p. 855) observes, though it may be difficult to draw reliable conclusions about the omissions, additions, and reductions in the translations published by most newspapers in the seventeenth century because there are few remaining copies of both originals and translated versions, these textual transformations were referred to at the time in the same way as now. Brownlees (2019), who analyzes a corpus of English corantos and newsletters published between 1622 and 1630 together with their sources, shows that while some texts were translated in full (and often referred to as "faithfully translated" rather than simply as "translated"), others were shortened to amend references to events in Britain or for reasons of space, while glosses and explanations were added for the British readers. Brownlees concludes that, even though in the case of Dutch news (as opposed to Italian or French news) the publishers' editorial and commercial objectives favored a translation that closely followed the content of the source Dutch text, there was no uniform mode of translation as regards early seventeenth-century news.

In order to refer to the kind of textual transformations taking place in newswriting, some authors have used the term "transediting" (e.g., Chen 2011b; Conway 2014; Gambier 2009; Hernández Guerrero 2009; Hernández Guerrero 2011; Pan 2014b; van Rooyen and Naudé 2009; Xia 2019; Zhang 2013), a term first introduced by Karen Stetting in 1989. Stetting did not restrict the use of the term to the journalistic context, but provided a list of five cases of transediting – i.e., "1. Shortening of text passages for subtitling; 2. Making the text of an interviewed politician idiomatic and well-structured; 3. Cleaning up inadequate manuscripts; 4. Journalists drawing on material in other languages for writing their own texts; 5. Extracting information from various documents for producing promotional company material in another language" (Stetting 1989, pp. 373–374). She distinguished between three types of transediting, also practiced in literary and religious translation, "although in a minor way" (p. 374). These are cleaning up (i.e., the "adaptation to the standard of efficiency in expression"), situational transediting (i.e., the "adaptation to the intended function of the target text"), and cultural transediting (i.e., the "adaptation to the needs and conventions of the target culture") (p. 377).

Since then, some have used the term transediting to refer to the practices of news translation as something different from translation "proper," others to refer to a type of translingual rewriting, not specific to news translation, that goes beyond the literal rendering from one language into another and implies "acts of ST rewriting, sometimes ST re-ordering" (Schrijver et al. 2016, p. 219). Outside of research in news translation, the term transediting has been used to refer to the translation of popular fiction by Hemmungs Wirtén, who uses the term transediting to refer to the Swedish editions of popular romance literature published by Harlequin. Hemmungs Wirtén (1998, pp. 125–126) argues that in the process of transediting "the categories of "translation" and "editing" close in on each other, and the line between translator and editor is unquestionably a fluid one". Baumann et al. (2011b, p. 137) instead discuss transediting as a separate journalistic practice on the same level as translation.

Bielsa and Bassnett (2009, pp. 63–64) argue that the concept of transediting is unnecessary as it implies the existence of another form of translating news, while Schäffner (2012a) maintains that the term translation is already inclusive of the types of activities comprised by transediting. She argues that that the term transediting, like transadaptation for screen/audiovisual translation (Gambier 2003) and transcreation for marketing and advertising translation (Pedersen 2014), is "meant to highlight processes which go beyond the aspects of pure language change" (Schäffner 2012a, p. 880), thus restricting the use of translation to its "proper" sense of literal interlingual rewriting rather than embracing a wider definition of it. Valdeón (2014) discusses the complex interrelationships between translation, transediting, and related concepts and argues the term transediting may become obsolete "because the original emphasis on language transfer and edition is of lesser importance than the political, economic and social implications of processes like adaptation and appropriation" (Valdeón 2014, p. 60).

While the term translation can certainly be used to cover a wider spectrum of practices than those which have traditionally been associated with literary and religious translation, the compound transediting nicely summarizes the combination between translating and editing that is typical of newswriting. Newswriting consists to a large extent in recycling and transforming previous text and intertwines the practices of intralingual editing with those of interlingual rewriting (aka translation "proper" in general parlance) since editing and translation are, in fact, jointly part of the process. In newswriting, the difference between inter- and intralinguistic translation acquires looser contours, and translation is better thought of as a process of textual transformation rather than of textual equivalence, as the source text is often replaced by a multitude of sources.

2.5.3 Gatekeeping

Gatekeeping theory originated in the late 1940s within communication studies and has since been accorded increasing favor in neighboring fields, including in translation studies. It refers to various actors involved in the selection and transmission of national and international news (White 1950) and includes concepts such as "the gatekeeper, gate, and forces around the gates, as well as channels through which information flows and sections within the channels, such as gathering information, writing messages, editing, graphics, and final approval" (Shoemaker & Riccio 2015, p. 1). Among the first studies of international news flows that consider the role of translation as part of gatekeeping are Henningham (1979), who categorizes the main topics in the news selected for translation in the major Japanese news agency Kyodo, and Fujii (1988), who looks at the translation into English in the newspaper *Asahi Evening News* of a news story first published in Japanese in the parent newspaper *Asahi Shinbun*. Fujii (1988, p. 37) argues that, besides literal translation, the translator carried out the four gatekeeping functions of "controlling, transforming, supplementing and reorganizing messages."

Wilke and Rosenberger (1994) discuss news production flows at the AP German service in Frankfurt, showing that translated stories that are more or less identical to the original were less than one in ten, whereas the vast majority of foreign news items were abridged and revised by reducing and transforming contextual details (Wilke & Rosenberger 1994, p. 430). Vuorinen (1997) instead maintains that what he refers to as "gatekeeping operations" and that include deletion, addition, substitution, and reorganization should "be considered part and parcel of the normal textual operations performed in any translation, and particularly in news translation" (Vuorinen 1997, p. 170). Hursti (2001) looks at news production of Finnish articles originating in English at the Reuters agency and translated by the Finnish News Agency (FNA), and argues that gatekeeping includes both selection and transediting processes. Song (2017) provides a quantitative analysis of the news items from *The New York Times* published by South Korean local newspapers between 2008 and 2013, arguing that the Yonhap News Agency, a de facto South Korean state news agency, functions "as the most prominent foreign news gatekeeper in Korea" (Song 2017, p. 659) by being more likely to select for translation articles that display a positive or neutral attitude towards the Korean president and government, and to filter out those that exhibit a negative stance. After reviewing some of these studies, as well as Cheesman and Nohl's (2011) distinction between gatekeeping and transediting, Matsushita (2019b, p. 30) argues that gatekeeping "deals primarily with selection" rather than with textual transformations, for which he prefers to use the term transediting. Valdeón (2020, p. 6) proposes a distinction between a first- and a second-level gatekeeping role of translation, the first referred to news selection and the second to news transformation, and Perrin et al. (2017, p. 468) suggest that "the relative (un)availability of translation experts can also be considered a type of gate-keeping mechanism".

Finally, Shoemaker and Riccio (2015, p. 3) note that, with the advent of the Internet and social media, the linear gatekeeping model originally envisaged after WWII has evolved into a complex, multidirectional and cross-national model in which "gate-keeping channels now cross and reach around the world in a web-like structure," and "multitudes" are now involved in the process of news selection and transmission, rather than "a few journalists." As mobile devices have increasingly become the main tool for accessing information, technology giants like Google, Facebook, and Twitter are replacing newspapers as gatekeeping channels. While user-tailored news-personalizing algorithms create "filter bubbles" (Pariser 2011) around newsreaders, troll factories threaten to supplant journalists in their role of gatekeepers (Marantz 2020).

2.5.4 *Localization*

In order to account for how the source text material is tailored to suit the needs and expectations of the target audience, the term localization has been applied to news translation by scholars in both translation and media/journalistic studies. Elaborating on Pym (2004), Orengo (2005) and Hernández Guerrero (2009, pp. 59–63) propose to extend the notion of localization to the study of news translation, arguing that the processes involved in the production and distribution of foreign news at news agencies, newsrooms, and other media outlets are similar to those of software or game localization. In both cases, the aim is the "simultaneous release of foreign-language versions of a product" (Orengo 2005, p. 171), and news reporting is treated as a "global" information product that is first globalized by international news agencies and then localized by national newspapers in order to be adapted to the local cultural context.

Similarly, in their discussion of translation in the BBC World service, Cheesman and Nohl (2011) argue that the news in English is first globalized – that is, "adapted to the (anticipated) expectations and comprehension of an assumed 'world public'" – and then localized by "adapting specific aspects of the coverage of the globalized event on the basis of assumptions made about the knowledge, comprehension, and cultural reference points of the target audience." Cheesman and Nohl (2011) argue that the localization of BBC news into its various Languages Other Than English services comprises both gatekeeping processes, by which they refer to the selection of news text for translation and its sequential order in the translated report, and transediting processes, by which they refer to textual transformations within the segments translated. Conway (2015b, p. 525) also sees transediting as a form of localization, described as having at its heart "a consideration for a community's shared process of meaning-making".

The concept of localization (together with that of domestication) is invoked, among others, by Nossek (2004, p. 363), who argues that journalists act as gatekeepers and that the selection and presentation of foreign news is determined by national political contexts, and by van Leeuwen (2006), who presents a case study of "globalizing" translation, whereby local news is translated by local translators/reporters from a local language (Vietnamese) into English and adapted to global conceptions and cultural frames of reference with the help of foreign subeditors.

3 Approaches to News Media Translation

3.1 Introduction

The area of enquiry covered by this volume is usually referred to as "news translation" (Bielsa 2020; Holland 2013) or "journalistic translation" (JTR, Valdeón 2015b). The two terms make reference to the professional field in which translation is practiced rather than to a specific type of activity; however, as noted by Davier et al. (2018, p. 154), the second term is more comprehensive, including the translation of not just news but also other journalistic products such as lifestyle magazines. By adopting the label "news media translation," I would like to propose an even more inclusive definition of news media as "forms of mass media that focus on delivering news to the general public or a target public. These include print media (newspapers, news magazines), broadcast news (radio and television), as well as digital media (online newspapers, news blogs, news videos, live news streaming, etc.)."[1] In this sense, the term news media translation highlights the role of translation in different media and by different actors, including nonprofessional translation of information.[2]

Though largely neglected until the end of the last century (but see Valdeón 2015b, pp. 640–641, for an overview of journalistic translation research in the 1990s), the translation of information has since been increasingly attracting the attention of researchers.[3] News translation now features entries in

[1] https://en.wikipedia.org/wiki/News_media, February 15, 2020 (last accessed on October 16, 2020).

[2] Some scholars, like Matsushita (2019b, p. 20), on the other hand, restrict the scope of "news translation" to specific outlets – i.e., news organizations – to specific news genres – i.e., hard news – and to specific modes – i.e., at the exclusion of audiovisual forms of news translation such as those involving voice-over, dubbing, and subtitling.

[3] The initial impetus to the study of translation practices in the area of news media was provided by the Warwick Project in the mid-2000s, led by Susan Bassnett, whose most influential research product was the book jointly written with Esperança Bielsa in 2009, focused on translation and news agencies. Equally important was María José Hernández Guerrero's (2009) monograph on translation and national newspapers. An especially important contribution to the field has been that of Roberto Valdeón, with a steady record of articles and editorships covering various aspects of research, from historiography to contrastive analysis and translation theory.

encyclopedias and handbooks (Bielsa 2020; Holland 2013; Palmer 2009; Valdeón 2012b; Valdeón 2018b; van Doorslaer 2010a), and the number of volumes dedicated to it is growing at a very fast pace – including monographs (e.g., Azodi 2016; Bielsa & Bassnett 2009; Conway 2011; Hernández Guerrero 2009; Károly et al. 2013; Károly 2017a; Liu 2019; Matsushita 2019b; Scammell 2018; Xia 2019); collected volumes (e.g., Conway and Bassnett 2006; Cortés Zaborras and Hernández Guerrero 2005; Davier and Conway 2019b; Valdeón 2010a); and special issues of journals such as *Language and Intercultural Communication* (Bassnett 2005b), *Across Languages and Cultures* (Davier et al. 2018; Valdeón 2010b), *Perspectives* (Conway 2015a; Valdeón 2020), *Meta* (Valdeón 2012a), and *Translation and Interpreting Studies* (Constanza Guzman 2019). Articles on translation in the news media have appeared, among others, in collected volumes and special issues of journals dedicated to translation, politics, and conflict (e.g., Federici 2016; Pérez-González 2012c; Schäffner & Bassnett 2010; Zhang & Munday 2018), inasmuch as these are the main topics of foreign news. Other scholars have investigated news translation as part of institutional translation, looking at newspapers as one type of "translating institution" together with companies, churches, literary publishers, etc. (Kang 2014; Mossop 1990; Pan 2014a). As Valdeón (2020, p. 10) remarks, "[f]rom Canada to China, from the USA to the Arab world, from Finland to Spain, journalistic translation research has gone truly global."

Many studies have focused on print media, and, in fact, the more specific terms "press translation" and "newspaper translation" have also been used (Schäffner 2012a, p. 876). A principal object of research has been translation practices at news agencies, operating both at global and national levels, but researchers have also focused on the translation of different written genres, ranging from news reports to opinion and feature articles in newspapers and magazines, both in print and online. The translation of speeches by and interviews with high-level officials – for example, presidents and prime ministers – is also treated as part of news translation, inasmuch as these speeches are indeed translated and disseminated through the media.

Much research has also been conducted on the role of translation and interpreting for TV and radio. Tsai (2005, 2006, 2010, 2012, 2015), for instance, has carried out extensive research on Taiwan's newsroom translation, while Conway (2014) has investigated reports in French and English in the bilingual Canadian broadcasting network. Haddadian-Moghaddam and Meylaerts (2014) discuss the translation policy of television programs in the province of Kurdistan in Iran, whereas Kang (2012) addresses the reframing of news on meat imports from the USA on a television news magazine in Korea. Studies on the Qatari news service Al-Jazeera channel include Ustad Figenschou (2012), who discusses Al-Jazeera English and both mainstream and alternative perceptions of it. Research on translation of news on the radio includes studies by van Rooyen and Naudé (2009) and van Rooyen (2013, 2018, 2019) investigating different settings such as public, commercial, and community radio in South Africa. Hernández Guerrero (2019) provides an overview of the role of translation in new forms of journalism emerging across digital media, mobile applications, social media, and multimedia platforms.

Insofar as news translation is carried out through audiovisual channels, news media translation research clearly overlaps with interpreting and audiovisual translation (AVT) research. The latter has traditionally focused on the entertainment industry and on the translation of fictional products, and only more recently began to include news media translation and interpreting within its remit (Abend-David 2014; Darwish & Orero 2014; Li 2020; Pérez-González 2014a). Research on interpreted news production and distribution in the media has been mostly known as media or broadcasting interpreting (Pöchhacker 2010; Straniero Sergio 2011, 2013), and includes analyses of modalities such as voice-over and subtitling, as well as of the performances of interpreters in both simultaneous and consecutive modes, in contexts ranging from the live transmissions of events like political speeches, debates, press conferences, weddings, and funerals (Colucci 2011; Dal Fovo 2012; Gu 2019; Gu & Tipton 2020; Kurz 1997, 2002; Liao & Pan 2018; Sandrelli 2015, 2017; Schäffner 2015) to televised interviews (Baker 1997), debates, and talk shows (Katan & Straniero Sergio 2001, 2003; Straniero Sergio 1999, 2003, 2007, 2012b, 2012a; Wadensjö 2008a), and sign language interpreted events on TV (Wehrmeyer 2015; Xiao et al. 2015).

Within translation studies, research in news media translation has been undertaken following different approaches and has been informed by a range of methodological and disciplinary perspectives, including those from linguistics, ethnography, and sociology. Most studies can perhaps be described as being either process or product oriented (Holland 2013, p. 335; Palmer 2009, p. 186). Process-oriented approaches focus on the agents and contexts of news translation and aim at describing the organization of work and the process of production of translated news, using ethnographic methods such as observation and interviews. Product-oriented approaches focus on text and typically compare translated news items with their "sources." Other studies – drawing on cultural, media, and journalistic perspectives – look at the role of news media translation in order to investigate national media systems, often in officially bilingual countries like Canada, Switzerland, and South Africa. Several studies, however, combine "a textual with a contextual analysis" (Schäffner 2012a, p. 870), looking at news translation both as product and process (e.g. Bielsa and Bassnett 2009; Manfredi 2018; van Rooyen 2018; Roumanos and Noblet 2019; Matsushita 2019b; Xia 2019) or adopt a methodological approach consisting in a combination of various data sources (Troqe & Marchan 2017). Davier et al. (2018, p. 156) suggest that "scholars need to combine textual analysis either with process research . . . or workplace ethnography", while Davier and van Doorslaer (2018) recommend that text analysis should be combined with fieldwork as a form of "methodological triangulation."

Various scholars have called for more interdisciplinary methodological collaboration with adjacent fields such as journalism and communication studies (Valdeón 2014, 2015b, pp. 647–648), transfer studies, and adaptation studies (Davier et al. 2018, p. 156). Scholars of media, journalism, and communication studies have only recently started to take an interest in the role of translation in international news production. A notable example is a special issue of the journal *Journalism*, edited by Baumann et al. (2011a), on translation in the BBC World service, though, as noted by Valdeón (2012b, p. 71), work carried out by translation scholars is hardly mentioned in the introduction to the volume. Media scholars' lack of interest in the role of translation in international news production is illustrated by Valdeón (2018a), who – after looking up the 186 occurrences of the term "translation" in a corpus containing all the articles published in four specialized journals in the field of journalism studies between 1994 and 2016 – contends that journalism researchers seem to take "translation" for granted and see it mostly as the literal interlingual rendition of a foreign text. Very few authors establish links between journalism and translation or problematize issues related to the role of translation, and they only refer to it as a technique at the same level as omitting or summarizing.

Finally, news media translation is increasingly attracting the attention of historiographic research (see Section 2.2), while news texts have also been used in applied and descriptive linguistics, including for language teaching (see Davier 2014, p. 54, and Valdeón 2015b, pp. 651–652, for an overview) and in research in language change (e.g. McLaughlin 2013, 2011; Siddig Abdalla 2018).

In this chapter, I review the main approaches to research in news media translation. I first discuss process-oriented research, followed by product-oriented and cultural-oriented research, and briefly touch on other approaches, bearing in mind that these perspectives are often considered jointly in research and illuminate mutually beneficial and often intermingled aspects. In fact, Conway suggests that these perspectives overlap to some extent and should be seen as complementary in the study of news translation. To better illustrate research methods and findings, I then provide a survey of case studies covering some of the main language pairs and journalistic genres.

3.2 Process-Oriented Research

Process-oriented research includes ethnographic studies of news production and studies in the translation process and has often been carried out by practitioners of journalism, including journalists-turned-researchers (e.g., Bani 2006; Fujii 1988; Haapanen & Perrin 2019; Hursti 2001; Matsushita 2019a, 2019b; Tsai 2005).

3.2.1 Ethnographic Approaches

Various studies are informed by an ethnographic approach that focuses on workplace practices and dynamics. Several scholars have investigated routines in practices involving translation at both global and national news agencies. Data collected for the analysis include institutional guidelines and style guides, direct observation of practices, and interviews with agency staff.

Though involved in almost every aspect of news production, in global news agencies style guides, translation is not treated separately from general reporting and writing, and it is only rarely referred to explicitly. However, "this should not be taken as a sign of the secondary importance of translation in news agencies, but rather as an indication of the extent to which translation has been integrated with other processes involved in the production of news" (Bielsa & Bassnett 2009, p. 70). For instance, the Reuters style guide (*Handbook of Journalism*, Reuters 2008) only mentions translation in two paragraphs, with reference to the translation of quotes, calling for them to be translated "in an idiomatic way."[4] Scammell (2018) examines indirect references to translation as regards "golden quotes" – i.e., direct quotations that are to be inserted in the first few paragraphs of a news wire to "best illustrate the main point of the story"[5] and that should be translated "in an idiomatic way rather than with pedantic literalness."[6] While the organization and division of work may vary considerably depending on the size and scope of a news agency, all authors underline how production speed and time pressure are among the main constraints in news translation practices.

Based on extensive data from semi-structured interviews and questionnaires, Bielsa and Bassnett (2009) describe translation practices at the regional desks of AFP and Inter Press Service (IPS)[7] in Montevideo, which mediate "between news gathering at the local level and the production of a coherent and comprehensive global information service" (Bielsa & Bassnett 2009, p. 77).

4 http://handbook.reuters.com/index.php?title=standards_and_values&oldid=32 (last accessed on October 16, 2020); http://handbook.reuters.com/?title=Accuracy (last accessed on October 16, 2020).

5 http://handbook.reuters.com/index.php?title=Reporting_and_Writing_Basics (last accessed on October 16, 2020).

6 http://handbook.reuters.com/index.php?title=Accuracy (last accessed on October 16, 2020).

7 Founded in 1964, the alternative global agency IPS has established itself as the largest supplier of information about the less developed nations, focusing on in-depth stories and issues such as human rights, environmental protection, and sustainable development (Bielsa & Bassnett 2009, p. 50).

They describe how editors process text produced by reporters, being responsible for editing texts before they are published, both in the language in which they are originally written and in another language. Interlingual translation is normally carried out in-house by the editors themselves, though in some cases it may be assigned to dedicated translators. This second model in which translation and editing are more clearly separated and assigned to different professionals is more commonly employed at IPS. Translation takes place from English (and French, in the case of AFP) for the Spanish newswire and vice versa, and translation amounts to approximately one-third of desk work.

Davier (2014, 2015) discusses work in the multilingual pressroom in Switzerland, looking at news items published in French and German by both AFP and Agence Télégraphique Suisse (ATS), which provides news almost exclusively for the Swiss market. Based on direct observation and semi-structured interviews with journalists and editors, Davier details a number of features relative to the Swiss context. For instance, she observes that multilingual newswires can either be produced in a sequence, whereby French reports are written after English reports and are – in full or in part – translations of one or more reports in English, or they can be produced in parallel when there is no time to translate important news. In Switzerland, journalists translate only into their native language, and while news is both produced and translated in German and French, Italian is only used as a language into which German and French news is translated (cf. also Perrin 2013).

Bani (2006) describes the various stages a translation goes through at the Italian weekly magazine *Internazionale*, which publishes translations from newspapers from all over the world. Once received from an external translator, the translation goes to the editorial office, where it is treated as a draft and is revised by several different people. A first editor checks the target text against the source text; then a second editor proofreads exclusively the Italian version. Then the translated text is edited by a copy editor, who decides on the placement of the translation inside the newspaper, and by the director. Only the first proofreader checks the target against the source text, which – according to Bani (2006, p. 41) – "shows that the final product that will reach readers is more important than fidelity to the source text."

Some studies investigate translation routines and attitudes on the part of foreign correspondents. Matsushita (2019b), for instance, conducted interviews with Japanese foreign correspondents stationed in the USA reporting on President Obama's speeches and explains that they started writing their articles while watching and recording the speech, and when "they wanted to insert a translation of Obama's words as a direct quotation, they either played back their recording of the speech to listen again or they made use of transcripts prepared by news assistants or external providers" (Matsushita

2019b, p. 57). In some cases, their comprehension was checked with a local assistant or an intern native speaker of English, and sometimes their articles went through a senior reporter before being transmitted electronically to Tokyo. The translation of direct quotes was then checked against the original English version, and any change had to be agreed upon by the author of the article. Additionally, fact checkers verified the accuracy of the article, including that of translated quotations, and before printing went ahead, proof prints were sent to all the parties involved.

Filmer (2014) discusses translation practices by journalists reporting on Italy for major British newspapers and Reuters and, on the basis of interviews conducted by telephone and email, reports that all foreign correspondents translate themselves from Italian sources when writing their articles. Bazzi (2009) describes translation practices at Reuters Arabic and Al-Manar[8] in Lebanon, based on interviews with representatives, editors, and translators. She explains that the production of translated texts is regulated by informal guidelines, making sure that a translated text conforms to the readers' assumptions. Translators into Arabic at Reuters are expected to produce text whose content, according to the editors, should be "tailored for the needs and interests of Middle East audiences" (Bazzi 2009, p. 8), "unbiased" (Bazzi 2009, p. 131), and show "a great deal of respect for the Arabic culture, ideology, and identity," with an eye to marketing considerations. Similarly, Al-Manar editors and translators have "fine grained policies" (Bazzi 2009, p. 131) guiding their translation strategies that, according to the organization, consist in relaying "credible" and "reliable" information to its audiences while adopting "firm ideological positions" (Bazzi 2009, p. 132).

Based on firsthand experience as a reporter at Taiwan's Formosa Television (FTV), as well as on interviews with former colleagues, Tsai describes news broadcasting translation practices in a series of articles. In TV, the translation of video news is part of the routines dominated by rapid turnaround times (Tsai 2005), and news texts are often based on several (written and/or oral) sources mostly provided by global TV news agencies and satellite network broadcasters (Tsai 2006, 2010). Tsai (2012) considers the translation of written text behind the verbal delivery accompanying the raw footage, while Tsai (2015) looks at the translation of humorous TV news programs.

Van Rooyen (2018) maps translation flows in multilingual community radio in the Free State province of South Africa, looking at the languages used in news broadcasting in twelve community radio stations and charting the languages that were allocated broadcast time in the presentation of news, together

[8] Al-Manar is a Lebanese leading satellite channel whose influential voice on the Palestinian–Israeli conflict in the Arab world is recognized internationally, even though the channel is ostracized in some Western countries.

with source languages and media, and the languages spoken by people in the newsrooms. Van Rooyen (2019) applies actor–network theory (ANT)[9] to the study of community radio news translation in South Africa. Van Rooyen relies on ANT as a framework to describe and systematize ethnographic data (field notes, photographs, interviews, etc.) collected from two community radio stations and to trace the interactions and translation processes between human and nonhuman actors, paying special attention to the role of new media technologies.

Ethnographic research has been carried out on translation work at *Reference News* in China by Pan (2014a) and Xia (2019). Pan (2014a) explores the impact of institutional guidelines and organizational practices on translation at the *Reference News* headquarters in Beijing, based on in-depth interviews with senior staff. Xia (2019) describes translation practices and routines at *Reference News* based on interviews with and direct observation of editors, news selectors, and translators together with close reading of "many in-house publications setting out regulations, principles and policies of the institution" (Xia 2019, p. 77).

At *Reference News*, the labor and responsibilities for selecting, translating, revising, and editing the news are distributed among distinct groups of people. First, several teams located abroad collect and provide a gist translation of selected items, which are then sent to the Chinese headquarters. Approved items are then sent to the translation department requesting full and "faithful" translations, and these are finally edited and provided with a headline by editors. According to Xia (2019, pp. 103–105), in the "pre-editing stage," news selectors work together with page editors to decide on the content of each page. Selectors search for news items on specific websites and on specific topics using news aggregators, and then send to the page editor selected items, together with notes in Chinese and possibly with indications of which sections of a report should be translated. Translations are carried out by novice translators and proofread and revised by senior translators, who train new staff with comments, corrections, and suggestions. Professional news translators are institutionalized through an in-house full-time training process, and institutional regulations, principles, and policies are also socialized through internal publications and regular staff meetings. While "fidelity and literal translation are advocated as the institutional guideline" (Pan 2014a, p. 555), an empirical

[9] ANT, also called "sociology of translation" (Callon 1986), is an approach developed by Bruno Latour (1987, 2005, 2012) and colleagues within the sociology of science, which posits that knowledge is constructed and interpreted through the interaction of shifting networks of human and nonhuman actors. Translation should be here understood not as the object of research but as a transformation process subsuming "all the negotiations, intrigues, calculations, acts of persuasion and violence, thanks to which an actor or force takes, or causes to be conferred on itself, authority to speak or act on behalf of another actor or force" (Callon & Latour 1981, p. 279).

survey of responses to a questionnaire administered to in-house full-time translators reveals that "faithfulness" is mostly interpreted as regarding adherence to hard facts rather than literalness, and translation strategies vary concerning, for instance, the translation of expressions with political or ideological implications.

In the final stage, translations are heavily edited to comply with guidelines, which explicitly instruct to avoid political, factual, and technical errors (Xia 2019, p. 111). For instance, whereas in foreign source texts Chinese leaders are usually clearly identified, their statements are generically attributed to a "party leader" in Chinese translation (Xia 2019, p. 138). Rather than as a country, Taiwan is referred to as a "region" or "area," and paragraphs and sentences projecting a negative image of China are edited out. Both Pan and Xia underline that editing is carried out by working exclusively with Chinese texts, without consulting the source texts, and most editors do not understand the source languages. Editors at *Reference News* are given technical as well as political guidelines through internally circulated material such as memos on sensitive matters and reference publications by the Xinhua News Agency's Proper Names Translation Office, which has regulated the standardization of foreign terms since 1956 by assigning them government-approved Chinese characters (Xia 2019, pp. 107–108). In 2011, *Reference News* set up its guidelines, "Specific Measures to Enhance Reporting Management in Reference News," providing "new regulations for the editing program, publishing process, filtering of political concerns, and focal points of error prevention" (Xia 2019, p. 137). Editors are required to be conversant with and observant of party (CCP) principles and are well aware of the need to stick to official policies and avoid mistakes. Any errors, which may range from using the "negligent translation of fixed terms" to "negligent reporting due to misunderstanding political and historical background" (Xia 2019, p. 112), can be sanctioned with penalties.

3.2.2 Process Research

Studies that describe the practical tasks and cognitive processes involved in news media translation practices are rare. Techniques include participant- or process-oriented methods such as verbal protocols (most commonly think-aloud protocols [TAPs]), eye tracking, screen recording, and keystroke logging, among others. In their study of the process through which articles are translated and published in the Italian magazine *Internazionale*, Troqe and Marchan (2017, p. 277) adopt a "hybrid methodological approach based on semiotic discourse analyses with textual corpora, think-aloud protocols with news editors and a survey among the readers of the translated texts." They integrate ethnographic methodologies (field observation and interviews) with an analysis of a corpus of original English, German, and French articles, their Italian translations as produced by freelance translators hired by the magazine, and the published versions – that is, the translations as revised by in-house editors, together with the verbalizations of *Internazionale* editors as they went about revising the translations, and a survey among the magazine's readership. The analysis of TAPs recorded by editors showed that most adjustments were made to adhere to the magazine style guide, and the most time was spent on online fact-checking. "Space and layout are the major constraints that account for summarizing and cutting strategies and this can partly explain the high number of omissions found in the text analysis" (Troqe & Marchan 2017, p. 301), and the published translation are, on average, 22 percent shorter than the originals. As a result of the readers' survey, they found that most readers are unaware of what happens when texts are translated and believe that "loyalty" and "equivalence" to the source text characterize the translations.

Most notable is the work carried out by Daniel Perrin and colleagues with reference to multilingual news media in Switzerland (Ehrensberger-Dow & Perrin 2009, 2013; Haapanen & Perrin 2019; Perrin et al. 2017; Perrin & Ehrensberger-Dow 2018). Drawing on research on the newswriting process at the multilingual public service broadcaster Swiss Broadcasting Corporation (SRG) (Perrin 2013) and arguing that the process of newswriting and translation can, in fact, be described in similar terms, Ehrensberger-Dow and Perrin (2013, pp. 79–81) have proposed to extend progression analysis to translation process research, in order to devise a method to trace the longitudinal development of the translation process, with the aim of documenting and describing its practices, routines, and procedures. Perrin et al. (2017, p. 465) apply this multimethod framework, which combines workplace ethnography (interviews, verbal protocols, participant observation) with keylogging to a case study of a journalist writing an editorial for the *Corriere del Ticino*, the main Italian-language newspaper in Switzerland, working from source material in English. The analysis of recorded data allowed the researchers to reconstruct how the journalist translated extracts from a speech by then UK Prime Minister David Cameron, sometimes integrating different pieces into a single quote and sometimes reformulating direct quotations. Noting that in the process there was no evidence of the journalist resorting to external resources (human translators, machine translation, or online dictionaries), they suggest that "media systems and society-at-large are challenged to adapt professional education in order to enable newswriters and their audiences to reasonably deal with the demands of multilingual glocalized newsflows" (Perrin et al. 2017, p. 478). Using the same methodology, Perrin and Ehrensberger-Dow (2018) discuss a case in which a journalist from a local Swiss television station translated a news text to be read aloud from standard German into the local dialect (Zurich German). The very close examination of the rewriting process showed that the journalist carried out considerable shifts in meaning, justified retrospectively by the need to adapt the text to the linguistic sensitivities of his audience. On the basis of this and other Swiss newsroom data, the authors conclude that, since translation is "intertwined with every aspect of news production, including how journalists handle their source materials, their target texts, and their social environment" (Perrin & Ehrensberger-Dow 2018, p. 179), knowledge and insights from translation theory and professional practice should be made available to media organizations and professionals in order to improve the quality and efficiency of their output. Finally, Haapanen and Perrin (2019) apply progression analysis to research on translingual quoting in Swiss television newsrooms, describing in considerable detail the stages the quotes go through before their final formulation. They show that the process of translingual quoting is not simple and linear but, rather, complex and often fragmented, and it affects and is in turn affected by the entire news production process, including practices such as searching for background information, negotiating between colleagues, and planning and performing interviews. They also distinguish between two types of interlingual quoting, based on whether or not the source of the quoted segment is an interview conducted by the same journalist who then writes the news text.

3.3 Product-Oriented Research

Product-oriented research focuses on translated news texts and may vary depending on the type of text under consideration and the approach and methodology used for the analysis. Differences by type of text relate to not only medium (i.e., printed, broadcasted, online) and genre (e.g., hard news, editorials, feature articles) but also the unit of text under analysis. Thus, as concerns written texts, some studies only consider headlines (e.g.. Guangjun & Huanyao 2015; Kadhim et al. 2013; Khanjan et al. 2014; Kontos & Sidiropoulou 2012b; Shi 2014; Sidiropoulou 1995b; Valdeón 2007b), while others deal with news stories, albeit of different length, from short agency wires to long feature articles, as well as with spoken and multimedia news genres. Furthermore, even though most studies adopt a comparative perspective pairing source and target texts, since translation strategies such as omissions and additions are rather common, and "journalists are more likely to draw from multiple sources than translate stories in their entirety" (Conway 2015b, p. 525), often what is compared is text fragments rather than full texts. Such fragments are either formally identified, as in the case of direct quotations – i.e., reported speech as signaled by quotation marks (see, e.g., Chen 2009; Kuo & Nakamura 2005; Matsushita 2019b) – or identified by the researcher in relation – for instance, to cultural concepts (Scammell 2018) and metaphors (e.g., Bazzi 2014; Bulut 2012; Sharifian 2011, pp. 195–218;

van Poucke & Belikova 2016) – as articulated in two (or more) news texts across paired paragraphs, sentences, or even shorter segments. On the other hand, some studies investigate particular language features across various types of small or large news corpora.

While some studies compare source and target text in order to identify strategies such as omission, addition, etc., others look in more detail at the language of the corresponding text and, through textual analysis, try to describe and explain what and why news texts change through translation. For example, Bielsa and Bassnett (2009, p. 110) show that a Reuters' "French text only shares about one-third of its content with the original English version, although it is of a similar length, pointing to the fact that, through translation, significantly different versions of texts are globally circulated." Scholars have classified the relations between source and target segments as the results of different translation strategies. Bani (2006, p. 42) distinguishes among four main strategies used at *Internazionale* – i.e., cutting or summary, inclusion of explanations, generalization, and substitution. When coding an aligned parallel corpus of source texts, translations, revised translations, and published translations, Troqe and Marchan (2017) adopt a wider array of categories from semiotic discourse analysis – i.e., omission, revolution ("[m]ajor variations that radically change the meaning of the original text"), emergence ("additions of content"), apparition ("expansions, clarifications and amplifications"), decline ("synthetic formulations, shortened versions and summaries"), fluctuation ("shifts in the vocabulary and semantic fields"), distortion (e.g., shift in point of view), adjustments (editors correct typos in the translation), and intensity (shifts that "increase or decrease euphoric or dysphoric intensity"). Kang (2007, p. 226) distinguishes among omission, addition, generalization, particularization, and re-perspectivization, whereas Matsushita (2019b) prefers to differentiate only three strategies – i.e., omission, addition, and substitution. Based on her extensive analysis of translated quotations (150 paired segments) from speeches of then US President Obama published by six top-selling Japanese newspapers, which shows that "omission was used in 53 percent of the TTs, substitution in 31 percent, and addition in 10 percent" (Matsushita 2019b, p. 102), and in line with what happens in news translation more in general (e.g., Bielsa and Bassnett 2009; Hursti 2001; Jiménez-Crespo 2012), she argues that omission is the predominant strategy in the translation of quotations. The reason for this lies primarily in the very short production times and "the need for conciseness, especially in the case of print media" (Matsushita 2019b, p. 102). Xia (2019) classifies instances of additions (where information is added – e.g., glosses or qualifiers), subtractions (where sentences are cut and information is otherwise omitted), and modifications in a corpus containing reports published in Chinese in 2012 by *Reference News*, together with their sources. She describes how sometimes a critical report may be transformed into an article filled with words of praise, and how information in conflict with official political and ideological views may be filtered out or omitted altogether, or sometimes replaced with or modified by "correct" information (Xia 2019, pp. 91–92).

Textual analysis in news media translation has drawn on different research frameworks, concepts and methods, ranging from critical discourse analysis (CDA) to narrative theory, from systemic functional linguistics (SFL) and appraisal theory to corpus linguistics, from anthropology to cultural studies and media studies. These approaches are not exclusive; rather, they are often combined. In what follows, I will briefly consider some of the main approaches informing product-oriented news translation research.

3.3.1 Critical Discourse Analysis

Much product-oriented news media translation research draws on CDA, a research tradition that comprises various schools or trends, all focusing on the ideological implications of discourse and seeking to find connections between language use and ideological, societal, or cognitive structures, with the aim of making visible the relations between language and power. According to Fairclough and Wodak (1997, p. 258) "CDA sees discourse – language use in speech and writing – as a form of 'social practice'. Describing discourse as social practice implies a dialectical relationship between a particular discursive event and the situation(s), institution(s) and social structure(s) which frame it."

CDA can be described as an approach rather than a methodology, as it "encompasses different methods of analysis and theories from a multidisciplinary approach" (Alvarez-Benito & Inigo-Mora 2015, p. 8), in the attempt to make connections between language and broader social theory. For instance, in her analysis of the representation of the Palestinian conflict in Lebanese newspapers, Bazzi (2009) draws on Michel Foucault's (1989) theorization of discourse and power, Lévi-Strauss's and Barthes's discussion of *myth*, defined as "a structured system of signifiers, whose internal sets of relationships are used to chart the structure of other sets of relationships" (Bazzi 2009, p. 28); Antonio Gramsci's concept of *hegemony*, whereby the elites rule by consent and individuals accept the dominant ideological influence which is supposed to embody their interests; Louis Althusser's *interpellation*, which refers to the way people are addressed and given a particular identity or subjectivity in a given society; and Herman & Chomsky's (1988) discussion of *worthy vs. unworthy victims*, in which the former are presented with ample detail while the latter are given meager coverage and are quickly dismissed by mainstream media.

Most studies in news media translation refer to work by van Dijk (1988), Bell (1991), Fowler (1991), and Fairclough (1995), who investigated news discourse and journalism – though largely overlooking the crucial role played by translation. Many authors – for instance, Schäffner (2005), Valdeón (2005a, 2007a), Kang (2007), Chen (2009), Pan (2015), Manfredi (2018), and Xia (2019) – make reference, in particular, to Fairclough's (1995) three-dimensional model of CDA, differentiating a textual level, which involves linguistic description and analysis; a discourse level, which provides for an interpretation of the relationships between text and discursive processes, i.e., translation practices; and a sociocultural level, which provides an explanation of the relationship between discursive processes and social processes, i.e., the broader institutional and social context.

An important concept derived from critical analysis of political discourse is that of recontextualization – whereby, in newspaper texts, events are represented either as direct or indirect discourse, by foregrounding or backgrounding particular elements, so that some elements become more or less salient (Blackledge 2006; Fairclough 1995). Schäffner (2008, 2010), for instance, applies the term to news translation research to refer to the way translated speeches, interviews, and press conferences are incorporated in news reports. Recontextualization through translation is seen here as a result of discourse processing, not different from monolingual recontextualization processes, in which "one event, or discursive practice (e.g., a Parliamentary debate, a state visit, a press conference) is incorporated, appropriated and transformed within the context of another event, or discursive practice (e.g., a news report, an editorial)" (Schäffner 2010, p. 255). Similarly, Kang (2007) draws on discourse studies, linguistic anthropology, and symbolic interactionism (Bauman & Briggs 1990) and argues that, in news translation, recontextualization takes place through a wide range of discursive strategies, since "parts of the prior discourse as manifested in the source text may be lifted from their original setting, re-perspectivized, differently foregrounded, blended with other voices and relocated in a new setting" (Kang 2007, p. 221). According to Kang, news translation is an instance of entextualization – that is, the process by which discourse is first decontextualized and then recontextualized into a different stretch of language. Kang shows how, for example, the production of translated news stories on North Korea in *Newsweek Hankuk Pan* involves resituating a *Newsweek* journalist's discourse, which is anchored in the specific discourse context of a *Newsweek* story for *Newsweek* readers, in the context of producing a translated news story for the South Korean readers of the *Newsweek Hankuk Pan* newspaper. Recontextualization involves shifts in meaning resulting from textual operations classified by Kang (2007, p. 220) as omissions, additions, re-perspectivizations, generalizations, and particularizations.

3.3.2 Systemic Functional Linguistics

As regards textual analysis, Fairclough and other scholars in the CDA tradition subscribe to a view of language as social semiotic (Halliday 1978), making reference to tools and concepts originating from M. A. K. Halliday's systemic functional linguistics (SFL) (Halliday 1985; Halliday & Matthiessen 2014). As a comprehensive theory of language in context SFL is indeed one of the most influential models of linguistic analysis in translation studies as a whole, especially as regards nonliterary translation (cf. Hatim and Mason 1990; House 2015; Zhang & Munday 2018). Pertaining to news translation, several authors make explicit reference to Halliday's model and/or appraisal theory (see what follows) – including Fattah (2020), Guangiun & Huanyao (2015), Manfredi (2018), Pan (2017a), Talebinejad and Shahi (2017), and Wu (2018), reviewed later – or adopt it implicitly as part of Fairclough's analytical approach.

According to Halliday, grammatical choices realize the meaning potential of language and are related to its ideational, interpersonal, and textual metafunctions. The systematic analysis of textual organization, clause combination, clause grammar, and vocabulary may thus offer a way to relate linguistic choices to larger ideological factors. Aspects typically investigated by researchers drawing on SFL include thematic progression (i.e., distinction between information presented as given – the theme – and information presented as new – the rheme), modality and transitivity patterns (i.e., the ways in which the participants in a process are represented in a clause), and cohesion and coherence as realized by explicitly and implicitly linked vocabulary. By reproducing or departing from such features – for instance, by inverting the order of theme and rheme in a sentence, by foregrounding or backgrounding certain actors in a clause, or by the choice of particular lexical items in cohesive chains – translators may perpetuate or deviate from a particular discourse and construct a representation of reality possibly diverging from that offered by the text(s) in another language on which a translated text is based. Thus, "[b]y identifying the lexicogrammatical structures employed in a target news text and contrasting these to those used in the identified source(s), specific representations can be analysed, interpreted, and evaluated with regard to a given socio-political context" (Skorokhod 2016, p. 162).

The highly structured theoretical and descriptive apparatus of Hallidayan linguistics has been further enriched by appraisal theory (Martin & White 2005), a development in the study of the interpersonal function of language. The appraisal framework provides a detailed and elaborate description of features of interpersonal meaning "such as evaluative epithets and modal expressions that indicate the speaker's attitude and commitment to a statement" (Munday 2018, p. 2). Extending Halliday's tripartite mapping of linguistic analysis, the evaluative language used for appraisal is described as relating to positive or negative assessment of three types of attitude – i.e., as related to "affect" (e.g., adjectives that convey an emotional reaction), "judgment" (e.g., adjectives which imply an ethical assessment of human behavior), and appreciation (e.g., adjectives that express an esthetical evaluation). These subtypes of attitude can be examined also with regard to values associated with "graduation" and "engagement." Graduation refers to the "force" and "focus" of evaluative language, as indicated, for instance, through adverbs that modulate the intensity of an adjective and expressions that sharpen or blur a semantic categorization, respectively. Engagement refers to how overtly "inscribed" positioning and indirectly "evoked" attitudinal stances, both by text authors and attributed to others as reported by them, are encoded in language through, for instance, the choice of pronouns, verbs, and modal particles.

Studies that adopt an SFL methodology typically use it as a toolbox to assess ideological manipulation in translated text through the analysis of translation shifts. Thus, shifts in the transitivity system can put actors either in a foregrounded or backgrounded position, while shifts in the translation of evaluative language will direct readers to align with an ideological stance that has been altered with respect to the source text(s) – for instance, by removing, mitigating, or amplifying criticism toward reported-on people and events.

3.3.3 Narratives and Frames

An approach that, though not solely and directly concerned with news media translation, has been highly influential on research interrogating the ideological implications of translated news texts is (socio-)narrative theory,[10] first introduced to translation studies by Baker (2006). According to this paradigm, storytelling is central to human understanding of the world, and narratives organize the experience and memory of human happenings (Bruner 1991, p. 5). Building on work by Fisher (1984, 1985, 1987), Bruner (1991), and Somers (1994), among others, Baker (2006, p. 19) defines narratives as "public and personal stories that we subscribe to and that guide our behaviour." Narratives simultaneously represent and construct conventionally acceptable perceptions of reality and one specific narrative may be contested by, or be in direct conflict with, other competing narratives. It is through the involvement of translators and interpreters that narratives travel across linguistic and cultural boundaries, and through translation that their elements may be reconfigured as part of divergent of conflicting narratives. Baker (2009), for instance, illustrates how translation activities carried out by activist groups of translators and interpreters, including independent online news and translation providers such as Tlaxcala, may challenge dominant narratives circulating in

[10] Harding (2012a, p. 13) used the term socio-narrative theory to distinguish this framework "from purely narratological approaches typically concerned with the structure of finite texts, and to emphasise its sociological perspective."

mainstream media. According to Baker, the main features of narratives – that is, the organizing principles that explain how events can be structured in a logically plausible sequence – are temporality (the chronological order of events), relationality (how independent events are connected as part of the same story), causal emplotment (how events are interpreted as part of a chain of causes and effects and, thus, given moral and ethical significance), and selective appropriation (which elements are excluded and which are privileged and made central to a narrative). Baker distinguishes between four main types of narratives: ontological or biographical, public, conceptual, and meta-narratives. Valdeón (2008, pp. 300–301) argues that public narratives and meta-narratives are of particular interest in the analysis of news translation – the first being narratives elaborated by and circulating among institutions such as the media, and the latter being "master" narrative such as "Progress," "Decadence," "Industrialization," and "Capitalism vs. Communism" in which individuals are embedded as actors of "epic dramas" in history (Baker 2006, p. 44).

Like CDA, narrative theory offers a general framework for understanding translation in the context of news media but does not in itself engage in textual analysis. Thus, Baker combines narrative analysis with the concept of frames, seen both as cognitive constructs and as pertaining to the social dimension, drawing on a sociological tradition that includes symbolic interactionism (Goffman 1974, 1981) and media and social movement studies (Cunningham & Browning 2004; Entman 1993; Gamson & Modigliani 1987). Of particular relevance are Goffman's notions of frame space, which refers to the interpretative framework afforded by the different roles and capacities in which participants engage in an interaction and the positions they take toward the event and other participants (Goffman 1981, p. 230), and frame ambiguity, defined as "the special doubt that arises over the definition of the situation" (Goffman 1974, p. 302). The concept of frames as elaborated within media studies stresses active participation in the construction of reality (Baker 2006, p. 106). According to Entman (1993), newsmakers present and define an event or issue according to specific frames, a frame being "a central organizing idea or story line that provides meaning to an unfolding strip of events, weaving a connection among them" (Gamson & Modigliani 1987, p. 143). Frames are constructed through the interaction among journalists, elites, and social movements (de Vreese 2005, p. 52), and framing means "to select some aspects of perceived reality and make them more salient in a communicating text in such a way as to promote a particular problem definition, causal interpretation, moral evaluation and/or treatment recommendation" (Entman 1993, p. 52).

Based on these concepts, Baker suggests a number of visual and verbal resources through which narratives can be (re)framed in translation. Key framing strategies proposed in relation to news media translation include the exploitation of frame ambiguity, selective appropriation, and labeling. Frame ambiguity may consist in framing a violent conflict in different ways in order to promote competing narratives – for instance, by referring to the actors and actions in the Basque conflict as either "separatist" or "terrorist," depending on the Anglophone or Spanish medium (Valdeón 2007a, pp. 99–118). "Selective appropriation" refers to patterns of omission and addition – that is, whether translators elect to include or supplement specific textual material in order to "suppress, accentuate or elaborate particular aspects of a narrative" (Baker 2006, p. 114). Finally, by labelling, Baker (2006, p. 122) refers to how lexical items, terms or phrases are used "to identify a person, place, group, event or any other key element in a narrative," in order to provide "an interpretive frame that guides and constrains our response to the narrative in question."

The concept of (re)framing descending from Baker can be seen as similar to that of (re)contextualization descending from CDA. Thus, Tsai (2015) discusses the translation of humor in TV news in Taiwan in terms of taking details from a certain context (decontextualizing) and recontextualizing them through reframing processes. Pan (2017a) – who combines CDA, SFL, and narrative theory – looks at news translation as "recontextualization and reframing," explicitly merging the two perspectives. Xia (2019) – who, like Pan, examines the concept of framing in connection with *Reference News* – argues that "a translator develops a particular conceptualization of a piece of news or reorients his interpretation of the news item. Decision-making in communication affects frames in thought and overall attitudes" (Xia 2019, p. 38). Liu (2017, 2019), who also investigates the translation of foreign news at *Reference News* as well as at *Financial Times Chinese*, introduces a related term, transframing, defined as framing mediated through translation. Liu argues that, in news translation, "'transeditors' recreate texts in view of the targeted context by reshaping facts for the target readers and viewers" in accordance with the ideology and goals of an organization or authority – in this case, the Chinese government.

3.3.4 Corpus-Based Studies

While (critical) discourse and textual analysis may provide insights into how power and ideology are instantiated as well as influenced by language and texts, corpus linguistics may provide the means to extend the study of linguistic (or visual) features beyond the individual qualitative case, in order to be able to generalize observation on the basis of repeated patterns of occurrence of a given phenomenon.

While a corpus is, generally speaking, a collection of texts put together according to some informed, ad hoc criteria, in corpus linguistics, corpora are generally assumed to contain "texts in electronic format which are processed and analyzed using software specifically created for linguistic research" (Zanettin 2012, p. 7). Since almost all news text is currently available in electronic format, and is thus available for processing through computer applications, corpus-based studies of news media translation may be distinguished on the basis of the degree of automation involved in the analysis. Some studies only involve search criteria for selecting texts (either verbal or audiovisual) from larger databases – for instance, all news reports belonging to the same genre and about a specific event (Valdeón 2019) or published by the same media outlet over a period of time (Caimotto 2016) – in order to manually analyze the resulting corpora. Other studies make use of word lists, concordances, or other automatically generated data as a starting point for systematic investigations, often attempting to combine qualitative analysis in the CDA tradition with quantitative methods from corpus linguistics (e.g., Aragrande 2015, 2016; Constantinou 2017' Gagnon et al. 2018; Gu 2018; 2019; Kim 2017; Romagnuolo 2009). Other studies (e.g., Gaspari 2013; Laviosa et al. 2017; Ondelli and Nadalutti 2018; Ondelli and Viale 2010) rely almost exclusively on statistical measures and techniques, and usually focus on language features as evidence of translation strategies, norms or laws, without attempting to relate them to ideological or cultural aspects of news media translation.

In translation studies literature, corpora usually belong to three main types, each involving two components or subcorpora (Zanettin 2012, pp. 10–39). They can be either "parallel" – that is, consisting of one subcorpus of source texts and one of their translations – or they can be comparable – that is, consisting of two subcorpora created according to the same design criteria (e.g., in terms of topic, time and date, and type of media outlet in the case of news corpora). Further, comparable corpora can be monolingual – i.e., consist of two subcorpora in the same language, one being of translated and one of nontranslated texts – or bi-/multilingual – i.e., consist of two (or more) usually nontranslated subcorpora in different languages. Depending on the research purpose, different types of corpora can also be combined in order to triangulate results, including with different types of reference monolingual corpora to be used as benchmark. Different approaches may privilege different corpus types; for instance, Davier and van Doorslaer (2018) suggest that multilingual comparable corpora are well suited as a base for the analysis of cultural translation (see Section 3.4), whereas monolingual comparable corpora are mostly used in studies focused on language features. However, research in news media translation challenges traditional corpus typology and methodology. Thus, Caimotto and Gaspari (2018) argue that parallel corpora are of limited use in news translation research, as most translated news texts do not have a straightforward source text, and call for the cross-fertilization and methodological synergy between discourse-oriented research based on multilingual comparable news corpora and studies in journalistic translation. Even if "not created by explicitly including translations from the start, multilingual comparable corpora can contain translations or translational elements" (Davier & van Doorslaer 2018, p. 247); thus, Davier and van Doorslaer suggest that the distinction between parallel and comparable multilingual corpora may not be relevant in a journalistic context. Hybrid "comparable-cum-parallel" (Zanettin 2012, p. 151) or "comparallel" (Gaspari 2015) corpora may, in fact, often be more suitable to news media translation research, for which distinctions between inter- and intralingual translation, as well as between translation and original, are often blurred.

The basic staple of corpus analysis is word indexes, either based on frequency information or used for the display of search results. The former includes wordlists and collocations; the latter includes concordances (i.e., all occurrences of "node" words surrounded by one line of context) and other display formats. Wordlists can be manipulated in various ways – for instance, in order to filter out very frequent words, such as articles and prepositions, or to highlight "keywords" specific to one corpus as opposed to another or to general language. A corpus can be enriched with linguistic and structural annotation, attaching semantic and grammatical information to each word, which can then be used to refine searches and generate automated lexical profiles. In order to extract information from wordlists about the relationships between words – e.g., about collocations, clusters of consecutive words, and other linguistic patterns – corpus software uses various statistical measures.[11]

3.4 Culture-Oriented Research

Culture-oriented approaches are informed by research frameworks traditionally associated with the study of culture, literature, and communication[12] rather than language and discourse, and focus on the role of translation and interpreting in shaping perceptions and interpretations of cultural and social identities. The object of investigation is the role of journalists, agencies, and audiences in the representation of culture. While this representation often involves the discussion of textual objects, studies carried out within this framework do not necessarily imply a discussion of linguistic features, or even the assumption of a specific source text. Rather than subscribing to a strict

[11] See Zanettin (2012) for an introduction to corpus-based translation research and methodology and Ji et al. (2017) for the application of advanced statistical techniques.

[12] Conway (2012) relates the concept of cultural translation to anthropology/ethnography and to cultural/postcolonial studies and argues that "the *cultural studies* or *sociological* approach asks how journalists understand their role in society" (2015b, p. 521) [emphasis in the original].

definition of translation as interlingual text transfer, culture-oriented approaches regard the production of foreign news as a translation phenomenon, independently of (a) traceable original text(s) in a different language. Researchers "do not look at the translation processes at play but compare media coverage" (Davier & van Doorslaer 2018, p. 246) of specific people, topics, or events by looking at their meanings or definitions in the languages in which they are covered.

Rather than looking at translation processes and products per se, scholars examine how these processes and products contribute, for instance, to the construction and reception of images of national identity, and "the way in which nations and nationalities are represented in news media" (Kim 2017, p. 36). Studies carried out using a "cultural translation" approach, defined as concerning "the explanation of how members of a foreign cultural community interpret an object or event" (Davier & Conway 2019a, p. 2), often look at "human interest stories and editorials, whose authors try to persuade rather than merely inform" (Conway 2015b), rather than at hard news. Several of these studies – which examine the role of translation in shaping "a community's interpretative horizon" (Conway 2015b, p. 526) and "the dynamic relationship between political actors, journalists, and the public as they negotiate questions of identity and shared meaning" (Conway 2015b, p. 527) – have been carried out in countries that are officially multilingual (e.g., Canada, Switzerland, and Belgium). In his extensive investigation of the public Canadian Broadcasting Corporation (CBC), Conway (2006, 2010b, 2010a, 2011, 2014), for instance, examines the various meanings attributed to the sociopolitical concept of "société distincte"/"distinct society" in newscasts from CBC and Ici Radio-Canada – the English and French language broadcasters, respectively. Conway analyzes the coverage of two key political events – i.e., the 1990 and 1992 constitutional accords that have helped shape the relationships between the Francophone and the Anglophone communities in Canada. While CBC and Ici Radio-Canada did not translate full stories from each other, Conway describes six categories of translation methods used in Canada's television news programs. He argues that the method of translation (e.g., dubbing vs. subtitling) has important consequences in the way television news is constructed and perceived. While other studies have concerned Belgium (e.g., van Doorslaer 2009, 2010b, 2012) and Switzerland (e.g., Davier 2015), the scope of research is not necessarily restricted to cultural communities defined as different primarily on linguistic terms. For instance, Maitland (2015) discusses the coverage of political and social conflicts in Northern Ireland by the British Pathé News newsreels screened in UK and US cinemas as a form of cultural translation. Hester (2002) discusses recipient design concerning the "same" set of events broadcast by three different national television channels – i.e.,

CNN World News, the BBC National News, and BBC Wales Today – using member categorization analysis (see Chapter 4).

Culture-oriented research of news media translation include studies that discuss translation in terms of gatekeeping and news flows, sometimes carrying out quantitative analyses of the coverage of specific topics in translated news (see Section 2.5.3). On the basis of an observation of news flows, Bielsa and Bassnett (2009) argue that the role of translation in globalization has been overlooked. Van Doorslaer (2009) compares the attention paid to different countries in Belgian newspapers written in French and Dutch, and he finds that Dutch-language newspapers focused on the USA, followed by European neighboring countries, while French-language newspapers focused on France, followed by the USA. This correlated to the news agencies used as sources, since reports in Dutch-language newspapers drew predominantly from AP and Reuters, whereas French-language newspapers drew almost exclusively from AFP.

Some studies draw on imagology (e.g., Caimotto 2016; Filmer 2016; Valdeón 2016a; van Doorslaer 2012), a research approach that– though mainly focused on literary discourse – has also been applied to journalistic texts and travel writing (van Doorslaer 2021). Imagology studies the representation of nations and nationalities by in- and out-groups and aims to describe national prejudices and stereotypes (van Doorslaer 2010c). Applications of imagological research to news media translation research focus on the role of translation in shaping perceptions of events – for instance, how the selection and deselection of certain news and topics for translation may be functional to the creation of certain images of foreign people and events and to the development of stereotypes. For instance, van Doorslaer (2012) investigates the coverage of neighboring countries by Dutch-language Belgian TV news and finds that Germany is less present than other countries and is typically associated with images of industrial and military power.

3.5 Other Approaches and Methods

While most studies can be described as belonging to one or more of the approaches described so far, the application of other theories and concepts to news media translation has also been explored. Matsushita (2019b), for instance, in her study of translingual quotations, combines the analysis of translation processes and products with the concept of risk management as applied to translation studies by Pym (2015) and Pym and Matsushita (2018), claiming that the theory provides a "convincing rationale for some of the translation strategies used by Japanese newspapers" (Matsushita 2019b, p. 26). She argues that foreign correspondents want to lower the risk of the target readers being presented with unfamiliar information or terminology, and that they take the risk of producing nonliteral translations of direct quotes even when the source is a high-ranking official such as the US president because the benefits of using quotations are higher than the risks. Benefits include the rewards of having an “inaccurate” but “catchy” quotation repeated in headlines and digests, whereas the risks of complaints by the parties affected (sources, journalists, target readers) are generally low, since translingual quotations are scarcely monitored unless they occur in special circumstances – for instance, in the case of translated statements at joint press conferences by heads of state.

Some researchers investigating news media translation from a communication studies perspective resort to the method of content analysis (see Section 2.5.1). For instance, Hanusch (2008) uses quantitative content analysis to compare the coverage of death in foreign news by two Australian and two German newspapers, respectively. He finds important differences in reporting, related to evidence that journalists primarily look for certain types of death in culturally proximate countries. He traces these differences to the use and translation of words such as “carnage” and “Massaker’” in the two languages. Hong uses content analysis in order to study changes in the meaning and function of attribution (i.e., the identification of sources of information) in a corpus of English translation of Korean-language news stories and argues that such a methodological approach can “bridge the methodological gap between Translation Studies and journalism” (Hong 2021, pp. 789–790). Some studies investigate the reception of translated news texts by the audience (e.g., Bulic 2011; Conway and Vaskivska 2010; Jaber and Baumann 2011; Thiranagama 2011; Tian and Chao 2012; Troqe and Marchan 2017). For instance, several studies in Baumann et al. (2011b) focus on viewers’ responses to BBC reporting in translation – including in Arabic, Serbian, Tamil, and Singhala. Jaber and Baumann (2011) discuss viewer/reader response to the BBC Arabic Service in light of correspondence from users and online questionnaires, and they find that the BBC’s claim to impartiality is often questioned. Bulic illustrates the techniques used by the BBC to present translated news as impartial and discusses the reaction of Serbian listeners, most of whom seem to regard news broadcasted by the BBC as an example of pro-Western propaganda. Thiranagama (2011) examines responses to BBC news in Tamil and Sinhala by listeners in Sri Lanka and contends that the two services contribute to the creation of ethnically discrete audiences. Finally, Chen (2011b) draws on Jauss’s (1982) and Iser’s (1978) reception aesthetics as a general analytical framework to investigate a case study on English-Chinese news “transediting” in the Taiwanese press.

3.6 Case Studies

This section presents an overview of research on some of the most represented language pairs and news media genres. While it cannot claim to cover exhaustively a research area that currently counts several hundred publications in numerous languages,[13] this overview aims to illustrate the range and breadth of the methodologies adopted and the languages and cultures involved. This section focuses on product- and culture-oriented research, both because most studies fall into these broad categories and because the organizations, practices, and processes involved in news media translation have already been examined in Section 3.2.

3.6.1 Spanish

Spanish is, together with English and French, one of the main languages used by global agencies, and news translated into Spanish has a large audience both in the Americas and in Europe. Scholars have analyzed a range of media outlets – including news agencies (e.g., Bielsa & Bassnett 2009); newspapers (e.g., Valdeón 2015a, 2016a; Hernández Guerrero (2009); and a variety of digital media, mobile applications, social media, and multimedia platforms (e.g., Hernández Guerrero 2019, 2020). In a series of articles, Valdeón (2005a, 2005b, 2007b, 2007a, 2008, 2009, 2011, 2019) has compared English and Spanish versions of reports posted on the websites of media organizations offering multilingual versions – such as CNN, the BBC, and Reuters – against the backdrop of news published in some British and Spanish online newspapers during the same time frame. For instance, he compares news texts (headlines and news stories) published on the CNN US and on the CNN Spanish websites in 2004, considering both the choice of texts translated (news flows and selection) and the content of paired source English and target Spanish texts, detailing omissions, additions, and reformulations. He argues that both the selection of texts for translation and the choice of which parts to include and which to omit in the translations constructs the world according to Anglophone norms and ideological agendas. According to Valdeón (2007a, p. 237), while "text producers often used one particular news report as a base," they often "translated, rearranged and complemented [it] with information from other texts published on the same day." He adds that "[e]ven if most of the original content remained, the texts underwent thorough transformations, such as the re-organization of the news events (including the order of the paragraphs) as well as additions, omissions and substitutions. These strategies allowed the translators to imbue the final product with their own ideological stance" (Valdeón 2007a, p. 240).

According to Valdeón, the Spanish versions of news reports from Anglophone-based media conglomerates tend to instill the ideological stance

[13] Most publications surveyed are in English; fewer are in Italian, Spanish, and French.

and linguistic norms of "inner circle" countries, where English is the native language of most speakers. For instance, while the CNN website did not state a clear editorial policy, the reports chosen for translation were seemingly not conceived specifically with a Spanish-speaking target readership in mind but, rather, tended to impose a source culture outlook on international events without taking into account the expectations of the Spanish audience. Similarly, the headlines used for the articles published by the BBC, the CNN, and Reuters Internet services in English and Spanish did not accommodate to the Spanish target norm by adopting a standard syntactical structure but, rather, maintained the elliptical style of English headline language (Valdeón 2007b). He argues that the information about agents in the CNN Spanish website translation tends to be consistent with that found in the English source texts rather than with that commonly found in Spanish newspapers. A textual comparison revealed, in fact, that the Basque organization ETA was labeled as "banda separatista" or "grupo armado" (*separatist group* in the English source text), whereas Spanish newspapers would refer to it as "grupo terorista," without any linguistic and ideological hedging (Valdeón 2005a, 2009). The terms Falklands and Malvinas – respectively, the English and Spanish words used to refer to the islands at the center of the undeclared war between the UK and Argentina in 1982 – have different patterns of use in news posted on the BBC News and BBC Mundo websites (Valdeón 2011). While BBC News, like other British media surveyed, almost exclusively uses the term Falklands, BBC Mundo predominantly refers to them using both terms as a binomial, which is in contrast with the norm in Spanish newspapers, which almost exclusively use the word Malvinas. Valdeón (2011, pp. 77–78) concludes that the Spanish translations "unashamedly imitate the linguistic conventions of the source texts, but also accept the ideological impositions of the source culture, thinly disguised as principles of impartiality." In a later study, however, Valdeón (2019) shows that different language versions in the same outlet may differ considerably. Valdeón examines a number of stories (including headlines and accompanying photographs) posted between March and April 2013 on BBC News and BBC Mundo covering Margaret Thatcher's death and funeral, pointing out that the Spanish translations deliver an image of the former British PM that is clearly divergent from that of the English texts. This is achieved by excluding events and actors that portray her in a positive light and emphasizing others that cast a darker shadow, both through the choice of words (e.g., the repeated use of words like "polémica" and "polémico") and pictures (e.g., a photograph of Thatcher together with Chilean dictator Augusto Pinochet).

Initially drawing on Fairclough's CDA, Valdeón's extensive research has also incorporated concepts from other perspectives. For instance, Valdeón (2008) adopts Baker's category of selective appropriation to discuss the selection of the news events posted on BBC Mundo together with the selection of the information included in those reports. He argues that, taken together, they contribute to project onto the target audience an ethnocentric a perspective of the world, "whereby Anglophone news is given prominence at the expense of other more international items" (Valdeón 2008, p. 303). In another study, Valdeón (2016b) discusses the translation of Paul Krugman's economic columns in *El País*, using Nord's (2005) functional model as a framework for textual analysis.

While most studies focus on translation from English into Spanish, some scholars have also considered the opposite translation direction. These include Valdeón (2016a), who draws on framing theory and imagology to discuss the construction of national images of Spain through translated texts and images published in *El País English Edition*, and Munday's (2007) analysis of the translations of political speeches by Latin American leaders such as Castro, Marcos, and Chávez published in the US press, as compared to their official translations and the Spanish source texts. Munday argues that the lexical choices of the translators are better explained in terms of "lexical priming" (Hoey 2005), based on their individual experience of language, and cannot be predicted on the basis of the ideologies associated with the specific media outlets in which the translations appear.

3.6.2 Italian

Studies involving the Italian language are also primarily concerned with texts translated out of, rather than into, English. Federici (2010, 2011) draws both on CDA and narrative theory to discuss the translation and use by Italian newspapers of the US official report about the killing, by US "friendly fire," of the Italian security agent Nicola Calipari in Iraq in 2005. He shows how Italian newspapers across the political spectrum reordered, summarized, and edited the report in the translation in order to provide support for their different internal political purposes. For instance, the translations by *Il Corriere della Sera* and *La Repubblica*, the two major Italian newspapers, offered an "heroic perspective" (Federici 2010, p. 128) and excluded "references to the complex responsibilities in the event" in order to "legitimize the Italian complaints against the hegemonic perspective given by the US report" (p. 134). While, in moderate and left-wing newspapers, the translation was used to "stress the US guilt and the Italian government's submission to the USA" (Federici 2011, p. 1406), the translation of the same documents was used by right-wing newspapers to support the (right-wing) government.

Caimotto (2010) examines Italian translations of an editorial published in the British newspaper *The Economist* containing an analysis of the economic situation in Italy after the national elections of 2006. After examining how the article was translated and incorporated in stories published in the Italian national newspapers, she argues that, through omissions and modifications, the meaning of the original article was "distorted" by focusing on the leaders of the two main parties rather than on the overall election results. According to Caimotto, the differences between source and target texts can be understood as the result of a strong tendency in the Italian media system toward infotainment value – i.e., the mixing of information and entertainment. Caimotto (2016) uses concepts and methods from corpus linguistics and CDA, as well as narrative theory and imagology, to discuss the influence of British newspapers in the construction of the image of Italy during the 1970s. She examines a few articles published in the Italian newspaper *La Stampa* between 1969 and 1976 containing translated quotations and summarized segments from articles by *The Times* foreign correspondents regarding political and social tensions in Italy. She argues that translation strategies such as selective appropriation, permutation, omission, and addition were employed in order to mitigate criticism and foreground positive comments present in the British articles, remirroring a highly domesticated image of Italy. Also adopting an imagological perspective and drawing on both narrative theory and CDA, Filmer looks at news media texts translated in the opposite direction – i.e., from Italian into English. Filmer (2016) examines the translation of taboo expressions reportedly uttered by the then Italian premier Berlusconi in the period preceding his resignation in 2012 in several British newspapers and argues that "translation is employed as an ideological prop to intensify convenient news narratives on the ex-premier" (p. 272). Filmer (2018) explores the themes of homophobia, sexism, and racism, which were given special prominence in news about Italy in the British press in the year 2013, and concludes that "the worst ideological legacies of the Berlusconi era continue to fuel stereotypes of Italians as culturally backward within newspaper discourse" (p. 17). Filmer (2019) shows how stereotypes of Italianness are introduced and reinforced in an interview with Berlusconi as well as in a nonfiction miniseries and a documentary about Italian matters broadcasted by the BBC through voice-over techniques such as revoicing, narration, and simultaneous interpreting.

The weekly magazine *Internazionale* has been investigated in a number of studies, examining translation processes (Bani 2006; Troqe & Marchan 2017), products (Manfredi 2018; Troqe & Marchan 2017), and reception (Troqe & Marchan 2017). Manfredi (2018) investigates and compares translated feature articles with the same and similar articles published on the online news website *Italiadallestero* (i.e., "Italy from abroad"). All items considered were translated from English language sources and dealt with Italian political affairs. Manfredi draws on appraisal theory to examine shifts in evaluative language, finding that, whereas translations published in *Internazionale* tended to omit or soften negative evaluations, attitudinal stances were mostly preserved in *Italiadallestero*. Interviews with translators and editors of the two news publications suggested that a higher or lower degree of intervention was not due to explicit translation briefs. However, different translation strategies seemed to comply with the respective editorial policies and practices. Whereas *Internazionale* is a professional news enterprise with a specific (progressive) editorial line, *Italiadallestero* was[14] a nonprofit enterprise containing articles translated by volunteer translators, claiming to have no political orientation but, rather, to have as its mission the verbatim, documentary translation of articles by the foreign press. Troque and Marchan (2017) combine process research and discourse analysis with a reader survey. Responses from 167 readers indicated that the generally highly educated readers of the magazine tend to expect and trust translators to hold to values of faithfulness and readability and are generally unaware of "the translational and editorial process texts go through before publication ... and unknowing of the backstage and the criteria supporting that process" (p. 304).

Several corpus-based studies have been conducted using a range of corpus types and methods. Aragrande (2015) combines aspects of corpus linguistics and CDA to investigate the representation of migrants in corpora containing the transcriptions of four sets of audiovisual news recorded at the same time, one of Italian newscasts from public Rai channels, one of British BBC newscasts, and two of news videos, in Italian and English, from the Euronews website. After manually looking at the collocational profiles of migration-related words, Aragrande argues that they correlate with the ideological positioning and political debates of Italy (RAI) and the UK (BBC), with Euronews data being the least ideologically biased in both languages. Other studies using monolingual corpora are primarily focused on linguistic features. Gaspari (2013) carries out a study of lexical bundles – i.e., recurrent four-word units such as "the end of the," in an English monolingual comparable corpus of news texts comprising texts published between early April and mid-May 2010 by two news agencies based in Italy (ANSA and Adnkronos) and by two news agencies based in English-speaking countries (Reuters and UPI). He finds that the English texts produced by the Italian news agencies have a larger repertoire of phraseological units, which tend to be used more frequently than those in Reuters and UPI texts. Gaspari hypothesizes that the reason for this is that English texts produced by ANSA and Adnkronos are more "mediated" than those produced by "native" English agencies, as the editorial process involves more translation and nonnative speaker writing. Ondelli and Viale (2010) and Ondelli and Nadalutti (2018) use a monolingual

[14] The website was closed in late 2017; see https://web.archive.org/web/20171130205027/http://italiadallestero.info/faq (last accessed on October 16, 2020).

comparable corpus created from Italian newspapers containing two subcorpora of translated texts (mostly from English) and nontranslated texts and find that the language of translated texts is more conservative than nontranslated language, and translated texts are more similar among themselves than nontranslated texts are, as regards different measures of lexis and syntax. They relate their findings to general tendencies of translated texts – i.e., so-called universal features of translation such as simplification, explicitation, normalization, and convergence (see Baker 1993; Zanettin 2012).

3.6.3 Arabic

News media translation into Arabic has been extensively studied by Bazzi (2009, 2015, 2019), who uses a varied range of tools and concepts from linguistics and related disciplines from a CDA perspective. Noting how a large part of Arabic news discourse is based on information from global news agencies, Bazzi (2009) examines news about Middle East conflicts as translated from English-language news agency sources and published in Arabic by either the Reuters and AFP newswire services or by media outlets in the Arab world. These include Al-Manar, Al Jazeera, *Assafir*, and Al-Mustaqbal, the two main Lebanese newspapers and two newspapers in Arabic from other countries. Translations are also compared with nontranslated texts from the same sources and with English translations of Arabic text provided by Al-Manar. In her primarily product-oriented study (though see Section 3.2.1), Bazzi illustrates how English and Arabic texts are oppositionally worded, and she relates semantic, structural, and pragmatic choices to contextual and ideological factors. She argues that the English source text (fragments) and their Arabic translations refer to the myths that dominate the narratives of the respective media. While the overarching myth that dominates the Reuters and AFP texts in English is that of "Israel security," whereby Israel is protecting itself against Palestinian terrorism, the myth in Arab media is that "Israel is a powerful occupying entity" (Bazzi 2009, p. 27), and Palestinians are the victims. Depending on the dominating myth, the aggressor is either "Palestinian attackers" or "the Zionist entity"; the worthy victims (Herman & Chomsky 1988) are either Israeli or Palestinians; and occupation can be offered or not, as the specific reason for the "violence." The system of meaning responsible for the construction and interpretation of news stories in the Arab world is built on binary oppositions in which, in the Arab–Israeli conflict, there is "one particular aggressor (Israel), one particular worthy victim (Arab victims) and one specific reason (occupation)" (Bazzi 2009, p. 32).

When translated into Arabic by Reuters and AFP, English texts are adapted to the commonsensical expectations, beliefs, values, and cognitive models of Arab readerships. For instance, "Reuters own Arabic texts tend to avoid as much as possible describing Palestinian acts as violent, and simultaneously legitimate a new discourse on occupation, thus maintaining the prevalent moral and political orders in the Arab world which commonly believe in the Palestinian's legitimate right to resistance" (Bazzi 2009, p. 108). Bazzi also shows that Israeli and Palestinian voices are selectively quoted in both English and Arabic Reuters; i.e., whereas English text quotes at greater length Israeli voices, Arabic text quotes at greater length Palestinian voices. In order to meet the expectations and mental representations about agents and victims as part of an in-group or of an out-group and display the relations of solidarity or enmity toward them that are typically found in Arabic newspapers, background information that conflicts with the representation of Palestinians in a favorable way is usually omitted in Reuters Arabic translations. Translations shifts include the use of assertive verbs (e.g., say) rather than evaluative verbs (e.g., allege, claim) to described what Palestinians do, and while Palestinian officials are quoted in full, descriptions of Israelis are stripped of expressive verbs and adjectives, and Israeli officials are quoted less fully. Hezbollah is consistently recategorized and, unlike in the English text, is not referred to as a terrorist organization, whereas official statements from Arab voices are often added together with more detail about Palestinian victims.

Translations published in Al-Manar go a step further, and classification of agents adapt more fully to naming practices found in Arabic newspapers, so that the English "Israeli forces" in Arabic become "the Zionist occupation army" – which, rather than "kill armed militants," "martyrs resistance fighters," while "suicide bombers" become "martyrs" (Bazzi 2009, p. 20). In contrast, Al-Manar's own English translations of Arabic reports are rather literal and maintain the naming system and conventions of Arabic reports. For instance, in both Arabic and English translations, full detail and relevance are given about Palestinian victims, and the terminology used is consistent with an ideological reading by which Israel is referred to as "the Zionist entity" or "the enemy" and "Northern Israeli border with Lebanon" as the "Lebanese border with occupied Palestine."

Barkho (2008) and Fattah (2020) examine BBC coverage of the Palestinian–Israeli conflict in Arabic and English, with similar findings. Drawing on CDA and communication studies, Barkho correlates data from interviews with BBC editors, their blogs, and BBC guidelines with patterns of omission, specification, nominalization, and transitivity in paired English and Arabic online reports. Barkho (2008) argues that, while attempting to appear impartial, BBC editorial strategies and policies resound with the unequal power and status of the parties in conflict. However, while the linguistic choices in English texts reflect "to a large extent the views, assumptions and norms prevalent in the corporation" (p. 278), translations into Arabic are "relatively tailored to cater for predominantly Arab and Muslim audiences" (p. 291).

Fattah conducts a detailed analysis of a pair of English and Arabic online BBC reports covering the same news story. Drawing on SFL and appraisal theory, the author shows that, while based on the same source (a statement issued by the Hamas Ministry of Interior about the execution of three prisoners in Gaza), the two hard news reports display divergent ideological and evaluative orientations, instantiated in different "patterns of attribution" (Fattah 2020, p. 136) and "ideational selections and translational transformations." Thus, as opposed to the Arabic text, the English text does not recognize the governmental status of Hamas, and while the former "portrays the executions as a legitimate matter of law enforcement and judicial process, faithfully citing direct quotations which forcefully justify the executions on legal and religious grounds," the latter "foregrounds Hamas's agency and responsibility for the executions, delegitimating its political and judicial authority and casting doubt on the fairness and validity of any judicial process in Gaza."

Interestingly, Franjié (2009) finds that similar shifts occur when Arabic texts are translated into French. She investigates news stories in Arabic translated in the *Courrier International*, which publishes daily selections of articles from the foreign press. A corpus of twenty-four articles from Lebanese and Palestinian newspapers is compared with twenty-one articles from international media and twenty-two articles from Israeli media, all published before and during the 2006 war in Lebanon. Franjié points to three main strategies at work – i.e., omission, mitigation, and explicitation. Omitted content includes statements overtly hostile toward the USA and Israel and references to Lebanese internal politics, while mitigated content include statements about Israel, Hezbollah, and political positioning with respect to the conflict. Whereas Israel is referred to as الكيان الصهيوني ("the Zionist entity") and العدو التاريخي ("the historical enemy") in Arabic, this becomes simply *Israël* in French, and "the Israeli aggression against Lebanon" becomes "les hostilités" (the hostilities).[15] In this way, argues Franjié (2009, p. 78), "la traduction française passe sous silence une prise de position idéologique de la langue-culture source" ("the French translation silences an ideological position of the source lingua-culture"). Similarly, المقاومة اللبنانية ("the Lebanese resistance") becomes "Hezbollah," and "Hezbollah" is referred to as "la milice" (the militia), while "a displaced person from the city of Ain Fiq in occupied Syrian Golan" becomes "une ancienne habitante d'un village du Golan annexé par Israël" ("an elderly dweller of a village in Golan annexed by Israel").

Several studies consider translation from Arabic in English-language media. Al-Mohannadi's (2008) analyzes BBC's and CNN's translations of Osama Bin

[15] Similarly, *The New York Times*, when quoting references to "the Zionist entity" in reports or speeches by sources such as the ISNA Iranian news agency reporting the translated words of Iranian president Ahmadinejad in 2005, rephrases it as "Israel" (Zanettin 2016b).

Laden's statements following Al-Qaeda's attacks against the USA of September 11, 2001, showing that, while the translation by BBC is rather literal, the one by CNN departs considerably from the Arabic text and contains "numerous mistakes, omissions, additions and inconsistencies" (Al-Mohannadi 2008, p. 539). Drawing on CDA, Al-Mohannadi argues that these changes amount to an ideological intervention but at the same time suggests that they are most likely due to a combination of time pressure and "linguistic incompetence" rather than to conscious political manipulation. In her discussion of talks by Saudi women translated by BBC News from Saudi Arabic into Standard Arabic and then into English, Al-Hejin (2012) draws on both CDA and narrative theory to argue that the translations provide "a good example of selective appropriation which sometimes went beyond that to include content that was basically invented." Hijjo and Kaur (2017b, 2017a) and Hijjo et al. (2019) use narrative and frame theory to support an extensive analysis of the representation of "Daesh" in Arabic editorials and their English translations published by the Middle East Media Research Institute (MEMRI), a press monitoring and analysis organization based in Washington. The authors argue that MEMRI publishes selected and decontextualized excerpts and mistranslations, and uses paratextual devices such as titles, images, and footnotes to reframe Arabic narratives on Daesh, in order to further the meta-narrative of the war on terror and its ideologically laden agenda of terrorist Arabs and Muslims.

3.6.4 Russian

Several authors have investigated translation out of and into Russian. Harding (2011, 2012b, 2012a) discusses in detail news reporting of the Beslan hostage crisis that took place in Southern Russia in 2004, during which more than 300 hundred people were killed. Harding draws on narrative theory to investigate the effects of the reconfiguration into English of the alternative Russian-language narratives of the state controlled RIA-Novosti news agency, of the oppositional, nonmainstream Kavkazcenter, the website of the Chechen armed resistance, and of Caucasian Knot, an independent Russian news site. She first investigates how the competing narratives are constructed in the Russian texts by a selection of details – which can be either appropriated, omitted, or given a different degree of significance. Narratives are also constructed through the choice of temporary narrators (correspondents, eyewitness accounts, officials, and other media), the way actors are characterized and events presented, and the way they are connected to other narratives. The narrative of RIA-Novosti is largely made up of official reactions to the hostage taking, while official sources are almost absent in the narrative constructed by Kavkazcenter, or only presented in a critical light. RIA-Novosti connects the events to the narrative of the war on terror, while Kavkazcenter connects them to the conflict in Chechnya. Caucasian Knot constructs a complex and multivocal narrative that includes eyewitness reports and avoids a reductionist characterization of narrators or actors as either "good" or "evil". In the Russian texts, eyewitness reports are selectively appropriated by both RIA-Novosti and Kavkazcenter to confirm and reinforce their competing characterization of the actors (Russian authorities, Chechen separatists). Caucasian Knot provides a larger number of eyewitness accounts, in which people openly express their anger and frustration "with both the authorities [omitted by RIA-Novosti] and the hostage-takers [omitted by Kavkazcenter]" (Harding 2012b, p. 240). Interviews were collected through the agency's own correspondents (RIA-Novosti), extracted from other newspapers (Kavkazcenter), or both (Caucasian Knot). Only two interviews were published in English translation by RIA-Novosti, the longest of which was based on the interview published in Russian in a different newspaper. No eyewitness reports were published by the other news sites. Harding argues that, in the case of RIA-Novosti, the English reports, which are "anonymously translated amalgamations of bulletins from the Russian text" (Harding 2011, p. 55), convey and even reinforce the narrative of the war on terror by selecting relevant bits from the Russian text and by adding additional information, while the two other news agencies fail to convey their oppositional narratives by omitting critical comments and the voices of a variety of temporary narrators.

Adopting a CDA framework, Schäffner (2008, 2010) discusses the ways in which an interview given by Russian President Putin to a group of international journalists in 2007 was translated and reported in media in various languages, including German, English, French, and Italian. While she does not analyze the source text, she compares the different target genres and types of contextualization. For instance, in some cases, the interview was presented as such; in others, it was transformed into a report. Schäffner considers features such as titles and subtitles used in the media in the four languages, as well as the way in which different pieces of information (including information possibly from other sources) were selected and presented to reflect what the different media had identified as the main focus of the story, as determined primarily by national political interests. She shows how, through lexical and syntactic transformations, or sometimes through the addition of metacommunicative comments, the readers of the different target newspapers "get a different impression of the topics discussed in the interview and of the way in which Putin expressed his views" (Harding 2010, p. 264).

As far as translation into Russian is concerned, Spiessens and van Poucke (2016) and Spiessens (2019) draw on CDA and narrative analysis to examine a corpus of 770 English and French news reports about the 2014 Crimean crisis and thirty-nine Russian translations posted on InoSMI, a website affiliated with the RIA-Novosti news agency. Spiessens and Van Poucke (2016) argue that through the systematic selection of articles that are critical of Western countries and appreciative of Russia (a minority in the corpus examined), lexical shifts and the removal or replacement of original photos accompanying the reports, InoSMI reframes the discourse of the news sources to align it with the Russian government's official viewpoints, so that "Russia emerges as a powerful yet honourable player on the global stage" (p. 319), while the morally ambiguous position and the divisions of Western countries are highlighted. Through a similar analysis of selective appropriation, translation shifts, and manipulation of visual material, Spiessen (2019) argues that InoSMI reinterprets translated reports on the Ukraine war through the lens of WWII narratives that trigger "deep collective memory" (p. 339) and activate schematic master narratives that oppose Russian "patriots" and Ukrainian "fascists."

Conway and Vaskivska (2010) focus on the reception of the Russian translation of a series of articles by Clifford Levy on contemporary Russian society. The articles were published in 2008 in *The New York Times*, their translation was posted on the popular Russian blogging platform LiveJournal.ru, and the author and the translators solicited comments from both readerships. This study examines reader reactions to a story on the evolving relationship between the Russian state and the Russian Orthodox Church. Conway and Vaskivska argue that four acts of translation are involved in their analysis – i.e. first, the interlingual translation of Russian statements incorporated in the English article; second, an act of cultural translation in that Russian matters were presented/mediated for a US readership; third, the translation of the whole article in Russian; and, fourth, the translation into English of comments in Russian. After describing the frames at work in the English version and how the article was reframed in Russian through omissions, additions (including of paratextual material such as pictures and videos), and various other transformations, the authors examine the structure and content of the profusion of comments the article gave rise to in both languages. Comments in Russian were highly interactive and self-reflexive, and most of them did not directly address Levy's article. The authors argue that most readers perceived what they were reading about themselves as distorted. English responses in *The New York Times* comments section, which incorporated translated comments that originally appeared on LiveJournal.ru, seemed instead to engage with other readers to a lesser extent.

Finally, drawing on Entman's (1993) framing theory, Kovalyova (2010) investigates news reporting of the 2004 Orange Revolution in the Ukraine appearing in US, UK, German, and French media, which includes translations from Russian (as well as from Ukrainian), arguing that a preelection unrest was transformed into a political revolution scenario in order to meet the readerships' expectations of a grand narrative of spectacular social transformations.

3.6.5 Chinese

Most studies of Chinese news media translation involve English as either a source or target language and directly address ideological issues within a primarily CDA approach. Several researchers who investigate translation into Chinese have focused on *Reference News* (see Section 2.3.2), including Li Pan (2014a, 2014b, 2015, 2017a), Wu (2018), Liu (2017, 2019), Xia (2019), and Ping (2019). Pan's (2014a) ethnographic study (see Section 3.2.1) was followed by other investigations by the same author that focused on textual analysis of source and target texts dealing with the representation of China with respect to social unrest in Tibet and China's human rights record. Pan (2014b) discusses two news items translated from *The Daily Telegraph* and *The Times*, respectively. Pan (2015) examines two sets of reports, one translated from articles collected on the BBC, Reuters, and *The Washington Post* websites, the other from the websites of AP and *The Washington Post*. Pan (2017a) considers two translated news reports – one from *The Washington Post*, the other consisting of two parts, translated from *The Daily Telegraph* and *The Times*, respectively. After providing a historical overview of the Chinese outlet, in her extensive study, Xia (2019) considers a sizable corpus of news related to China translated from English sources and published between January 1 and April 30, 2012, focusing on news about the conviction of Bo Xilai, a top-level politician charged with corruption and sentenced to life imprisonment. Both researchers adopt Fairclough's macroanalytical CDA model, attempting to link a description of textual products – i.e., source texts and translations – to an interpretation of the discourse processes – i.e., the translation practices at the Chinese government's official news agency – and to an explanation through the wider sociocultural contexts – i.e. Chinese government and party policies.

To describe "deviation patterns" of translation with respect to source texts, Pan integrates concepts such as reframing by labeling, frame ambiguity, and selective appropriation with appraisal theory. Examples include divergence in the labeling of people and locations. For instance, "the closed city of Lhasa" is rendered simply as 拉萨 ("Lhasa") and "Kathmandu, the capital of Nepal" as 加德满都 ("Kathmandu"), while events in Tibet described as "riots" in English are either reframed as 打砸抢烧事件 ("beating, smashing, looting, and burning incidents") or not qualified at all. Chen Shiqiu, the source of a positive comment on China's human rights situation, is defined as a "Chinese government-appointed adviser to U.N." in the source English text and as "an expert from the Advisory Committee of U.N. Human Rights Council" in the translation published in *Reference News* (Pan 2015, pp. 221–222). Selective appropriation deviations include omission and additions – for instance, the omission of references to monks taking parts in the "riots." These "deviations," which "often have ideological implications and construe distinct positioning in the translated texts" (Pan 2015, p. 221), are explained, in appraisal theory terms, as different graduations of "focus" and "force," which lead to scaling up positive descriptions of China (for instance, Reuter's "economic performance" is turned into 经济成就 – "economic achievement" – in *Reference News*) and scaling down negative values (e.g., people who "protest" in relation to events in Tibet according to *The Washington Post* only "disturb" in Chinese translation).

Xia combines a classification of linguistic "adjustments" based on Nida (1964), who distinguishes between "addition," "subtraction," and "alteration," with Baker's (2006) framing strategies of labeling and selective appropriation. Additions include comments, explanations, headlines, and subtitles. Subtraction refers to the omission of text containing descriptions and comments on government and party leaders and sensitive events and topics. For example, while English source texts refer to Bo Xilai using phrases such as "pugnacious Chinese politician," "son of a Communist revolutionary leader," "once an ambitious member of the elite Politburo," and "former rising star of the ruling Communist Party," any descriptive labeling is omitted in translation. "Alteration" refers to a variety of textual replacements, modifications, and manipulations. Xia notes that omission, in particular, is "the linchpin of censorship" and that "[n]otable censored subjects include, but are not limited to, democracy, corruption, social unrest, party monopoly, political reform, governmental transition, and the 1989 Tiananmen Square protest" (Xia 2019, p. 92).

Both Pan and Xia relate textual "deviations" or "alterations" to institutional routines and practices collectively implemented at *Reference News* that, in turn, are shaped by a different ideological understanding of the events and people involved, which determine a different stance toward the news reported. While *Reference News* officially upholds values of "faithfulness," this is generally to be interpreted as faithfulness to the correct ideological interpretation of events. "Faithfulness" is thus mediated by the perception of source texts as ideologically biased, and translators are not expected to reproduce this biased perspective. Pan argues that the choice of words is indicative of the different ideological affiliations of the authors of English and Chinese texts, and that "contrary to the general expectation of objectivity in news reporting, both the original news and its translations are not free from deploying linguistic resources to make judgments and express attitudes implicitly in representing news 'realities'" (Pan 2015, p. 233).

Wu (2018) also combines frame analysis and appraisal theory in the analysis of the translation, in *Reference News*, of a set of stories on a Sino-Japanese territorial dispute centered on a group of uninhabited islands, while Liu (2019) offers a book-length analysis based on a theoretical model called "transframing" (i.e., "translation-mediated framing"), which attempts to combine insights from translation studies with concepts from frame analysis (based primarily on Entman 1993) and techniques of content analysis developed within communication studies. Liu codes source texts according to story "tone" (i.e., displaying a neutral, positive, or negative attitude toward the topic), "type" (hard vs. soft news) and "sensitivity" (i.e., whether or not they deal with issues perceived as sensitive – e.g., human rights, Tibet, Taiwan, etc.). These so-called "influencers" are correlated to so-called indicators of transframing, which are coded into the target texts and attributed a positive, negative, or neutral value. "Indicators" include framing "tone," "meaning," "degree," and "device" – e.g., use of metaphors or of "certain words, phrases or catchwords" (Liu 2019, p. 36), which "are realized through strategies in news transframing" (Liu 2019, p. 36), including additions, omissions, and various other types of transformation. Liu finds that stories with a "neutral tone'" do not undergo many changes, whereas positive tones are amplified, and negative tones are neutralized. Hard news is modified more often than soft news, and stories covering sensitive topics are "transframed," whereas neutral stories are not. Liu's (2017, 2019) analysis is based on translations published in both *Reference News* and British-owned *Financial Times Chinese*, which are "managed by different institutions with disparate ideological viewpoints and cultural perspectives" (Liu 2019, p. 10). She finds that, by and large, both outlets resort to the same types of reframing operations, though stories published in the former "yield more changes in framing tone, framing meaning, framing degree or framing device" than those published in the latter. The translation of news in *Financial Times Chinese* is also the subject of a study by Guangjun and Huanyao (2015), who compare the headlines of a set of source and target articles concerning South China Sea disputes, and after analyzing strategies of "substitution," "omission," "explication" as well as changes in modality and agentivity (within a CDA/SFL framework), conclude that the priority of Chinese translators lies in "producing translations suitable to target readers and censors' ideology, rather than linguistic equivalents" (p. 407).

Ping (2019) compares data from *Reference News*, *EJ Insight* from Hong Kong, *The New York Times Chinese* from the USA, and BBC Chinese from the UK, which address different target readers (the BBC and *The New York Times* websites are blocked in mainland China). Ping's study focuses on a controversy involving two elected legislators in Hong Kong who, during the oath-taking ceremony, expressed their disagreement about admitting Hong Kong as part of China. Ping (2019) compares the type and amount of framing strategies and argues that "consistent patterns of selection and framing can be found in the narratives produced by different media outlets" (p. 15), reflecting the respective "ideologies and power relations" (p. 16). Like Ping, Luo (2015) uses narrative theory and framing strategies to discuss translations published by a network of volunteers on Yeeyan.org, the "largest User Generated Content" translation community in China (p. 831). Originally motivated by an interest in "translating news from Western media which exposes the evil aspects of Chinese society" (p. 842), after a shutdown in 2009, Yeeyan's managers and translators "have become stricter in self-censorship" (p. 843). The author focuses on stories about the 2012 London Olympics published in the Sport section to investigate how certain narratives about China and Chinese sport in stories translated from Western media were reframed through selective appropriation (both concerning the choice of stories translated and regarding patterns of omission and addition within texts), labeling, temporal and spatial (re)framing, and repositioning of participants. Luo sees these framing devices "as the direct reflection but also as an effective indicator of the translators' socio-political positioning" and argues that, contrary to previous practice, Yeeyan translators infused the news with ethnocentric undertones and projected a very positive image of China and Chinese sport.

Zhang (2013) compares news headlines about international celebrities and events from the BBC, CNN, and Foxnews with headlines about the same events in Chinese media such as Youku.com and Sina Sports. Drawing on appraisal theory, she argues that English headlines display different stances and attitudes than those of "transedited" Chinese reports, which are "heavily mediated and recontextualized" (p. 408) in order to adapt them to the knowledge and values of Chinese readers. Kuo and Nakamura (2005) and Chen (2009) draw on CDA to discuss translation into Chinese in ideologically opposed Taiwanese newspapers. Kuo and Nakamura's study aims to uncover the ideological motivations behind the contrasting linguistic choices and editorial transformations in the translations of an interview with Taiwan's first lady. Chen (2009) looks at the translation of quotations from *The New York Times* and *The Washington Post* and argues that the different target newspapers use similar strategies to manipulate quotations and choose "those quotation contents congruent with [their] ideological viewpoints, and [delete] those incompatible with [their] ideologies" (Chen 2009, p. 228). Tsai (2005, 2006, 2010, 2012, 2015) investigates production practices and routines in the translation of international news in Taiwan's Formosa Television (FTV) newsroom (see Section 3.2.1).

Finally, Yun Pan (2017b) and Hu and Wang (2019) provide two studies on the training of students translating news texts from English into Chinese, while Laviosa et al. (2017) carry out a computerized sentiment analysis on a corpus of environmental news published in BBC Chinese.

Studies involving translation from Chinese into English are fewer; they include research in news reports in agencies and newspapers, as well as interpreted press conferences. Qin and Zhang (2018), for instance, compare reports on the Edward Snowden case published in Chinese by Xin-hua.net, Huanqiu.com, and *China Daily* with the English versions collected from Ecns.cn, all of them being state-owned news outlets. Qin and Zhang discuss their findings using a narrative approach, carrying out a qualitative and quantitative analysis of translation strategies in a corpus of forty-seven paired news items published in 2015. In particular, they look at selective appropriation (i.e., omission and addition) and labeling (i.e., generalization and specification) strategies, and they argue that news published on Ecns.cn is reframed and adapted to the target readership for diplomatic reasons too, as the USA is the second-largest subscriber to the agency. Thus, whereas in Chinese texts, "the US is projected in a negative light and is strongly condemned for its massive surveillance programme" (p. 273), critical or hostile stances toward the US government are omitted or played down in English translation, while the neutral attitude of the Chinese government toward the Snowden case is emphasized through textual additions. Drawing on van Dijk's (1988) socio-cognitive approach to CDA and on appraisal theory, Chen (2011a) analyses translation shifts in a corpus of twenty-six Chinese commentaries about the economic cooperation between Taiwan and China published in the *Liberty Times* and their English translations in *Taipei Times* (both published by the same media group in Taiwan but aimed at different readerships; see Section 2.3.2), and the author argues that source text writers (who check and approve the English versions produced by translators) construe different solidarity relations and "align with the Taiwanese readers in the source text, but with the diverse foreign readers in the target version" (p. 702). Drawing on Conway's (2010a) characterization of cultural translation as a form of cultural resistance, Tian and Chao (2012) discuss news trustworthiness and media credibility by examining readers' responses to a report of civil unrest in China in 2009 by *The Economist* and argue that the British weekly provided biased and unreliable coverage. Drawing on Fairclough's CDA model and SFL, Li (2009) compares *The New York Times*'s and *China Daily*'s reports of two events that marked moments of crisis in US–China relations – i.e., the NATO bombing of the Chinese embassy in Belgrade during the Kosovo war in 1999 and the air collision between a US and a Chinese airplane in 2001. Li discusses the respective ideological constructions of specific understandings of national identities and positions, arguing that while *The New York Times* "constructs an image of China caught up in wild nationalism with its irrational, fanatical, and essentially ineffectual protests to the bombing ... [and as] a potential threat to the US's politics and military" (p. 114), *China Daily* projects China as a nation that "promotes peace and justice through a condemnation of NATO's aggression and a heroization of its citizens" and "respects international regulations in its political and military activities."

Gu (2018, 2019) and Gu and Tipton (2020) analyze a computerized corpus containing twenty years of televised and interpreter-mediated China's Premier-Meets-the-Press conferences (1998–2017), where preselected and vetted questions by the national and international press are answered. These annual events are one of the main means of international diplomacy and show "the dynamic, mediat(is)ed and necessarily negotiated nature of the political press conferences ... [and] the potential mediating role of the interpreter as an additional subjective actor" (Gu 2018, p. 138) in constructing the public image of China. Starting from a list of English keywords obtained from the corpus of transcriptions of interpreted discourse and looking at the source texts of occurrences of forms of the present perfect containing the words "we," "China," and "government," Gu (2018) finds that most of these can be classified as optional shifts, – i.e., shifts not triggered by explicit Chinese temporal markers. The preference for these structures over the equally possible past tense forms on the part of the government-affiliated interpreters emphasizes the current and future relevance of past actions, enhancing the rhetorical force of the Chinese premier's statements and leading to a more positive image of the government and its achievements. Gu and Tipton (2020, p. 7) find that the frequency of these self-referential items in English "is almost double of that in Chinese," indicating "the interpreters' strong alignment and strengthening of the government's institutional hegemony." Gu (2019) investigates the word "people" when referred to the Chinese people as a collective, in order to determine "how hegemony and consensus is (re)mediated in English" (Gu 2019, p. 467). Interpreters tend to opt for the word "people" as a way to render not only the straightforward equivalent 人民 "renmin," but also related lexical items such as 大家 (dajia, "big family") and 群众 (qunzhong, "the masses"). Furthermore, 30 percent of all mentions of "people" in English are not triggered by a related lexical item in Chinese. Gu (2019, p. 481) argues that this "can be explained by the interpreters' active ideological mediation to avoid items that carry negative connotations in English," such as, for example, the word "masses." Collocational patterns such as "our people" and "of/to/for/by*people" are also more common in interpreted speeches than in comparable English corpora, showing that "the Chinese government is (re)presented as the benefactor and servant to the Chinese people" (Gu 2019, p. 490). The interpreters' words are often picked up and quoted verbatim in news articles by domestic and international media outlets, thus cumulatively contributing "to the discursive legitimisation and the further consolidation of the dominant position of the Chinese government as the chief social actor capable of delivering concrete benefits domestically and effecting change on an international scale" (Gu 2018, p. 146). Similarly, using data taken from eight Chinese–US joint press conferences held between 1999 and 2014, together with 125 segments presented as direct quotations and 279 segments presented as indirect reporting in eighty-five related news reports (totaling approximately 100,000 words in total) from a variety of sources and media institutions, Zheng and Ren (2018) show that selectively quoting interpreted discourse leads to considerable changes in meaning so that, for instance, omitting a reference by the Chinese Minister of National Defense to a statement by his US homologue results in what amounts to a groundless claim by the Chinese government (Zheng & Ren 2018, pp. 697–698).[16]

3.6.6 Korean

Several studies have discussed translation from English into Korean, focusing in particular on articles published in *Newsweek* and their translations in a version of the magazine published in South Korea, *Newsweek Hankuk Pan* (Kang 2007, p. 226; see Section 2.4.2). Kang (2007) examines three 2003 news stories on North Korea, while Kang (2010) considers a story, published in the same year, based on an interview conducted with the then newly elected South Korean President Roh Moo Hyun, and Kim (2017) investigates a bilingual corpus of 626 stories about China published between 2005 and 2015. Kang (2007) explains translation shifts in terms of recontextualization and reframing, and she argues that "the exceptionally negative representations of Kim Jong Il and North Korea are mitigated, and in some instances even nullified" (p. 236) in translation, stressing that shifts in meaning, achieved through cumulative re-perspectivization, are the result of collaborative work and institutionalized routines. She also observes that as tension with North Korea rose between 1998 and 2003, the percentage of original stories published in *Newsweek Hankuk Pan* during the period also grew with respect to those translated from *Newsweek*, possibly in the attempt "to resolve the problem of having to mediate between the intrusive discourse of the foreign voice, which constructs North Korea as the Other, and a local discourse that is more receptive and accepting of North Korea as Self" (pp. 239–240). With respect to the articles on President Roh Moo Hyun, Kang (2012) argues that, through its selection of translated interview parts, *Newsweek Hankuk Pan* blurs the boundaries between source and target text and constructs a different narrative of events from its English counterpart, evoking "a distinct and independent ... voice which explicitly comments on and questions" the *Newsweek* article (Kang 2010, p. 176), strategically downplaying the image of sameness between the two magazines and distancing itself from the views expressed in English. While, in the *Newsweek* article, Roh is portrayed

[16] On the English translation of Chinese political speeches, see also Li and Li (2015) and Wang and Feng (2018), who, however, do not address their treatment in the news media.

"as uncooperative and critical with respect to the US and as siding with anti-Americans" (p. 177), in translation, the focus is shifted "to convey Roh's opinion in an accurate and balanced way in relation to a range of social, economic, political, diplomatic and personal issues." Kim (2017) draws on methods from CDA and corpus linguistics and starts from the most frequent collocates of the words "Chin*" and "중국ㅁ*" (Chinaㅁ*")[17] in the English and Korean components of the corpus, respectively, focusing on "countries, cities, and regions" appearing in the top five hundred list. Kim notes, for instance, that "North Korea" and "Africa" feature as much stronger collocates of "China" in Korean translations than they do in English source texts, and goes on to examine the most common patterns in concordance lines in the two languages, which include a preference for "China" appearing as a modifier of the words "people" and "US" in Korean translations. Kim suggests that this exploratory study points to the way subtle linguistic changes are used to construct a different perspective in translation.

Kang (2012) examines the subtitling of sound bites from interviews and video footage in English in a 2008 episode of a television news magazine, namely "PD Swuchep" ("PD Notebook"), broadcast by a major Korean network. The episode, about the safety of US meat imports, created social uproar and "played a significant role in touching off many months of massive street rallies against the government" (p. 441). Kang argues that this was largely a consequence of how the subtitles explicitated, emphasized, and generalized the dangers of being infected with mad cow disease through reframing strategies, including shifts in referring expressions and epistemic modality, omissions, additions, and summarizations, whereby a distinct narrative was constructed in translation.

Lee (2006) compares the translation into English of broadcasting and newspapers reports. After discussing differences in summary lead structure between Korean and English, he shows that, while both reduction and expansion occur in translation for both broadcasting and newspapers, reduction through deletion or replacement of information is comparatively more frequent in the former, while expansion through the addition of background information is more frequent in the latter. He argues that this is because broadcasting places greater emphasis on brevity and simplicity, while translators are able to exercise more latitude in the case of newspapers. Park (2016) addresses translation in photojournalism, with a study on the translation into English and Japanese of photo captions. First, based on the analysis of photos of events occurring outside these cultures but covered by news media in the USA, the UK, Korea, and Japan, Park outlines major differences between agencies and

[17] The small square box is used to represent suffixes and other particles attached to the main lexical item.

newspapers in the different cultures. Korean and Japanese media source international news photos from global agencies and independently recaption them according to the national norms and styles. However, while Japanese outlets – like Anglophone media – privilege a "hard news" approach – e.g., captioning pictures of "conflict" in a denotative manner using words such as "protest," "violence," "clash," and "turmoil" – Korean media show a "softening" trend; i.e., captions tend to appeal emotionally to readers by describing the actions of people represented in the photos or the editor's interpretation of their thoughts. Then Park examines news photos from Korean agencies used by Anglophone and Japanese media and shows that, while "soft" captions are "hardened" in both Anglophone press agencies and daily newspapers, the features of hard news are only prevalent in Japanese agencies, while some Japanese newspapers appear to share the journalistic norms of Korean ones.

Kim (2014) examines a corpus of almost seventy million words including all reports containing the word combination "North Korea" published between 1998 and 2010 in *The New York Times*, CNN, and *Newsweek*. While not explicitly addressing results in a translation framework, this study can be considered an investigation in cultural translation, inasmuch as it aims at identifying discursive practices relating to the image of North Korea in US mainstream media. Combining a CDA approach with corpus linguistics methods, Kim examines nouns and adjectives related to countries and cities appearing in the top 300 collocate list of "North Korea." Based on a qualitative analysis of related concordance lines, Kim argues that the US media outlets, considered as a whole, polarize the world into specific sets of countries, and the association of a country with North Korea as well as with a positive or negative collocational profile depends on its pro- or antipolitical leaning toward the USA. Finally, Hong (2019, 2021) investigates the attribution of translated news to information sources (see Section 2.4.1) and the visibility and recognition of news translators in South Korea.

3.6.7 Other Languages

To conclude this survey, I offer a summary overview of a few studies on the translation of news involving Greek, Farsi, Ukrainian, Hungarian, German, and French. Translation into Greek has been investigated in a number of studies by Sidiropoulou (1995b, 1995a, 1998), Kontos and Sidiropoulou (2012a, 2012b), Loupaki (2010), Constantinou (2017), and Floros (2012). Sidiropoulou (1995b) and Kontos and Sidiropoulou (2012b) focus on headlines of articles translated from English language newspapers. Sidiropoulou contrasts structural and rhetorical formats in the two languages, arguing that Greek headlines are more descriptive, showing a preference for directness exemplified by the inclusion of direct quotations and the use of direct forms of questioning and first- and second-person pronouns, making use of figurative language to a lesser extent than English headlines. Kontos and Sidiropoulou blend narrative theory and CDA to examine how shifts in narrative features implement diversified perspectives on sociopolitical narratives of progress and civilization, justice, liberty and rights, and democracy. For instance, Greek headlines seem to display a preference for highlighting a binary conceptualization of the world. Sidiropoulou (1995a) observes a preference for explicating relationships of cause and effect between ideas in a sample of stories translated from English sources and hypothesizes that this is due to cultural differences in the way abstract relations are signaled in discourse. Sidiropoulou (1998, p. 320) argues that, in order to conform to the target ideological perspective and preferred conception of the world, even numerical quantities are adjusted in translation. Kontos and Sidiropoulou (2012b) discuss shifts in metaphor use and collocational meaning in two 2007 articles on the then British Prime Minister Tony Blair translated from *The Guardian* and *The New York Times* and published in the quality broadsheet *Η Καθημερινή* ("*I Kathimerini*"), and they argue that these are related to different communications styles and reveal alternative conceptualizations of the world. Loupaki (2010) also draws on CDA and narrative theory and examines four paired stories on the topic of terrorism published in similar source and target outlets. She discusses translation strategies used to strengthen or undermine particular features of ideological conflict in terms of lexical framing devices, suggesting that "the translator tries to comply with the ideological profile promoted by the [target] publication" (p. 72). Constantinou (2017) combines CDA, narrative theory, and corpus linguistics methods to investigate ideological placements and stance taking in the media coverage of terror attacks in articles translated from French and English into Greek and published in newspapers of different political orientation. Finally, Floros (2012) shows how, in the very conflictual Cypriot context, highly interventionist and manipulative news translation practices are used to "satisfy public feeling and disseminate national ideology" (p. 937) and argues that such practices ultimately challenge ethical norms.

Studies that investigate translation from English into Farsi include Kalanzade et al. (2013), Hosseini (2016), Talebinejad and Shahi (2017), and Sanatifar and Jalalian Daghigh (2018). Both Kalanzade et al. and Talebinejad and Shahi investigate translation practices at the Iranian Students News Agency (ISNA), a voluntary organization funded by the Iranian government and one of the major news sources in Iran. Kalanzade et al. provide a study of translation quality assessment involving the rating of a set of translations according to criteria of appropriateness, accuracy, naturalness, cohesion, and style. Drawing on CDA, SFL, and narrative theory, Talebinejad and Shahi (2017) show examples of how the news about Iranian nuclear negotiations underwent a series of "motivated and patterned manipulations" (p. 101), the main strategy being deletion. They argue that these practices contradict the ethics of journalistic translation. Sanatifar and Jalalian Daghigh (2018, p. 15) analyze translations into Farsi published in 2013 by *Diplomacy-e Irani*, an independent outlet that translated media from around the world for Farsi speakers in Iran and elsewhere, abiding by the media policies of the Islamic Republic of Iran. Drawing on narrative theory, they examine excerpts from news stories about Iran's nuclear program originally issued by Reuters and various other sources, and they show how they are reframed through selective appropriation, labeling, repositioning of participants, and temporal and spatial framing strategies in order to align them with the Iranian government's ideologies. Drawing on van Dijk's CDA model, Hosseini (2016) instead compares the translations of two sets of texts related to Iran's internal affairs published on the websites of BBC and Euronews, along with their English sources. He quantifies strategies of hyperbole, polarization, euphemism, and vagueness in the translated texts, and concludes that the only difference was that the BBC's translations have a higher degree of vagueness than those by Euronews. Shahi and Talebinejad (2017) and Pormouzeh (2014) consider instead the opposite translation direction, both drawing on narrative and framing theory. Shahi and Talebinejad examine a statement delivered in Farsi by an Iranian general and its translated versions included in reports published by the BBC, Reuters, *The Guardian*, Bloomberg, *The New York Times*, Al Jazeera, and Al-Monitor. They conclude that the idea of translation as "faithful representation" is challenged by the way the text is reframed through strategies of selective appropriation, overstatement, labeling, temporal framing, and inclusion of temporary narrators. Similarly, Pormouzeh considers a set of fifteen news stories originally broadcasted by Iranian media between 2000 and 2012 and translated by (mostly) US media – including *The New York Times*, MEMRI, and others. He compares features of narrativity in source and target texts and concludes that the framing strategies used result in the "renarration of Iran in the western media and news agencies" (2014, p. 618). Finally, a much-investigated incident is the translation and mediatization of a statement by the then Iranian president Ahmadinejad in 2005, supposedly calling for the annihilation of the state of Israel (Schäffner 2010; Sanatifar 2015; Zanettin 2016b).

Kamyanets (2017) draws on pragmatics and, more specifically, on Sperber and Wilson's (1995) relevance theory to discuss a series of ironic statements selected from three opinion articles published between 2010 and 2014 in a quality Ukrainian magazine, *Ukrainskyi Tyzhden*, whose English version, *The Ukrainian Week*, is distributed to foreigners via channels such as international airlines, embassies, and hotels, as well as through the magazine's website. Kamyanets (2020) investigates shifts in attitudinal strength in the English translations of ten opinion articles that appeared in the same publication.

Drawing on appraisal theory and narrative theory, she argues that the English translations are more restrained in their criticism of the Ukrainian political establishment than the source Ukrainian articles. This comes as the result of selective appropriation, whereas the translations mitigate the strength of the attitude toward Ukrainian actors and events by omitting evaluative adjectives and nouns, as well as entire sentences with a strong evaluative value. Similarly, she argues that there is an overall tendency to reduce the intensity of evaluative strength in translation, as some metaphors are omitted or translated with idioms, and ironic remarks are often edited out.

Károly (2012, 2017a, 2017b) and Károly et al. (2013) carry out a detailed investigation of cohesion and coherence in a small corpus of twenty paired "analytical articles" – i.e., the English translations of the summary sections of Hungarian news stories published in the online news magazine *Budapest Analyses*, together with their sources. The English translations published in this bilingual news site of local news stories in Hungarian were apparently carried out by nonnative speakers of English (Károly 2017a, p. 99). Károly bases the analysis on her so-called Complex Translational Discourse Analysis (CTDA) model, which integrates Halliday and Hasan's (1976) and Halliday's (1985) discussion of cohesion as realized by words in texts with work by other linguists such as Mann and Thompson (1986), Lautamatti (1990), Bell (1991), and Hoey (1991). Károly combines quantitative measures of lexical cohesion (grouped according to the main types of cohesive devices – i.e., reference, substitution and ellipsis, conjunction, and lexical cohesion), referring expressions (e.g., pronouns and demonstratives), and repetition (based on Hoey 1991) with an in-depth, qualitative analysis of cohesive shifts between source and target texts. The parallel corpus is mostly used as a basis for contrastive linguistic analysis and for testing the explicitation hypothesis (Baker 1993).

News translation into or out of German has been investigated in a number of studies by Schäffner (2005, 2008, 2010, 2015). Schäffner (2005) discusses the reason behind the "domesticating" selection of articles translated into English from *Der Spiegel* and made available online, arguing the aim was to "provide fluent, transparent texts that conform to the expectations and reading habits of the English-speaking addressees" (p. 160). Schäffner (2008, 2010) provides examples of different types of translated and mediatized political discourse – including interviews, press conferences, and political speeches. In particular, she discusses a 2006 joint press conference by the German Chancellor Angela Merkel and the US President George W. Bush held in Germany. Schäffner (2015) looks instead at two joint press conferences between Merkel, the British Prime Minister David Cameron (2010), and the French President Nicolas Sarkozy (2012), respectively. Matsushita and Schäffner (2018) conduct a detailed analysis of two translingual quotations from a speech by the Japanese prime minister and from reports about it in

German media, most of which contained the quotations. A comparison with English translations and media is also included in the study.

Research on news media translation involving French includes studies discussing the AFP news agency and French-language news stories translated into various languages, as well as research focused on France and countries where French is one of the official languages, such as Switzerland and Canada. Several of these studies (e.g., Conway 2006, 2010b, 2010a, 2011, 2014: Davier 2014, 2015; Ehrensberger-Dow and Perrin 2009, 2013; Franjié 2009; Perrin and Ehrensberger-Dow 2018; Perrin et al. 2017) have been considered in previous sections. Other studies include Gendron et al. (2019) and Davier (2019), both on the Canadian Broadcasting Corporation; Demers (1994), who compares headlines in French and English language newspapers; Gagnon (2012) on the translation of political journalism in Canada; Gagnon et al. (2018), who investigate inter- and intralingual translation in a French and English financial corpus of Canadian newspapers; and Bugnot (2012), who investigates the representation of Islam in French and Spanish newspapers.

4 Ethnomethodology and News Media Translation

4.1 Introduction

In this chapter, I introduce a novel approach to the study of news translation, which is intended to complement the various approaches surveyed in Chapter 3. Ethnomethodology is a field of sociology that focuses on conduct as the foundation of social order and studies "the commonsense resources, procedures, and practices through which the members of a culture produce and recognize mutually intelligible objects, events, and courses of action" (Heritage 1993, p. 856). An ethnomethological approach to news media translation is concerned with an analysis of the conventionally available textual options that orient the reader to understand a text as an objective reproduction of reality. How does a specific textual realization – for instance, a translation – make it possible to understand a newspaper article as a commonsense account of reality, and how is this account different from a very similar account of the same event – i.e., the source text(s) for the translation? While this chapter focuses on translation products and detailed textual analysis, ethnomethodology has also clear implications for process research, in that it can also be used to investigate workplace practices and routines (Perrin et al. 2017, p. 468).

After a short introduction to the main concepts of ethnomethodology, I examine a first line of research primarily based on this theoretical perspective – i.e., conversation analysis (CA) – and its application to the analysis of news media translation. Then I focus on membership categorization analysis (MCA), a related strand of ethnomethodology, and consider in particular research on newspaper texts. In the last section of this chapter, I look at the application of MCA to news media translation through two case studies. In the first of these, I consider the translation of a story first published in *The Observer* and later translated in the Italian magazine *Internazionale*. In the second case study, I look at how a range of different news outlets, in English and in Italian, reported on an "incident" that took place in Gaza in February 2020, focusing in particular on two sets of reports, published on two consecutive days by *The Guardian* and *La Repubblica* – one of the latter being the translation of the text published by the former the previous day. It is proposed that corpus tools and resources can be used to supplement MCA in the analysis of how different narratives are instantiated in translated news texts.

4.2 Ethnomethodology

The term ethnomethodology was coined by the US sociologist Harold Garfinkel – after cognate anthropological terms such as ethnobotany and ethnomusicology – as a label for the study of "the rational properties of indexical expressions and other practical actions as contingent ongoing accomplishments of organized artful practices of everyday life" (Garfinkel 1967, p. 11). Ethnomethodologists have developed a distinct notional and terminological arsenal in order to describe and explain their analytical approach, using concepts that are often interlocked – i.e., used in a circular way so as to define one another. In order to provide a summary overview of ethnomethodology, I offer a discussion of some of the main terms used in this field of research, starting with the word ethnomethodology itself.

The term ethnomethodology comprises the word "methodology," in which the "methods" that are the object of study are the routines and procedures produced by participants in social interaction as properties of the context that is being created through their actions, while the suffix "ethno-" is used to "mark that these methods are used by a community with shared knowledge and language" (vom Lehn 2014, p. 82). It is important to underline that the "methods" are not preexisting rules that have been internalized and are applied on specific occasions, but, rather, they are common sense practices that are used by social actors for the "managed accomplishment of organized settings of practical actions" (Garfinkel 1967, p. 32). It is insisted that actions are to be understood as being "accomplished" or achieved locally "rather than being predetermined by a semantic code" (Hammersley 2018, p. 149), and that the "methods" are the procedures and policies that make sense for those enacting them in any particular context and endeavor. The shared agreement foregrounded in the suffix "ethno-" does not refer to a common understanding of the propositional content under consideration, the "substantive matters" (Garfinkel 1967, p. 30) of something being discussed but, rather, points to a common understanding of the reasoning procedures that are used to interpret that something. That is, the agreement concerns the need not to explain to other participants in the interaction what was meant. The subject matter of ethnomethodology is thus "the body of common-sense knowledge and the range of procedures and considerations by means of which the ordinary members of society make sense of, find their way about in, and act on the circumstances in which they find themselves" (Heritage 1984, p. 4).

Two crucial and interrelated notions that characterize the understanding of what is meant by context in the ethnomethodological perspective are indexicality and reflexivity. According to Garfinkel, meaning is created through processes of social interaction that both depend on and shape context. That is, any communicative action is "doubly contextual" (Heritage 1984, p. 242) in that it can only be interpreted in relation to its preceding and following actions, and at the same time, each action constantly redefines its context. In other words, the meanings of actions follow "a hermeneutic circle" (Heritage 1984, p. 83), in that they are locally constituted (indexicality) over time through prospective and retrospective processes, and at the same time, they are context renewing (reflexivity), because "the means by which any action is made sense of involves reciprocally identifying features of its context" (Hammersley 2018, p. 135). That the meanings of social actions are indexical and reflexive means not only that they are locally variable and context dependent, but also that they are intersubjective; that is, they depend on whether the status of actions is confirmed or challenged by how others respond to them, on how they are accounted for by social actors.

The concept of accountability is, in fact, another central tenet of Garfinkel's thinking. In order for orderly social processes to occur and be mutually intelligible, the meaning of social actions must be publicly displayed and be accessible to all parties involved. Social reality is constituted through the accountability of actions – that is, "their meaning is displayed and recognised by actors via shared methods and practices, in the course of ongoing processes of social interaction" (Hammersley 2018, p. 89). Meaning is generated by actions that are recognizable and can be described by participants as well as the analyst. In fact, there is no necessary distinction between social actors and analysts other than that social actors usually take mutually intelligible actions for granted and, thus, without the need to be explained, whereas analysts interrogate the means by which these "ordering practices," which are "open to direct investigation" (Hammersley 2018, p. 93), are taken for granted. The focus of ethnomethodological enquiries is on explicating how participants themselves understand their mutual actions, based on the assumption that the methods employed by social actors for making sense of the world are perceived by them as natural, as the way things are, as common sense. The task of the researcher is to describe the practices designed to make sense of what is going on and to find out what in the description negotiated by participants is taken for granted, how something is methodically assumed to be the case, in order to reveal how social order is generated and maintained through intelligible patterns of interaction. Unlike mainstream sociological tradition, ethnomethodology is interested in systematically investigating the role of "the obvious," of what "goes without saying," what "stands beyond question," or what "can by supplied by the hearer/reader" (Sharrock 1989, p. 662), without assuming that social institutions and structures exist independently of and determine the perceptions and practices of social actors. Since meaning is locally produced through "methods that are reflexively embedded in concrete social situations, the precise nature of that achievement cannot be determined by the analyst through a priori stipulation or deductive reasoning" (Maynard & Clayman 2003, p. 175). In this sense, ethnomethodological work refrains from "all forms of decontextualization of its materials in order to derive generalizable analyses of the *endogenous* methods of their production by the agents who produce them" (Jalbert 1999, p. xvi).

Ethnomethodology was first conceived and developed by Garfinkel in the context of a study of jury deliberation, and the centrality of this setting can be seen in its ethical tension, its preoccupation with moral implications implied in the use of terms such as accountability in reference to mundane knowledge and reasoning procedures that are observable and reportable. The commonsense character of sense-making procedures involves not just empirical regularity but also an underlying moral dimension, since the disruption of states of affairs perceived as "normal" may provoke sanctions (Maynard & Clayman 2003, pp. 178–179).

Ethnomethodological research has concerned itself with a variety of investigations of practical reasoning in action, taking place in a variety of settings and including a range of human activities. Studies have considered practices enacted in formal work contexts by, among others, optometrists, lawyers, and quality assurance inspectors, as well as nonoccupational activities and individual experiences such as learning to play jazz piano or to practice kung fu. Garfinkel's approach to the study of social action has inspired different lines of enquiry. Ethnographic studies of human behavior include the application of legal and bureaucratic rules in settings like police stations, courtrooms, and welfare agencies, the establishment and maintenance of queues, the production of mathematical demonstrations and the teaching of science, and human–computer interaction.[1]

Shared knowledge and understanding are achieved to a large extent through the specific type of symbolic action that is linguistic behavior (though, of course, natural language occurs in situated physical contexts and along with other symbolic actions perceived and processed through all the sensory systems). Perhaps the most notable development of ethnomethodology stemmed from the work of Harvey Sacks on conversation analysis (CA) and membership categorization analysis (MCA), which focus primarily on one specific type of social behavior – that is, the use of natural language. In particular, CA focuses on spoken language as the most potent tool of social

[1] Another important theoretical development influenced by ethnomethodology, as well as by semiotics, is actor–network theory (ANT; see Section 3.2.1).

action and on the mechanisms that regulate conversation as they are used to accomplish social goals. Before examining in more detail CA and MCA and considering their applicability to research in news media translation, in what follows, I outline some of the similarities and differences between the different perspectives on text, discourse, and translation conveyed by analyses informed by ethnomethodology, symbolic interactionism, critical discourse analysis (CDA), and narrative theory – these latter being, as seen in the previous chapter, the most common approaches adopted in product-oriented news media translation research.

CDA, narrative theory, symbolic interactionism, and ethnomethodology share a constructivist approach to reality, in that they do not take reality as a given that has to be uncovered but as something that is construed as it is being described and explained. Thus, while there are certainly major differences between these theories, it could be argued that, as compared to the differences that bear between any of them and essentialist and positivistic views of reality and social research – for instance, any mechanistic view of translation and interpreting practices as the "neutral" transfer of information – these differences simply amount to a diversity of emphasis. As opposed to social constructionism, however, ethnomethodology stresses its reliance on the analytical categories displayed by members rather than on theories elaborated by professional analysts (Eglin & Hester 2003, pp. 6–9).

Ethnomethodology has been defined as a "micro-sociology" in that, like symbolic interactionism (see Section 3.3.3), it is interested in describing the underlying patterns of everyday social practices and methodical actions by means of which people constitute social phenomena rather than in devising abstract theoretical accounts of social structure, which are the object of macro-sociological models (Hammersley 2018; Tyulenev 2014). Both ethnomethodology and symbolic interactionism focus on processes of communication and ordinary social interaction. However, whereas Goffman provides formal conceptual analyses using metaphorical abstractions, Garfinkel is interested in providing literal descriptions using the participants' own categories. Thus, while both investigate everyday social interaction and are concerned with "practical intersubjectivity" (Maynard & Clayman 2003, p. 196), symbolic interactionists "tend to focus on comparatively broad meanings and persistent definitions of the situation rather than singular actions and the sequences in which their meanings emerge" (Maynard & Clayman 2003, p. 174), whereas ethnomethodological investigations subject such practices to "sustained empirical analysis" (Maynard & Clayman 2003, p. 196) based on very detailed observation.

As opposed to ethnomethodology and symbolic interactionism, CDA and narrative theory are macro-theories. CDA emphasizes the social embeddedness of texts, how ideology and the political and social setting of communication affect the form and meaning of messages. Thus, while Fairclough and Wodak's (1997) CDA model, for instance, emphasizes the mutual impact of and dialectical relationship between discursive events and the wider social context in which language is used, whereby events are framed by institutional and social structures and at the same time contribute to shape them, there is a clear hierarchical relationship between the two, insomuch as texts are ultimately interpreted and explained in light of social structures. The notion of "discourse," as conceived in CDA, bears similarities to that of "narrative," as defined in sociological narrative studies. According to Baker (2018), however, while the former refers primarily to the way knowledge is constructed and mediated through (oral and written) text, the latter is more versatile in that it lends itself more readily to its realization through different media as well as nonverbal and paratextual material. Furthermore, she argues, while CDA emphasizes abstract social structures of knowledge, "narrative theory also pays considerable attention to the detailed, concrete stories of everyday life and the personal dimension of experience. It further acknowledges that individuals can and do exercise agency and are not mere products of discourses nor of dominant narratives" (Baker 2018, p. 189). Conversely though, it has been argued that CDA is not a homogeneous theory but, rather, a research agenda or paradigm that does not rely on a single approach or methodology (Wodak 2011). In this respect, CDA can be seen as neither in opposition to nor in agreement with analytical approaches such as narrative theory, symbolic interactionism, and ethnomethodology, but as potentially inclusive of them as long as they serve its critical research perspective. Similarly, some proponents of narrative theory suggest that ethnomethodology looks at the methods through which local narratives are created, and that CA and MCA allow a detailed investigation of the procedures by which people actually construct narratives through linguistic accounts of actions and persons (Herman 2009, pp. 446–454). Practitioners of ethnomethodological approaches, on the other hand, often insist on their radical and paradigmatic difference from other theoretical frameworks (Hammersley 2003) and maintain that ethnomethodology is not interested in being incorporated into a macro-perspective, disavowing any correlation between micro and macro social structuring. Be that it as it may, an engagement with the different theoretical positions – which, of course, critically depends on the definition of discourse and narrative, as well as on the understanding of concepts such as paradigm, approach, theory, method, etc. – is beyond the scope of this book, whose aim is primarily to foreground the insights that can be brought by ethnomethodology to the study of news media translation.

Thus, the approach proposed here is based on an ethnomethodological understanding and definition of context, according to which context is never a given, something that exists independently of and determines a text, but it is always locally constituted through the participants' actions. Rather than looking at how a narrative is instantiated into translated news texts or try to explain the meaning of a discursive event on the basis of external social structures, it considers the interpretation of events that it is preferably oriented to by a translation as the outcome of locally accomplished and contingent methods of production. This type of textual analysis may be able to deal with some of the nuances and ambiguities often intrinsic in news texts.

4.2.1 Conversation Analysis and News Media Interpreting

Conversation analysis has grown out of the founding work of Harvey Sacks (1935–1975) and his colleagues, and is a rigorous empirical approach within the ethnomethodological tradition, though it has also been influenced by other approaches to the study of verbal communication, most notably including symbolic interactionism (Goffman 1974, 1981), but also generative linguistics (Chomsky 1965), anthropology, and ethnography.[2] In particular, CA and symbolic interactionism share a common interest in the study of "social life in situ and from the standpoint of societal members themselves" (Maynard & Clayman 2003, p. 173). CA offers tools for a detailed analysis of the local production of social order and of the resources that are drawn upon in structuring participatory frameworks (Goffman 1981, pp. 124–159) in face-to-face human interaction.

As opposed to other approaches to the study of spoken discourse, CA relies on the notion of locally organized context. Rather than looking at how a given social and cultural environment influences the way speakers behave, it looks at how conversational identities and roles are co-constructed in interaction through systematic methods or practices. CA attempts to explain communicative transactions in the same terms used by participants to reach a shared understanding about what they are doing in the course of interaction. By looking at naturally occurring (interpreted) data in as much detail as possible, CA reveals the resources participants systematically have recourse to in negotiating and constructing meaning to perform social actions. These can be analyzed not only in terms of the underlying structural organization of talk, but also in terms of the interplay between this underlying organization and recurring patterns of nonverbal behavior, including body language and interaction with the environment (Goodwin 2000). Initial work in CA focused on the basic mechanisms that regulate conversation in different settings of ordinary life, looking at how participants in mundane conversational

[2] Sacks was a student and then a colleague of both Garfinkel and Goffman. See Silverman (1998) for an overview of Sacks's view of the social sciences. See Lynch (2019) and Maynard and Clayman (2003) for a discussion of the relationship between ethnomethodology and CA.

interaction shape their contributions in terms of their relevance to the ongoing-conversation (Atkinson & Heritage 1984). Later research has also investigated communication in institutional and work-related settings, where conversational rights are distributed asymmetrically among participants (Drew & Heritage 1993).

In order to provide a description of the regular mechanisms that make an orderly conversation possible and allow for the co-construction of meaning, CA relies on the meticulous analysis of interactional data, which are carefully recorded, transcribed, and annotated. Practitioners of CA have developed a very specific set of transcription conventions that take into account not only the linguistic features but also the finest details of verbal as well as nonverbal communication practices (e.g., Jefferson 1973, 1996; Schenkein 1978). These symbolic notations are intended to capture phenomena such as overlapping speech, interruptions, pauses, and backchanneling; suprasegmental features such as length, intonation, stress, and tone; vocal and nonvocal behavior, including sighs, breath intakes, laughter, gaze, nods, and smiles, among other features. Based on the analysis of recordings and transcriptions of naturally occurring conversational exchanges in a variety of social settings, CA researchers have identified three main types of phenomena that structure conversation: turn taking, sequential organization, and repair management (Maynard & Peräkylä 2003; Sacks et al. 1974; Silverman 1998).

Conversational exchanges are highly structured verbal actions whose workings often go unnoticed and whose flow is thus taken for granted; however, they are, in fact, regulated by conventional procedures whose organization can routinely be observed and reported. Speaker selection is the main mechanism that regulates conversational exchanges, allowing interlocutors to carry out orderly interaction, negotiating and co-creating meaning, and ensuring that only one interlocutor is speaking at any one time. Sacks et al. (1974) show how conversational turns are allocated through a series of consecutive and recursive options. It is the current speaker who selects the next speaker in the first instance. Failing that, the next interlocutor may self-select, and, failing that too, the first speaker may resume speaking. This mechanism is cyclically reenacted at each transition-relevant point – that is, each time a potential completion is projected in the next turn. The moment at which speaker transition may take place is determined by the participants in a conversation through a series of clues. The transition between one turn and the next may become a relevant option when an utterance can be treated as grammatically complete, when the end of a turn is signaled by intonation, or if an utterance is perceived as completing a sequence initiated by a previous turn. These mechanisms allow for the minimization of pauses and overlaps in conversation (Jefferson 1973). Short overlaps may occur, for instance, when the current speaker does not select the next speaker at a transition-relevant point and two interlocutors self-select at the same time. Such overlaps, however, usually last only very briefly, as one speaker interrupts their turn before completion (Maynard & Clayman 2003, p. 189). Overlaps may also occur when a speaker self-selects and begins to talk without waiting for the end of the current speaker's turn, having projected its completion. When, at a transition-relevant point, none of the speakers talk, there is a pause in conversation. A long pause can be perceived as silence, a violation of the rules of interaction.

Participants structure their contributions as sequences of actions whose basic form is that of adjacency pairs (Schegloff & Sacks 1973) – for instance, greeting and greeting, question and answer, invitation and acceptance. Adjacency pairs are characterized by conditional relevance, as conversational turns are understood in light of what has been said and of what follows. Thus, the lack of a reply to a question is understood as meaningful, perhaps as being caused by a misunderstanding of the question, and may initiate a repair sequence. Sequences of turns accomplish specific courses of action, such as accepting or declining an invitation, reaching an agreement, or negotiating a transaction. Each turn potentially represents a completion of the sequence initiated in the previous turn as well as the beginning of a new sequence that is projected on the following turn. Such rules enable the flow of conversation so that interlocutors can engage in meaningful interaction and reach some kind of understanding on what is being said.

In ordinary conversation, turns are not allocated in advance; rather, their distribution is locally produced as participants engage in making sense of their own and the other participants' contributions. Utterances and turns do not have a predefined extension; they may consist of a minimal verbal response or a nod or of a rather extended turn involving multiple utterances. Extended turns, as in the telling of a story, are often prefaced by a pre-sequence in which a speaker negotiates the extended turn and a temporary deferral of the turn allocation system with the other participants, thus preventing them from starting to talk at the first transition-relevant point (Jefferson 1978; Sacks 1974; Schegloff 1980). Participants may contribute to the conversation by interjecting minimal vocal responses and other continuers at possible transition-relevant points. In order to be complete, a story must typically be proposed by the teller and subsequently "accepted by the recipient by recognition of completion and display of understanding" (Schegloff 1984, p. 45).

The first part of an adjacency pair does not only project a second part but may also present the interlocutor with the option of alternative actions, which have been shown to be routinely structured according to what Pomerantz (1984) calls preference organization. The concept of preference organization does not refer to a psychological inclination but, rather, to what is routinely projected as preferred by the first turn in an adjacency pair or other sequence. It refers to the implicit evaluation carried out in the conclusive part of the sequence rather than to the reply favored by a speaker. Thus, a short pause, when occurring at the beginning of a reply to a yes/no question or an invitation, and even if followed by acceptance, may be perceived as signaling a dispreferred activity, while an indirect expression of disagreement may be perceived as preferred in response to a negative evaluation or judgment. The turn allocation system provides participants with the resources for accepting, acknowledging, or repairing communication problems, thus enhancing intersubjectivity and mutual understanding (Jefferson 1974, 1987; Schegloff 1979; Schegloff et al. 1977). A dispreferred response in a question/answer adjacency pair may therefore open up a three-turn repair management sequence in which the second turn is used by the current speaker to first assess comprehension and then possibly initiate a repair activity in the following turn, or in which the next speaker may either correct the current speaker or ask for repair work, such as a clarification or a reformulation.

CA has been applied to research based on empirical data from interpreting performances, providing insights into how interpreters contribute to the effectiveness of service in multiparty interactions and the construction of participants' roles and identities by negotiating conversational rights, managing coordination, and promoting participation. One of the first applications of CA in translation studies was Wadensjö's (1998) study of interpreting as interaction, in which she discusses the role of the interpreter in public service interpreting as consisting of both relaying propositional content and coordinating the exchange. Wadensjö points out that the interpreter's task does not simply consist of filling in slots in preallocated second turns of talk by providing translated utterances. Rather, a major part of the interpreter's work consists of the management of talk organization and includes utterances that do not have a corresponding source-language stretch. These often feature in dyadic exchanges where the two principal interlocutors orient their contributions toward the interpreter rather than each other, and they often address metacommunicative issues, including requests for clarifications, reformulations, and repairs. Similarly, Davidson (2002), in relation to institutional discourse, discusses interpreted-mediated interaction as a turn-taking system in which interpreters are involved as active participants in the construction of conversational meaning. Davidson (2002, p. 1277) looks at how "conversational common ground" might be constructed by different participants, including interpreters, as they negotiate the meaning of the various utterances produced within an ongoing conversation.

Baraldi and Gavioli (2012) show how verbal activities that are primarily renditions may also serve the function of coordinating talk, while reflexive behavior focusing on interactional coordination also contributes to the effectiveness of the translation activity. Thus, renditions not only serve a basic coordinating function in that it is through them that the interpreter selects a speaker for the next turn, but also often contribute to the unfolding negotiation of meaning – for instance, by elaborating propositional content through reformulation or simplification. On the other hand, nonrenditions play a function in contributing to the mutual alignment of the parties and in achieving smooth communication or, conversely, in highlighting points of friction deriving from interpreters' loyalties to and affiliations with either party.

CA has informed much research in the growing area of community and public service interpreting in a wide range of professional and nonprofessional settings, including in health and mental care contexts (e.g., Baraldi & Gavioli 2014; Bolden 2000; Gavioli 2012, 2015b; Pasquandrea 2011; Wadensjö 2001; Zorzi 2012), at the police and other legal institutions (e.g., Mason 2012; Nakane 2007, 2011, 2014; Wadensjö 2010), in educational settings (Vargas-Urpi 2015), in the contexts of guided tours (Gavioli 2015a), in nonprofessional contexts involving language brokering by family members (Traverso 2012), and in situations involving sign language interpreting (e.g., Roy 2000; Metzger 1999).[3]

CA has also been applied to studies of televised dialogue interpreting, which differ from postproduction news media translation based on revoicing modes such as voice-over and dubbing or subtitling, in that interpreting is carried out live, regardless of whether it is broadcast in real time or at a later date. Research has investigated different types of such settings, including press conferences (e.g., Sandrelli 2015, 2017; Straniero Sergio 2003; Liao & Pan 2018) and talk shows (e.g., Straniero Sergio 1999, 2007, 2011, 2012a, 2012b; Wadensjö 2008a, 2008b). Research in dialogue interpreting has often availed itself of conceptual tools introduced by Goffman (1981), who distinguished between different normative specifications of appropriate conduct for the commonly described roles of speaker and hearer in conversation. He decomposes speech production and reception into finer categories, discussed in relation to the concepts of production format and participatory framework. Thus, on the one hand, Goffman differentiates between the different capacities involved in the production format of an utterance – namely those of animator, author, and principal (Goffman 1981, p. 226) – which, though commonly

[3] Studies discussing verbal practices in interpreted encounters have considered, for instance, the function of interpreters' minimal response in achieving coordination (Gavioli 2012), of replies to yes no/questions in securing conversational space (Wadensjö 2010), and of evaluative sequences in negotiating the identity of interpreters as ratified participants in mediated encounters (Zorzi 2012). Other studies have focused on nonverbal behavior. Mason (2012), for example, suggests that gaze not only reflects and influences patterns of participation but also conveys the interpreter's affiliation or disengagement, while Wadensjö (2001) observes that the position and physical orientation of the participants affect the management of the interaction and the synchronization of talk.

present in one speaker, may be separated when, for instance, someone reads aloud or delivers a memorized speech by a different author. On the other hand, the concept of participation framework also refers to the status and capacity in which recipients are selected (or not) to participate in the interaction, according to recipient design (Sacks 1992b; Sacks et al. 1974). Thus, possible recipients are the person(s) directly addressed in a conversation but may also include other parties, who may be either ratified – i.e., acknowledged as recipients but not directly addressed – or not ratified – i.e., someone else listening to the conversation, either internationally or not.

In both talk shows and press conferences, interpreters may be physically present and on-screen or feature only as off-screen disembodied voices. Straniero Sergio (1999, 2007, 2012b) discusses several examples of interpreting taken from a large corpus of Italian talk shows, which are "info-tainment" programs mixing together the features of information, entertainment, and opinion. He shows that participants may engage in complex and dynamic changes of footing (Goffman 1981, p. 227); i.e., they may change their alignment with respect to a particular utterance both as concerns production format and participation status. Thus, host-initiated repair sequences may engage interpreters as ratified participants in the interaction (Straniero Sergio 2012b), and interpreters may switch between different recipients and orient the utterances they produce either to the direct addressees or to the secondary audience. Such alignment work is, in fact, characteristic of broadcast talk, "which is designed for (absent) overhearers" (Wadensjö 2008b, p. 122). Interpreters do not simply act as animators of someone else's propositional content, but also as authors, in as much as they take responsibility for the words they themselves utter as appropriate renditions of the interpreted parties. Furthermore, an interpreter sometimes may be required to take on the more active role of discussant and entertainer, therefore acting as principal – i.e., "someone who believes personally in what is being said and takes the position that is implied in the remarks" (Goffman 1981, p. 167).

While Straniero Sergio's examples are taken mostly from "tabloid" and "lifestyle" shows, Wadensjö (2008a, 2008b) discusses a political interview with the former leader of the Soviet Union Mikhail Gorbachev conducted by a BBC journalist. An interpreter is sitting next to Gorbachev and translates into English for the benefit of the host and the audience and into Russian for Gorbachev, in whispering mode. Wadensjö shows that, even though – as opposed to examples discussed by Straniero Sergio (1999) – the interpreter does not align himself with the host and declines to participate as an interlocutor, he may still be seen as acting as a principal. Through his "precisely timed self-selection, and the pragmatic characteristics of his renditions" (Wadensjö

2008b, p. 142), in fact, the interpreter "provided Gorbachev with the resources needed to locate upcoming places to begin speaking and to keep the turn at talk." Wadensjö argues that through his (non)renditions of the participants' contributions and paired sequences and his nonverbal behavior, the interpreter manages turn allocation at transition-relevant points in a way that tacitly supports Gorbachev's communicative project rather than that of the program's host.

Straniero Sergio and Wadensjö illustrate how interpreters are often ratified and active participants in talk shows, rather than fitting the traditional image of interpreters as invisible translating machines. The case studies they discuss, however, involve primarily dialogue interpreting in the consecutive mode, in which a physically present interpreter is entitled to a turn of talk distinct from that of the primary participants. Thus, the discursive and physical spaces available to them provide interpreters with several resources that allow them to become full-fledged participants in the interaction. In a forthcoming work, Caniglia and Zanettin focus instead on off-screen simultaneous media interpreting, in which the interpreters do not share a physical space with hosts and guests, reproducing the arrangement of conference interpreting. Contrary to what the physical arrangement of such programs as well as some literature (e.g., Viaggio 2001) seem to implicitly suggest, simultaneous interpreters are active participants in the context of political talk shows and play a central role in the accomplishment of the interactional practices of which such shows are made of.

Caniglia and Zanettin discuss the communicative actions of simultaneous interpreters in two political talk shows broadcast on Italian TV: a 2018 panel interview show featuring, among other guests, the British Eurosceptic politician and future leader of the Brexit Party Nigel Farage and a 2007 interview with Tariq Ramadan, a Swiss Muslim academic, philosopher, and writer. According to Hutchby (2006, pp. 65–80), contemporary political talk shows are largely based on creating the "spectacle of confrontation" – i.e., what has been referred to as "confrontainment" (see, e.g., Lorenzo-Dus 2009) rather than "infotainment." The main interaction modality of these shows, which owe their success to the heated debates taking place between participants, is conflict. Interviews and panel discussions often turn into real disputes, with participants giving free rein to their disagreements and staging verbal combats, which are fueled not so much by the presentation of opposed arguments and views but by communicative actions that turn disagreement into conflict. Typically, conflictual interactional modalities include the competition for turn space and control; the exchange of rapid quips and retorts; the production of adjacent pairs such as accusations and defenses, sarcastic laughs, point-blank questions; and so on. Hosts usually allow this to happen without intervening, or even instigate confrontations between guests or take an active part in them (Clayman & Heritage 2002).

Turn-taking competition is one of the most apparent aspects of talk show dynamics. Rather than talking one at a time, guests and hosts try to take the floor away from each other talking over someone else's turn, and persistent competitive overlap is, in fact, characteristic of televised talk shows (Schegloff 1988/89). Participants prevail or make the best impression when they manage to gain the floor, to not let themselves be overtaken by their opponents, or to confound them. In these situations, interpreters are often driven into the fray, invisibility notwithstanding, and their behavior has relevant consequences. Thus, for instance, in Excerpt 1, while Farage is talking (line 1), another guest cuts in (line2), and the interpreter interrupts his rendition of Farage's utterance (line 3) rather than overlapping with the other guest, who thus manages to continue undisturbed (line 4), while Farage is suddenly silenced.

Excerpt 1 F (Nigel Farage), I (interpreter), G (other guest)[4]

1	F:	[(*inaudible*)
2	G:	[le chiedo scusa io non ho detto che è forte ho detto
		I beg your pardon but I didn't say that it is strong I said
3	I:	(1.2)
4	G:	che voi per paradosso rischiate di rafforzarla (0.1) rischiate nella vostra ottica
		that you paradoxically risk to reinforce it (0.1) you risk from your perspective

In another instance, however, the interpreter doesn't stop so that Farage keeps his turn and manages to bring his argument to a proper ending. Interpreters thus take upon themselves the task of dealing with the various issues originating from the confrontainment format, and they play a crucial role as regards retaining the turn of the guest when faced with an attack from other participants. More in general, a foreign guest is completely dependent on the interpreter each time a turn-taking competition arises.

In the context of stiff turn-taking competition and increasingly faster cross talk, however, the contribution of interpreters may make it more difficult for primary participants to get the upper hand on their rivals and leave them without a valid response. The task of the interpreter is therefore not so much that of coordinating participation by ensuring the orderly flow of interaction but rather that of assisting the interpreted guests in their attempt to accomplish

[4] Transcription conventions:

[one bracket placed on top of another indicates the start of overlapping talk
? questioning intonation (usually with rising tone)
(1.0) one second of silence
( ) inaudible words.

the actions they wish to carry out. When a confrontation involves expressive resources such as sarcasm, irony, and forms of provocation, conflictual actions may be conveyed by prosodic patterns over and above the linguistic expression of disagreement. For instance, in Excerpt 2, Ramadan provocatively asks the host whether he has read his preface to a controversial book. The question is not simply a request for information, since the host had previously declared he had not read the preface. Its purpose is rather that of inconveniencing the host. The interpreter tries to convey Ramadan's provocative action by mimicking and stressing his prosody, producing a repetition whose first occurrence is marked by an upward intonation pattern. Then, she translates the sarcastic remark by Ramadan, bringing to a close the exchange started by his previous question. It should be noted that the Italian rendition is more face-threatening than the French utterance, since Ramadan's inclusive impersonal pronoun "de quoi *on* parle" (line 6) has been replaced by a more direct form of address (line 7).

Excerpt 2. R (Tariq Ramadan), I (interpreter), H (host)

1	R:	mais vous avez même pas lu la préface
		but you haven't even read the preface
2	I:	ma lei non l'ha neanche letta la prefazione:
		but you haven't even read the preface
3	R:	avez vous lu la préface
		have you read the preface
4	I:	lei l'ha letta la prefazione?
		have you read the preface
5	H:	no non l'ho letta
		no I haven't read it
6	R:	alor vous ne savais de quoi on parle
		then you don't know what we are talking about
7	I:	ah e allora? allora lei non sa di cosa sta parlando
		well then then you don't know what you are talking about

The interpreter's rendition in line 7 should not be understood as affiliative, as she is not siding with Ramadan but, rather, she is translating the meaning of the *action* performed by the guest. Interpreting in the context of the conflictual dynamics typical of political talk shows requires the display of involvement in the conversation, without which the interpreter may in fact not be as effective and efficient. In the example considered, the primary participants are opponents in a dispute, and this is what the interpreter is attempting to convey through her translation. Finally, interpreters can be sidelined – or let themselves be sidelined – by the primary participants, who directly address each other in fast-paced quarrels. However, such backing-out is not a mere absence but, rather, what makes it possible for disagreement to escalate into conflict.

4.2.2 *Membership Categorization Analysis*

Membership categorization analysis (MCA), a research strand also initiated by Sacks, can be defined as "a formal analysis of the procedures people employ to make sense of other people and their activities" (Leudar et al. 2004, p. 244). In other words, MCA is concerned with accounting for how communication actions are logically organized and made intelligible to the parties involved. Whereas CA has been highly influential in linguistics and discourse studies, as well as informing the media interpreting studies reviewed in the previous section, MCA has hardly been used as a methodological tool in news media translation studies (nor in translation studies more in general).[5]

In this section, I provide an introduction to the methodological tools and concepts of MCA research. In the next section, I present an overview of MCA research in the news media, focusing on written texts. In the rest of the chapter, I apply these methods and principles to news media translation, focusing on two case studies – one using as data a story about a Colombian reporter published in *The Observer* and then in translation in *Internazionale*; the second looking at set of news reports about an incident that took place on the border between Israel and the Gaza Strip in the Occupied Palestinian Territories, published in English and in Italian. Corpus tools and resources are also brought to bear in the exploratory analysis carried out in this second case study.

The aim of MCA is to describe "the apparatus through which members' descriptions are properly produced" (Silverman 1998, p. 77). Sacks "was concerned about the conditions of description, that is, what makes it possible for us to produce and understand descriptions of people and their activities" (Peräkylä 2008, p. 873), and, therefore, with the mechanisms used for the selection of categories that are used to refer to people "and about the conditions and consequences of this selection" (p. 873).

For instance, Sacks posits that a speaker may refer to an absent person using two main types of identification, namely a first type that consists in identifying a person as someone who is already known to the interlocutor – for instance, by calling that person by their first name – and a second type, which consists in identifying a person that the direct addressee is not supposed to know – for instance, by referring to this person as "someone." The rule for use of these identification types is to use the first type if possible; if not, use the second type (Sacks 1992b, pp. 444–448). Silverman (1998, pp. 145–152) shows how personal pronouns can be used to refer to a recipient either in a personal capacity or to indicate their institutional or corporate identity. MCA may also assist in the analysis of how people select formulations for locations. Schegloff

[5] Though see Zanettin (2016a), on which Section 4.4.1 is based.

(1972) suggests that these formulations are always indexical, and there seems to be a preference for using formulations that are related to members (e.g., Joe's place) rather than geographical knowledge (e.g., a street address).

In order to describe the mechanisms through which participants in a social interaction understand, make sense of, and respond to descriptions by other participants, Sacks introduced the concept of membership categorization device (MCD), by which he refers both to a collection of categories and to the rules for their application by members in the culture. These categories are not assumed to exist a priori but, rather, are the result of an empirical investigation of the application of descriptive practices in actual verbal interaction and textual instances. Sacks (1963) emphasizes that description is an action and that accounts of activities are themselves social practices. The classical example of how membership categorization works is the analysis by Sacks (1972b) of the beginning of a story by a four-year-old: "The baby cried. Mommy picked it up." Sacks observed how all members of the culture in which these two sentences are uttered are likely to understand them in the same way, and to consider it as something which does not deserve further explanation. What is understood is that the person who is described as the mommy is the mother of the baby, and that the mother picked up the baby because it was crying. We understand the story in this way because we associate the categories of "baby" and "mommy" with the membership categorization device (MCD) "family."

Two rules of application are at work here. The first is the economy rule, which says that one categorization is referentially adequate for a particular purpose. The young person in the first sentence could have been referred to also as the boy, and the woman could have been categorized also by age, marital status or occupation. However, one categorization is usually enough in a given context to understand what is happening. The second rule of application is the consistency rule, which says that "If some population of persons is being categorized and if a category from some device's collection has been used to categorize a first member of the population, then that category or other categories of the same collection *may* be used to categorize further members of the population" (Sacks 1972b, p. 333). A consistency rule corollary, or hearer's maxim, follows from this, concerning what is relevant for the hearer: "If two or more categories are used to categorize two or more members of some population, and those categories can be heard as categories from the same collection, then: Hear them that way" (Sacks 1972b, p. 333). According to the hearer's maxim, then, if two categories are mentioned in the same context, they may be heard as belonging to the same collection.

Sacks observes that there are different types of MCDs. A first type of device consists in collections of categories that any individual will fall into – for example, sex and age. That is, any and each person can be categorized according to a category in these collections.[6] A second type of MCD is what Sacks calls teamlike MCDs – that is, collections such as football team, family, orchestra, etc. An important property of teams is duplicative organization – that is, a collection of membership categories in which "potential members are . . . treated as a unit, not as countable individuals. When one category from that collection is used, then it will be inferred that any other category from that device can be used to construct an adequate description simply by virtue of occupying a position within that device" (Lepper 2000, p. 194). A third type of collection is the standardized relational pair (SRP), in which one category references the other to such an extent that the mention of one of the categories may include reference to the other – for instance, mommy and baby and wife and husband. Some collections may involve positioned categories – i.e., categories that can be seen as being placed along a scale from higher to lower positions within a certain MCD (for instance, baby, adolescent, and adult in the MCD "stage of life"). This "creates the possibility of praise or complaint by using a higher or lower position to refer to some activity" (Silverman 1998, p. 84).

Categories are "inference-rich" (Sacks 1992a, p. 41) so that, for example, what is known of a category can be attributed to someone described as an incumbent to that category. If a man cries, he can be described as a baby. An important concept is that of category-bound activities – that is, activities that are linked to certain categories "are expectably and properly done by persons who are incumbents of particular categories" (Hester & Eglin 1997a, p. 5). For instance, the activity of crying in Sacks's example is linked to "baby" in the device "stage of life," and therefore, "baby" can be seen as simultaneously belonging to the device "family" and the device "stage of life." Sacks proposed two viewers' maxims related to category-bound activities. The first maxim says that if one sees a category-bound activity being done by a member of a category to which that activity is bound, it should be seen as being relevant to the identification of that person as a member of that category (Sacks 1992a, p. 259; Silverman 1998, p. 85). The second maxim says that two activities are seen as related and sequentially ordered if both can be seen as bound to a category invoked by those activities (Sacks 1992a, p. 260; Silverman 1998, p. 86). Furthermore, categories are protected against induction (Sacks 1992a, p. 336; Schegloff 2007a, p. 469), in the sense that if someone does not "fit the description" of a category, the category itself is not invalidated.

Membership categorization was initially used by Sacks to refer to the categorization of people – i.e., the social types that are used to describe individuals such as teacher, father, or former politician – but categories have

[6] Sacks (1972a, p. 33) refers to these as Pn-adequate devices.

been extended to include "collectivities" such as named physical institutions as well as abstract constructs identified by designators such as "the legal system" or "the middle class" (Hester & Eglin 1997a; Jayyusi 1984). The scope of descriptions has also been widened beyond the description of people to include the description of actions, events, and behaviors.

Other developments concern the concept of category-bound activities, the recognition of different types of membership categories, and the use of lists as a way to constitute categories and collections of categories. The concept of category-bound activities has been extended to that of category-tied, category-constitutive, category-implied, etc., predicates or features. In other words, what is predicated of a category can include not just activities but also obligations, rights, habits, beliefs, knowledge, competences, etc. Jayyusi (1984, pp. 26–27) argues that "[c]ategories orientably and conventionally carry with them a cluster ... of expectable features [that] provide procedures for situated inferences" and argues that "the use of categorizations is not only descriptive of persons, but it is through and through an ascriptive matter" (Jayyusi 1984, p. 27). Through our descriptions, we also express evaluations and moral judgments, and "how we define an activity is morally constitutive of it" (Silverman 1998, p. 85). Thus, categorization practices are used to accomplish the local organization of moral order and display of social norms (Housley & Fitzgerald 2009) and are actively used by members to formulate or contest the meaning of activities and identities. Categorization through description is a way to exercise social control and, in fact, "contested categories are one way that one does 'rebellion'" (Silverman 1998, p. 17).

Membership categories belong to different types. For example, some categories may be presupposed by, while some may be implicated in, other categories. The description Catholic presupposes Christian, while the description Arab may implicate Muslim, though it does not presuppose it. While initial investigations have focused on individual descriptor designators – that is, categories such as son, dropout, or doctor – later studies have remarked on the difference between these and categories that refer to self-organized groups, such as football fans, political parties, or the Hell's Angels. One basic difference is that the actions of one member of an organized collectivity are projectable to other members of the group, who can be held morally accountable for these actions as a collectivity. A still different type of description is type categorization – for instance, dropout type, Hell's Angel type, girl-next-door type – which accounts for guarded implications and predictions.

Descriptions of people are primarily obtained through noun phrases, though verb phrases that describe the actions that are predicated of category members may also "convey the sense ... of being deployed as categories" (Schegloff 2007a, p. 480). Lists can be used to organize categories according to conventionally agreed collections such as family members, nationalities, etc., which, however, must be locally validated or according to a locally occasioned purpose – for instance, "food I don't like" or "enemies of my enemies." Lists can also be embedded in other lists and organized hierarchically (Jayyusi 1984, pp. 75–101). Categorization is locally accomplished, and collections of categories are established in and through textual practices rather than consisting in the application of preexisting categories.

As remarked by Housley and Fitzgerald (2015, p. 6), MCA should not be seen as a self-contained methodology but, rather, as "a collection of observations and an analytic mentality." The method of MCA is to "make problematic" what is taken so be common sense and therefore seen as unproblematic by the participants in a communicative exchange. By way of concluding this section, I offer a summary list of key analytic concepts emerging from the work of Sacks and other scholarly research in MCA (from Stokoe 2012), namely membership categorization devices (MCDs), category-bound activities, and other category-tied predicates that refer to features and characteristics of a category. Some MCDs, such as mother and baby or wife and husband, may be characterized as standardized relational pairs, and some – for instance, a family, may work in a unit or "teamlike" way – i.e., they may be duplicatively organized. Categories may be positioned – i.e., some collections of categories may be placed in a lower or higher hierarchical relationship with respect to another. Categorization work may involve solving category-activity "puzzles," which refers to (un)expected combinations of categories, the puzzle being the reason for the categories being together. Finally, there are the economy rules and the consistency rules, which concern how descriptions are accomplished, and the hearer's and viewer's maxims, which concern how the recipient of a description arrives at an interpretation of that description. According to the economy rule, a single category may be sufficient to describe a person. According to the consistency rule, if a category from a membership categorization device has been used to characterize a first member of a population being categorized, it may then be used to categorize further members of that population. According to the hearer's maxim – a corollary of the consistency rule – if two or more categories are used next to each other, and both belong to a standard collection or MCD (e.g., family), then the categories referred to should be heard as members of the same device: as each other's mommy and baby, or father and daughter. The viewer's maxims are related to category-bound activities and to their relevance for formulating an identification of the incumbents of the categories to which they are bound.

4.3 MCA and the News Media

Both conversation analysis and membership categorization analysis were conceived by Sacks as part of the same enterprise, which was largely focused on conversational interaction. While the applicability of MCA to research on written texts – as well as its status as a strand of ethnomethodology or as part of CA – has been a matter of some debate among scholars (see, e.g., Fitzgerald 2012; Schegloff 2007a, 2007b; Silverman 1998, 2012; Stokoe 2012), MCA has since then been extended not only to a variety of institutional contexts such as legal settings, counseling, and interviews, but also to monologic text types such as TV commercials (Francis & Hart 1997) and political speeches (Collet 2009; Leudar et al. 2004). Thus, Leudar et al. (2004) have looked at categorization work through the use of first- and third-person plural pronouns and particles in speeches by US president G. W. Bush, the UK prime minister Tony Blair, and Al-Qaeda leader Osama Bin Laden in the wake of the events of September 11, 2001, in the USA, while Collet (2009) analyzes a corpus of public addresses given by President Bush during the three years following the same events, looking at occurrences of the noun "civilization" and the related adjective "civilized." Her approach combines MCA with narrative theory and rhetorical analysis, showing how the construction of the standardized relational pair comprising the collective membership category civilization/civilized (world) and its negation "(uncivilized) terror," together with their predicates, are used by the US president in the activation of the "clash of civilizations" frame that was used to support the narrative of the so-called war on terror.

As regards news media texts, MCA has been applied to research on different radio and TV programs and formats, as well as printed news. For instance, Thornborrow and Fitzgerald (2004) analyze data taken from print and TV news and suggest that categorization practices are the primary mechanism used to organize and present news events and develop them into news stories. Roca-Cuberes and Ventura (2016) discuss a TV news item concerning the running of the bulls at the San Fermín festival in Pamplona (Spain) and how participants are categorized according to MCDs of nationality, race, and gender.[7] Several studies have combined CA and MCA in the analysis of the sequential and categorial organization of news media texts such as interactive radio programs (e.g., Fitzgerald & Housley 2002; Thornborrow & Fitzgerald 2013) and televised political debates (e.g., Bovet 2012; Gotsbachner 2009).

Watson (2009) discusses categorization practices in written texts as a way of rendering reading and writing practices intelligible, suggesting that MCA can be used as a powerful tool for carrying out fine-grained textual analysis. In particular, newspapers can be seen as "fragments of a culture" that show the "obvious-but-unstated connections between 'identifications' (ways of referring

[7] Interestingly, while the transcriptions of excerpts from the TV story are offered in English, these are presumably translations from Spanish, since the story was broadcast by TVE1, the public television channel (Roca-Cuberes & Ventura 2016, p. 570). However, this is not acknowledged or problematized in the article.

to persons) and 'activities' (ways of referring to what they did)" (Rapley et al. 2003, p. 433). The analyses of media materials can shed light on how descriptions are used to render persons, places, and events "intelligible, rational, sensible and logical" (Stetson 1999, p. 79) in a way that can be generalized beyond a particular newspaper account, since the media make use of resources that are shared by the wider public. Since Lee's (1984) groundbreaking analysis of newspaper headlines, several scholars have focused on newspaper headlines and reports, including Jayyusi (1991), Hester and Eglin (1997b), Stetson (1999), Eglin and Hester (1999, 2003), Rapley et al. (2003), Watson (2009), and Caniglia (2009).[8]

Headlines play two main functions; on the one hand, they summarize the content of the article and, on the other, they attempt to capture the attention of the reader. In so doing, argues Lee (1984), they provide a set of instructions on how to read the article that follows: "In so far as they are able to achieve all of this: headlines must be so constructed as to allow readers to employ a variety of methods and techniques of sense-assembly which enable them to decode the heading so as to discover the message and instructions which they impart" (Lee 1984, p. 69). Headlines create a series of expectations and orient the reader to a specific interpretation of the article, which may be disproved by the subsequent reading, but in this case, this may be attributed to, or blamed on, the author – or the translator – of the article.

Newsworthiness is derived from something being described as not normal, and newspaper headlines can often be seen as a kind of "referential puzzle" (Schenkein 1979, p. 190): for example, the headline "Girl Guide Aged 14 Raped at Hell's Angels Convention" discussed by Lee (1984) presents a puzzle in that a reader may wonder what a "girl guide aged 14" is doing at a "Hell's Angels convention," given that the pairing of these two categories is rather unconventional (and therefore newsworthy). When presented with such a headline, the reader may plausibly infer, even if this is not explicitly stated, that the girl guide was raped *by* Hell's Angels, because this is something that Hell's Angels do. Lee's discussion of this headline provides an illustration of the concepts of category-activity puzzle and category-bound activities. The headline "Wife Found Murdered at Home" can instead be seen as "guilt-implicative" (Watson 2009, p. 17) in its organization. This is because the victim is described as a wife, a categorization that is part of a standardized relational pair whose second part, the "husband," is also evoked by the conventional location of this pair – i.e., the "home" also mentioned in the

[8] Other studies of news stories, in both video and print media, carried out from an ethnomethodological perspective, which do not, however, adopt membership categorization as the primary analytical method, include Schenkein (1979), Barthélémy (2003), Jalbert (1984, 1992, 1994), and Jaworski et al. (2003).

headline. Thus, the husband "may (rightly or wrongly) be deemed by readers the favourite candidate for the additional category 'culprit.'" Similarly, in the headline "Drunk Irks Woman, Killed by Train" (see what follows), we understand the drunk person to be a "man" – i.e., to be part of the standardized relational pair implied in the categorization of the other person as a "woman," mutually constitutive and co-members of the "gender" MCD (Stetson 1999). Hester and Eglin (1997b) discuss two newspaper headlines in order to show how categories, predicates, and contexts are reflectively constituted. The terms used to ascribe people to categories do not have some "fixed referent outside of the occasion of their use" (Rapley et al. 2003, p. 431), and the predicates of these categories are deployed to accomplish moral judgments. For instance, the headline "Officer's Suicide at Girlfriend's Grave" can be read as a newsworthy item in that it presents an unusual situation, that of a police officer who does something unusual for the category of police officers (he kills himself) and that the tragic story is motivated by the death of his girlfriend. It does so because we hear the word "girlfriend" as paired in a standardized relation with "boyfriend," and since the relations predicated between boyfriends and girlfriends are such that that they may explain a suicide, the officer is understood as being the boyfriend and as having committed suicide because of the death of his girlfriend, which is what her "grave" stands for. Thus, the notions of standardized relational pair and predicate features "provide formal means by which the reader can assemble for these words on this occasion a locally ordered, relationally configured and reflexively constituted sense" (Hester & Eglin 1997b, p. 46). Caniglia (2009) systematically applies MCA to a corpus of headlines from Italian newspapers. He compares headlines about the same events taken from different newspaper reports or provides alternative formulations, thus exposing the mechanisms responsible for producing certain effects, which are otherwise hidden in their taken-for-grantedness. For instance, a headline such as "Ragazza stuprata da 5 rumeni. Arrestati grazie ai tatuaggi" (literally: Girl raped by 5 Romanians. Arrested thanks to their tattoos) treats a category-tied feature such as ethnicity or nationality as a category-constitutive feature, suggesting the inference that raping girls is something that Romanian men conventionally do. This may be interpreted as an indicator of bias or prejudice, as shown by a rewriting of the headline in which "Romanians" is replaced by "young men" ("Ragazza stuprata da 5 giovani. Arrestati grazie ai tatuaggi" [Caniglia 2009, p. 176]), which would be an equally factually accurate description of the perpetrators.

Some studies go beyond the analysis of headlines and discuss organizational aspects of newspaper stories as reported in one or more articles and editorials. One newspaper report (or more reports on the same event) may provide alternative descriptions of the people referred to in the story, and the way these descriptions appear and are systematically arranged in the text directs the reader to understand a particular report as a specific type of story. Jayyusi (1991) analyses a news report published in *The New York Times* in 1986, about the seizure and disappearance of a guerrilla leader in Argentina. Jayyusi (1991, p. 197) aims to investigate "how it is that a news text provides for its 'objective' character, by which it is encountered as an 'objective account of actual reality' rather than as just some subjective version of reality." According to her, the report is equivocal in its construction of the story in that, though not explicitly saying so, it orients the reader toward a particular reading of the text, namely that the police may have been responsible for the seizure. The equivocality and seeming objectivity of the report are achieved because the text's structure provides for the mapping of the police as the collective entity accountable for the disappearance, regardless of the denial of any knowledge of it. Such a categorization is achieved by the relevance and/or visible absence of category-bound features as described in the text.

Several studies have highlighted the working of an MCD that is typically found in news stories – i.e. "parties to an offence." This collection typically includes the categories of "victim" and "offender" that, as noted by Eglin and Hester (2003, p. 15), are part of a standardized relational pair and, as such, provide for the relevance of each other's actions. Stetson (1999) argues that the categories of victim, offender, and witness (another category usually found in the collection) are made available together as soon as one of these categories is introduced by ascribing someone to it. Stetson examines several newspaper articles and editorials about a man who got killed in a railway station in Tokyo. In the headline of one report – i.e., "Drunk Irks Woman, Killed by Train" – "irking" is predicated as a category-bound activity of drunks, and this description also provides and explanation of what happened – i.e., that the man was killed as a consequence of his behavior. An initial description provided in a newspaper's story may, however, be open to equivocation and change, introduced by further reports. Category collection assignment may be reversed, and journalistic accounts of events may undergo "storied category shifts" and "storied category-collections expansions" (Stetson 1999, p. 84) when reported in other texts. Thus, in an editorial, the train station incident becomes tragic when other categories are introduced in the description of the man – i.e., those referring to him as a "polite" and "popular teacher." In a later editorial, the category "public" is introduced as an expansion of the MCD "parties to the offence" in order to extend blame from the (unhelpful) witnesses to cultural bystanders, whose behavior is characterized as culturally inappropriate, and the incident is explained as a consequence of the public's tolerance of public intoxication. The editorialist attempted a "reconceptualization of excessive drinking, thus changing the way that drunks are viewed and subsequent constraints enforced" (Stetson 1999, p. 94).

Eglin and Hester (1999, 2003) and Rapley et al. (2003) discuss as case studies the press coverage of the mass killing of several people by one shooter in a public location. Eglin and Hester (2003) extensively examine the coverage, by two Canadian newspapers in the weeks following the attack, of the "Montreal Massacre" of December 6, 1989, in which a gunman killed fourteen women and then shot himself dead, leaving a suicide note explaining his action. They discuss three types of accounts, namely descriptions of the people involved provided by the reporters, descriptions and formulations found in the commentaries, and descriptions in the gunman's reported speech. They show how the Montreal Massacre story comprises a number of different story lines – namely "the crime story, the horror story, the stories of public disaster and private tragedy, the gun-control story, the story of the killer, the killer's story, and the story of violence against women" (Eglin & Hester 2003, p. 5) – the last becoming the main story as reports give way to commentaries. They point out how category organization and category predicates are procedural resources that allow news readers to recognize the relevance of the actors and actions mentioned in the text of the articles as related to a particular story line. Thus, for instance, the standardized relational pair "victim" and "offender" activates the crime story, featuring the appearance of police and of police-predicated activities, whereas place formulations related to the setting "University of Montreal" provide for the relevance of identifying persons at the scene as part of the duplicatively organized MCD "university personnel" (e.g., students, professor, dean, etc.), which – together with the incongruous appearance of an incumbent of a category belonging to a different collection (i.e., a "shooter,") – invoke the horror story.

Rapley et al. (2003) discuss the Port Arthur massacre of April 28, 1996, in which a gunman shot thirty-five people, based on a corpus containing all reports and editorials from seven Australian quality newspapers in the eight months between the date of the shootings and the conclusion of the trial. They illustrate how the media represented "mental illness" using selected examples from the corpus, which invoked both "lay" and "professional characterizations of "mental states" and "psychiatric" categories. They argue, in particular, that the categories made available by the media to characterize the perpetrator as an incumbent of the categories of "madman," "monster," and "child" produce a paradox in that, in categorizing him as not a "madman" but rather as a "child," he is to be held morally and legally responsible for his actions – which, however, being predicated as the actions of a madman, cannot be ascribed to an ordinary member of society. The tension between these "incongruous" candidate membership categories is resolved by placing him in "a technically contrived third space, a no-man's land" (Rapley et al. 2003, p. 440) through the use of diagnostic categories that describe him as a madman and yet not enough of a madman to be exculpable.

4.4 News Media, Translation, and MCA

The focus of MCA on close and detailed textual analysis is well suited to the study of news media translation, since the comparison of source texts and translations can be used to understand how the same people, actions, and events may be described differently through local categorization practices in the respective texts. On the other hand, translated news provides suitable material for the analysis of categorization practices. In order to uncover how it is that something is presented as "objective reality" rather than as discursive construction, MCA relies on the "problematization of sense" (Hester & Eglin 1997a, p. 15), which consists in making commonsense understanding strange by taking categories out of their context of occurrence and "entertaining the possibility of their having alternate meanings." Translated news offers examples of actual "alternate meanings" – that is, of how people, objects, and events can be categorized in sometimes rather different ways when a report or editorial is translated into a different language. Differences in meaning are often the result of the accumulation of minimal translation shifts whose analysis can be instrumental in bringing to light the taken-for-granted aspects of what is being reported on.

The application of MCA to the analysis of news translation can, in a way, be seen as a cultural-oriented approach (see Section 3.4), in the sense that it looks at how the "same" events are presented to different readerships. However, culture is here understood as the result of practical actions by specific people – i.e., the people responsible for a particular translation – rather than a set of preexisting norms or mental processes that are activated by features of the situation. At the same time, this approach can be seen as product oriented, in that it aims to investigate the categories that are used in the text to describe people and events. In order to do so, it considers the local procedures through which these descriptions are accomplished rather than trying to explain linguistic choices on the basis of some preexisting overarching social constructs.

4.4.1 Case Study 1: Journalist or Woman?

In order to illustrate the application of MCA to news translation, I first offer the analysis of a story in which the identity of the main character is constructed as that of a journalist in the source text and as that of a woman in the translated text. This study is a case of "stable" news translation, in which the translated text is acknowledged as such, and both the name of the author of the source text and that of the translator are provided. The story, by Ed Vulliamy, was originally published in the Sunday British newspaper *The Observer* on December 14, 2013, and then in Italian translation, by Giusy Muzzopappa, in the weekly *Internazionale* on March 28, 2014 (the two articles are reproduced in full in the appendix). The translated story can be seen as an interpretation of the original

Table 4.1. *Source text and translation*

The Observer	*Internazionale*	English translation
Colombian reporter Jineth Bedoya Lima gives voice to abused women	Jineth Bedoya Lima. Mai più in silenzio	*Jineth Bedoya Lima. Never in silence anymore*
Journalist tortured and raped by paramilitary fighters is now working to raise awareness of sexual violence in warfare	Nel 2000 è stata sequestrate e torturata dai paramilitari Colombiani. Tre anni dopo è stata rapita dai guerriglieri delle Farc. Ora ha lanciato una campagna contro la violenza sulle donne	*In 2000 she was abducted and tortured by Colombian paramilitaries. Three years later she was kidnapped by Farc guerrillas. Now she has launched a campaign against violence on women*

story, which creates a sort of dialogue with it and provides a backdrop against which the source story can be understood. At the same time, the source story provides a formulation against which the transformations displayed by the translation can be gauged.

The Italian magazine, which contains almost exclusively translations, has been the object of several investigations (see Section 3.6.2). Articles published in the magazine are mostly opinion and feature stories, to the exclusion of "hard news." The publication process includes four different readings by editors, copy editor, and director, and translation issues are given paramount attention.[9]

In what follows, I first compare the headlines and blurbs of the two articles and then look briefly at the stories themselves in relation to the respective headlines. Figures 4.1 and 4.2 reproduce, respectively, snapshots from *The Observer* and *Internationale*.[10]

Table 4.1 contains the English title and blurb from *The Observer* and the Italian title and blurb from *Internazionale*, together with a literal translation of these latter into English.

9 As exemplified in the following comment by one of the magazine's editors, Elisabetta Zoli (2012), while responding to a reader's comment about two competing translations for the name of the Greek party Golden Dawn in a weekly column on editorial matters: "A *Internazionale* l'adozione di una certa grafia può scatenare dispute roventi tra i redattori, l'uso delle maiuscole risvegliare rancori mai sopiti, la traslitterazione dei nomi russi riaprire antiche ferite. Ma nessuno vuole che i lettori siano costretti a interrompere la lettura per chiedersi se Alba d'oro e Alba dorata sono lo stesso partito. Lo sono, e d'ora in poi lo chiameremo Alba d'oro" [At *Internazionale*, the adoption of a certain spelling can unleash hot spats/arguments among the editors, the use of capital letters awakens old animosities, the transliteration of Russian names reopens old wounds. But nobody wants the readers to stop reading to ask themselves if Alba d'oro and Alba dorata are the same party. They are, and from now on we'll call it Alba d'oro]."

10 It should be noted that in *Internazionale*, the photograph of Jineth Bedoya Lima is printed on a full page fronting the story.

Colombia
The Observer

Colombian reporter Jineth Bedoya Lima gives voice to abused women

Journalist tortured and raped by paramilitary fighters is now working to raise awareness of sexual violence in warfare

Ed Vulliamy

Saturday 14 December 2013 12.43 GMT

Shares
952

Figure 4.1. *The Observer*

Ritratti

Jineth Bedoya Lima
Mai più in silenzio

Ed Vulliamy, The Observer, Regno Unito

Nel 2000 è stata sequestrata e torturata dai paramilitari colombiani. Tre anni dopo è stata rapita dai guerriglieri delle Farc. Ora ha lanciato una campagna contro la violenza sulle donne

Quando Jineth Bedoya Lima ha cominciato a lavorare per la radio nazionale co- … tici e promuovere il suo nuovo movimento chiamato No es hora de callar, non è il momento di tacere.

La sua figura esile nasconde l'energia di un uragano. Quando le chiedono perché, dopo tutto quello che ha passato, non abbia deciso di lasciare tutto, lei risponde: "Come avrei potuto sconfiggere la mia paura in un momento in cui la mia vita sembrava finita? Come avrei potuto andare avanti, come donna e come giornalista, avendo questo muro nero davanti a me? Avevo bisogno di sapere cosa fosse successo a me e a tante … donne. Ma oggi mi rendo conto del fatto che oltre a essere furiosi per quello che scrivevo, si sentivano offesi dal fatto che una donna ficcasse il naso nei loro affari". Continuando a occuparsi delle guerre colombiane, Bedoya è passata al quotidiano El Espectador, e nel maggio del 2000 è riuscita a intervistare il leader di un gruppo paramilitare, detenuto a La Modelo e noto con il nome di El Panadero, "il panettiere".

Come un business

"Sapevo dei traffici di armi gestiti dai dete-

Figure 4.2. *Internazionale*

The first thing that can be noted, when looking at one headline in light of the other, is that they provide very different descriptions. While in the English headline the proper name of the person referred to is preceded by a noun and an adjective (Colombian reporter), in the Italian headline, it is found by itself, and neither the rest of the headline nor the blurb provide any other categorization for this person. In other words, while in the Italian story, personal identity is considered enough to describe Bedoya Lima, in the English story, the reader is guided to understand her identity through her additional ascription to two further categories, namely a national/ethic category and a professional category, which are provided as relevant for the description.

In *The Observer* headline, Jineth Bedoya Lima's national identity is presented not in terms of being a woman, but as a journalist, and the rest of the headline introduces the category "abused women" (itself part of the MCD "women"), while what is predicated of her is "giving voice," a type of activity which can be readily be interpreted as related to her professional identity. There is some ambiguity in that Bedoya Lima can be seen as an incumbent of both the category of (Colombian) reporters and of that of (abused) women – and, in fact, she is both of them. That is, to what extent does Bedoya Lima give voice to abused women as an abused woman, and to what extent does she do so as a reporter? This ambiguity could be seen as being reinforced in the blurb, in which it is said that she was "tortured and raped." However, here she is referred to by the word "journalist," and this co-referent is clearly part of the same MCD as "reporter," a device that could be defined as "media professional" and that also includes "commentator," "correspondent," "columnist," "editor," and "photographer." It is not that Bedoya Lima's categorization as an abused woman is not allowed but, rather, that the reader is oriented to favor the description of her identity as media professional as the one that is most relevant for the purpose at hand.

It should also be noted that "reporter" and "journalist" are near synonyms and that "reporter" could be seen as a type of "journalist" – the difference being that the features predicated of a reporter are those of being an employee of a newspaper/media entity whose primary duty is "reporting," whereas the features associated with "journalist" convey a higher intellectual and professional status. However, I suggest that they are not used in this sense here; that is, "reporter" is not constructed as a member of the category "journalist," but rather, both terms are expected to be perceived as members of the category collection "media professional." Their sequential order can be heard as promoting a hierarchy (Jayyusi 1984, p. 80), by which "journalist" as the second item in the list can be seen, in fact, as a further specification, which provides Bedoya Lima with a higher status than that she was initially credited with by defining her as a "(Colombian) reporter." The activities "torture" and "rape" are predicated as a type of abuse that Bedoya Lima suffered as an incumbent of the category "journalist" rather than "woman." The sequential order of the two predicates can be interpreted as a case of embedded categorization, whereas "rape" is treated as category of the collection "sexual abuse," a reading reinforced by the formulation provided at the end of the blurb, namely "sexual violence" (in warfare).

The Italian reader is offered different reading instructions. In the *Internazionale* headline, Bedoya Lima is identified only through her name, so the only relevant identity is possibly that related to her gender. Though a national identity (Colombian) can be indirectly established by relating the linguistic features of the foreign- (Spanish-) sounding name and the adjective "Colombian" used in the blurb to refer to the paramilitary fighters, that description is not provided as relevant to the description of the main character of the story. While in the English headline Bedoya Loma is categorized as belonging to the media professional collection, in the Italian headline, in which it is not said that Bedoya Lima is a journalist, the identity of the woman is predicated as that of being the victim of the activities "abducting," "torturing," and "kidnapping," and as the active agent of "launching a campaign against violence on women."

The collection, the organizing principle of this categorization, is her role with respect to gendered violence. It should be noted that all references to "sexual" violence that appear in the English text (i.e., the terms "rape" and "sexual violence") are not present in the Italian text, where Jineth Bedoya Lima is described as a woman (whereby "gender" is the relevant category collection) and what is predicated of her is that she will not be silenced anymore. Therefore, she is not a media professional that acts in her professional capacity as a reporter based on her experience as a (sexually) abused woman but a woman victim of (gendered) violence who takes on a proactive stance and contrasts violence on women.

The standardized relational pair "victim" and "offender" is featured in this story in relation to the collection "parties to violence," though it is organized in different ways in the two languages. While in the English blurb the "offender" category is occupied by the collectivity "paramilitary fighters," in the Italian blurb, we find two different incumbents – i.e., the collectivities "Colombian paramilitaries" and "FARC guerrilla fighters," which – according to the consistency rule – are part of the same collection, which could be defined as "militia groups." The two groups differ on ideological grounds, a component that gets deleted in their being grouped by the device "self-organized military groups." Bedoya Lima is the victim of violence (and an active agent against violence) as an incumbent of the category "woman" in the standardized relational pair "gender" so that, in the Italian text, the principle organizing the categorization is "parties to gendered violence." The collectivity collection "militia groups" can thus also be heard not only as the second part of the standardized relational pair "parties to violence" but also as projecting the category "man" as the second part of the standardized relational pair "gender" in as much as Bedoya Lima is an incumbent of the category "woman."

The reader of the English text is instructed to interpret the collectivity "paramilitary fighters" as an incumbent of the category "professional fighters" and as part, together with the collection "media professionals," of the collection "parties related to sexual violence during a conflict," where the sexual element is salient. Bedoya Lima as a journalist is a witness of war as a context in which sexual violence occurs, as opposed to the Italian text, in which – as a woman – she is a first a victim and then a vocal opponent of gendered violence.

In the Italian blurb, Bedoya Lima speaks out as a woman. What is predicated of her is being kidnapped and tortured, and launching a campaign against violence on women, where the organizing principle of this collection is "role played in relation to gender-based violence."

Both headlines have in common as a categorization device the standardized relation pair "victim" and "offender" that make up the collection "parties to violence." However, while the English headline and blurb orient the reader toward "professional" categories such as "media operator" and "soldier," the Italian headline and blurb map the paired categories onto another standardized relational pair – i.e., women and men as part of the collection "parties to gendered violence." What is predicated of Bedoya Lima in English is that she performs what is expected of her as a journalist – that is, "report" on "sexual violence in warfare." In Italian, there is no explicit mention of sexual violence, only of physical violence more in general. Whereas the context evoked for the violence is that of wartime in English, it is that of gender-based violence in Italian.

In her analysis of the translation process at *Internazionale*, on the basis of her experience at the newspaper, Bani (2006, p. 41) explains that the headlines of translated articles are often "completely different from the original ones, and through them the editors guide Italian readers' comprehension and interpretation." The headlines of the Jineth Lima Bedoya story provide the respective readers with two different sets of instructions and based on the headlines the readers can make certain predictions on the story that, if not fulfilled, may be blamed on the inconsistency of the author or translator. Bani writes that the editorial board members "adjust the translation and modify the text according to the needs of the target medium, reorganizing the text fully, cutting, changing the paragraph structure, altering the syntax according to editorial stylistic norms or inserting explanations where they are believed to be necessary." The analysis of the headlines and blurbs suggests, that through these changes, the translation orients the reader to construct a different narrative out of the events and people described.

The interactional uses of categories in newspapers are textually achieved (Eglin & Hester 2003, p. 9). Context is created by textual organization, by the deployment of categories as part of categorization devices. Thus, newspaper headlines have a dialogic relationship with the content of the article

(Lee 1984), as category-bound activities posited in the headline of a report can be confirmed or disproved by how the story is developed in the report itself. For instance, a different orientation to the way people are categorized in the headline of a translated article may or may not be found to be congruous with how a story is narrated in translation through cuts, additions, omissions, lexical choices, and other translation strategies that reveal the use of different categorization options. The next step in the analysis is, then, to verify whether the two texts are consistent with the respective headlines – i.e., whether and to what extent the divergent readings offered by headlines and blurbs are warranted by the body of the articles.

Figure 4.3 provides a visual snapshot of the two articles displayed one fronting the other.

The English text is about one-third longer than the Italian translation (1,641 and 1,171 words, respectively). Several blocks and segments (highlighted in the English text in Figure 4.3) are omitted in the translation. The four main omitted blocks of text are reproduced here, all containing descriptions of actions carried out by Bedoya Lima (emphasis added).

1. "After that first day, when **I had been the only reporter granted access to the jail**, **I began to work** on what **I found out there**: complicity by the army in many of the massacres carried out by the paramilitaries, and ways in which the military were arming the paramilitaries – some members of the military were even selling weapons to Farc," Bedoya said last week.
2. When **I wanted to pursue my own case**, and **contacted the police hospital** for the evidence, it had all been destroyed."

   Bedoya's discourse goes beyond Colombia – it addresses the crisis of the misogynisation of warfare. "It happens in all wars now, the abuse of women's bodies as a weapon of war," she says. "But in Colombia, after decades, women had come to regard their bodies as weapons of war as almost normal. It was only when **we began to document** the abuse of women's bodies as a weapon of war that we understood the scale."

   Speaking in London at the Frontline Club, which focuses on **conflict reporting**, Bedoya said: "There are dramatic cases in rural areas in Colombia where women have been beaten, where their breasts have been cut off, where they've been amputated, where – and this is especially a practice of the paramilitaries – they've been abused and beaten to serve as a warning."
3. **Reporting** from Colombia this year, on the much-trumpeted resurrection of Medellín, I stumbled into a drama workshop run for displaced and violated women, who are encouraged to act out their stories. **I spoke to** Rosney and Blanca, who had been serially raped and who told me such violation was ubiquitous.

Jineth Bedoya Lima

Mai più in silenzio

Nel 2000 è stata sequestrata e torturata dai paramilitari colombiani. Tre anni dopo è stata rapita dai guerriglieri delle Farc. Ora ha lanciato una campagna contro la violenza sulle donne

Quando Jineth Bedoya Lima ha cominciato a lavorare per la radio nazionale colombiana a Bogotá, le è stata affidata una notizia che sarebbe diventata la sua vita. Quel giorno, nel dicembre del 1996, le hanno chiesto di occuparsi di una ribellione a La Modelo, probabilmente la prigione più pericolosa del mondo, uno snodo cruciale per il traffico di droga e armi tra le forze dello stato, i cartelli e le milizie rivali. Meno di quattro anni dopo, il 25 maggio del 2000, Bedoya è tornata in quella prigione dopo il massacro di 42 prigionieri compiuto da altri detenuti che appartenevano a gruppi paramilitari di destra, in quel periodo responsabili di una campagna di terrore in tutto il paese. È stata sequestrata all'ingresso della prigione, torturata e stuprata dagli uominidi un gruppo paramilitare.

Tre anni dopo, Jineth Bedoya Lima è stata rapita e tenuta prigioniera di nuovo, stavolta dai guerriglieri delle Forze armate rivoluzionarie della Colombia (Farc). Poi, nel 2009, Bedoya è riemersa da questo tunnel di violenza e, con una forza che va oltre ogni immaginazione, è diventata la voce di migliaia di donne vittime del più grave crimine nascosto della Colombia, descritto così in un rapporto pubblicato a dicembre: "L'abituale, diffuso e sistematico" rapimento e stupro di donne nel quadro delle guerre interne al paese.

Nel dicembre del 2013 Bedoya è andata nel Regno Unito per fare pressione sui politici e promuovere il suo nuovo movimento chiamato No es hora de callar, non è il momento di tacere.

La sua figura esile nasconde l'energia di un uragano. Quando le chiedono perché, dopo tutto quello che ha passato, non abbia deciso di lasciare tutto, lei risponde: "Come avrei potuto sconfiggere la mia paura in un momento in cui la mia vita sembrava finita? Come avrei potuto andare avanti, come donna e come giornalista, avendo questo muro nero davanti a me? Avevo bisogno di sapere cosa fosse successo a me e a tante altre donne".

Bedoya è nata nel 1974 da genitori che - come milioni di altri colombiani provenienti dalle campagne - sono stati costretti a trasferirsi a Bogotá a causa della lunga guerra civile conosciuta come La Violencia. È cresciuta tra le conseguenze di questa guerra, mentre il narcotrafficante Pablo Escobar portava avanti la sua guerra contro lo stato e la società. Bedoya ha cominciato a lavorare come giornalista dopo cheEscobar è stato ucciso e il suo impero si è frammentato in un labirinto di unità paramilitari e nuovi cartelli, mentre le forze armate dello stato, la guerriglia marxista e le gang chesi definiscono *combos* scatenavano ulteriore violenza. A quel tempo, racconta la giornalista, non si occupava "di violenza sulle donne. Ma oggi mi rendo conto del fatto che oltre a essere furiosi per quello che scrivevo, si sentivano offesi dal fatto che una donna ficcasse il naso nei loro affari". Continuando a occuparsi delle guerre colombiane, Bedoya è passata al quotidiano El Espectador, e nel maggio del 2000 è riuscita a intervistare il leader di un gruppo paramilitare, detenuto a La Modelo e noto con il nome di El Panadero, "il panettiere".

Come un business

"Sapevo dei traffici di armi gestiti dai detenuti dei gruppi paramilitari con la complicità dello stato", dice. "El Panadero voleva raccontarmi le ragioni del massacro nella prigione. Quello che non sapevo è che quei passaggi di armi nella prigione si verificavano con l'autorizzazione di persone ai massimi vertici delle forze armate e della polizia. Quando sono arrivata all'ingresso della prigione, una donna mi ha chiesto se fossi una giornalista. Stavo per rispondere, quando è arrivato un uomo che mi ha messo un braccio attorno a un fianco, mi ha appoggiato una pistola sull'altro e mi ha detto che mi avrebbe uccisa se non avessi iniziato a camminare".

Bedoya è stata "condotta in un magazzino dove c'erano altri uomini. Mi hanno legato mani e piedi, mi hanno bendata e mi hanno messa in un camion. Abbiamo viaggiato per molto tempo fino a raggiungere un luogo dove mi hanno violentata, torturata e tenuta prigioniera". Dopo un po' di tempo Bedoya è stata condotta in un altro posto dove "è arrivata una telefonata. Penso si trattasse di un avvertimento sulla portata delle operazioni di salvataggio". È stata subito scaricata, nuda, al bordo di una strada. Era "libera". Due settimane dopo era di nuovo al lavoro, stavolta per il quotidiano El Tiempo.Continuava a occuparsi di crimini ma, aggiunge, "mi sono anche messa in contatto con altre donne che avevano avuto esperienze simili".

Nel 2003 Bedoya si stava recando a un incontro con le Farc in compagnia di un fotografo: "Ma non avevamo il permesso di entrare in quello che i guerriglieri consideravano il loro territorio. Siamo stati rapiti e tenuti prigionieri. Stavolta non mi hanno stuprata, ma mi hanno umiliata e picchiata. Dopo otto giorni ci hanno liberati". Per altri sei anni Bedoya ha continuato a lavorare solo come giornalista, "e non ho detto una parola su quello che mi era successo". Ma nel 2009 ha rotto il silenzio. Lo ha fatto, racconta, perché "avevo incontrato tante donne che avevano avuto esperienze simili alle mie, senza che lo stato ammettesse l'esistenza di questi crimini. Nessuno voleva occuparsene, nemmeno parlarne".

Bedoya spiega che la violenza sulle donne non è solo una conseguenza del conflitto. È anche un affare, un'opportunità commerciale che va di pari passo con gli sforzi compiuti dalla Colombia per garantirsi gli investimenti delle multinazionali. "Oggi succede che un autobus arrivi a Medellin pieno di ragazze tra i 12 e i 16 anni. Vengono portate nei campi dell'estrazione mineraria, poi i loro corpi sono venduti e vengono violentate per quattro giorni prima di tornare a Medellin". Queste ragazze sono chiamate "prepagate", dice Bedoya, "come se fossero delle schede telefoniche".

Continua la giornalista: "In Colombia il 98 per cento dei crimini sessuali resta impunito". Questo accade in parte perché "oggi in Colombia quelli che si occupano di traffico di droga e di sfruttamento e traffico di donne si muovono come una holding. Molti sono ex paramilitari che hanno accettato di deporre le armi per consolidare i loro interessi nel traffico di droga, e ora offrono i loro servizi alle multinazionali; a volte sono assunti come responsabili della sicurezza per le aziende che investono nel paese".

Durante le sue visite nel Regno Unito, Bedoya ha cercato di mettere in relazione le iniziative del governo britannico sulla violenza sessuale nei contesti di guerra e la responsabilità sociale d'impresa. In Colombia alcune star della nazionale di calcio hanno aderito alla campagna contro il sequestro e la violenza sulle donne.

Bedoya oggi vive con una scorta armata. "Qui sono libera di camminare per strada", dice. "Quando torno a casa ho una macchina blindata e molte guardie del corpo. Ma è la mia vita, è quello che ho scelto". Tuttavia, aggiunge, "il peggio che poteva succedermi miè già successo. Ricevo minacce, e ogni giorno esco sapendo che potrei non tornare a casa. Ma il massimo che possono fare è uccidermi, e preferirei morire per un proiettile in Colombia che per il dolore in esilio".

Colombian reporter Jineth Bedoya Lima gives voice to abused women

Journalist tortured and raped by paramilitary fighters is now working to raise awareness of sexual violence in warfare

On the first day that Jineth Bedoya Lima arrived for work at the offices of Colombia National Radio in Bogotá, she was assigned to cover a story that would become her life. That day, in December 1996, her task was to report on a riot at what is probably the most dangerous prison in the world, La Modelo, infamous as a focal point for trafficking in drugs and arms between the forces of state, cartels and rival militias.

Less than four years later, on 25 May 2000, Bedoya returned to the jail after the massacre of 42 prisoners by inmates belonging to rightwing paramilitary groups, who were terrifying the country. This time, she was seized at the prison gates, kidnapped, tortured and raped by the paramilitaries' men on the outside.

Three years later she was kidnapped and held again, this time by the leftist militia that the fascists claimed to be fighting – the Fuerzas Armadas Revolucionarias de Colombia, or Farc.

Then, in 2009, Bedoya emerged from this wind tunnel of violence and violation and – with resilience that defies imagination – became the voice of the many thousands of survivors and victims of Colombia's greatest hidden crime: described by a report published this month as the "habitual, extensive and systematic" kidnap and rape of women in the country's internal wars.

Earlier this month, Bedoya toured Britain and Ireland to lobby politicians and rally supporters as a new movement calling itself Now Is Not the Time to Stay Silent bursts defiantly into the open – and to promote the report, compiled by the London-based ABColombia.

She is slight of frame in a way that belies her gale-force energy. Asked why she did not, as most would, crawl away into a cave after these experiences, she says: "How did I overcome my fear, when it looked like my life was over? How did I continue as a woman and a journalist when faced with this black wall? I needed to know what happened. When I leave this world, I need to have known what happened to Jineth Bedoya, to my colleagues and so many other women."

Bedoya was born in 1974 to parents who were – like millions of other Colombians – displaced to Bogotá from the countryside by the long civil war the country calls La Violencia. She grew up in the fallout of that war, as the narco lord Pablo Escobar waged his cartel's battle against state and society. And she began her work as a reporter on the slipstream of that war, after Escobar was killed and his empire fragmented into a labyrinth of paramilitary units and new cartels, while the state armed forces, Marxist guerrillas and gangs calling themselves *combos* mobilised further murderous forces.

"After that first day, when I had been the only reporter granted access to the jail, I began to work on what I found out there: complicity by the army in many of the massacres carried out by the paramilitaries, and ways in which the military were arming the paramilitaries – some members of the military were even selling weapons to Farc," " Bedoya said last week.

She was not, she says, "working then on the violation of women. But I can see now that as well as being furious at what I was writing, they were offended by the fact I was a woman – young, pretty, petite, but sticking my nose into their affairs."

Honing in on the corrupt and vicious duplicities of Colombia's wars, Bedoya moved to the newspaper *El Espectador*, and secured, in May 2000, an interview with a paramilitary leader, jailed in La Modelo, who went by the name of El Panadero – "the Baker".

"I knew about arms trafficking to the paramilitary prisoners with state complicity," she says, "and he wanted to tell the story of why the massacre in the prison happened. What I did not know then, but do know now, was that gun-running into the jail was happening on the authority of people high up in the military and police command.

"When I got to the prison entrance, a woman asked if I was the journalist. I was about to answer when a man came, put his arm round my waist, a gun to my side, and said he would kill me if I did not start walking." Bedoya was "taken to a warehouse where there were other men. They tied my hands and feet, blindfolded me and put me in a truck. We drove for a long time to a place where they raped me, tortured me and held me kidnapped, prisoner."

After some time, Bedoya was driven to another location when "a phone call came. I understand that it was a warning about the scale of the rescue operation." And she was suddenly dumped, naked, on a roadside – "freed".

Two weeks later, she was back at work – "though I cannot believe it, and cannot think why" – writing now for the prestigious newspaper *El Tiempo*. Her work reporting on crime did not change, but "I began to contact other women to whom the same had happened, for my own reasons, not for work."

In 2003, Bedoya "was travelling to meet the Farc with a photographer. But we didn't have permission to enter what they regarded as their territory. We were kidnapped, held – this time not raped, but humiliated and beaten. After eight days, they released us."

For six more years, Bedoya continued to work only as a journalist, "and said not a word about what had happened to me". But in 2009 she broke her silence. She did so, she says, because "I had met so many women who had experiences similar to mine, yet the state would not recognise these crimes. No one wanted to look into it, or even talk about it. When I wanted to pursue my own case, and contacted the police hospital for the evidence, it had all been destroyed."

Bedoya's discourse goes beyond Colombia – it addresses the crisis of the misogynisation of warfare. "It happens in all wars now, the abuse of women's bodies as a weapon of war," she says. "But in Colombia, after decades, women had come to regard their bodies as weapons of war as almostnormal. It was only when we began to document the abuse of women's bodies as a weapon of war that we understood the scale."

Speaking in London at the Frontline Club, which focuses on conflict reporting, Bedoya said: "There are dramatic cases in rural areas in Colombia where women have been beaten, where their breasts have been cut off, where they've been amputated, where – and this is especially a practice of the paramilitaries – they've been abused and beaten to serve as a warning."

But the crisis transcends war. "Violation against women is not just a result of the conflict," she says. "This is also a business, a commercial opportunity" that accompanies modern Colombia's efforts to secure investment by multinational corporations. "I can tell you that, today," says Bedoya, "a bus will arrive in Medellín, and girls aged 12 to 16 will be taken to camps for miners and their bodies will be sold and they will be abused for four days and then returned to Medellín." Such girls are known as "the pre-paid", she says, "like a phone card".

Reporting from Colombia this year, on the much-trumpeted resurrection of Medellín, I stumbled into a drama workshop run for displaced and violated women, who are encouraged to act out their stories. I spoke to Rosney and Blanca, who had been serially raped and who told me such violation was ubiquitous.

Bedoya said: "In Colombia, the levels of impunity for crimes of sexual violence have reached 98%. Of the 150,000 rapes of women that had been recognised by the paramilitary groups, only 2% have resulted in guilty verdicts."

Apart from being endemic in all societies, this happens partly because "in Colombia today, those in charge of drug trafficking and the exploitation and trafficking of women are like a holding company. Most of them were paramilitaries, who agreed to disarm so they could consolidate their drugand business interests, and now they offer their services to a corporation; they may be the heads of security for a new multinational investment.

"Nothing is allowed to get in the way of the arrival of the multinationals," says Bedoya, "but what happens in reality is that the multinationals fund the crime and exploitation. So that any action we demand goes against the investment, which will not happen – so we're back to square one. It's a vicious circle, catch-22."

Or, to be fair, it was catch-22 until Bedoya recently published a report on mining interests. Until then, she says, "of the majority of the mining companies, all of which are foreign, none had any kind of plan to prevent sexual exploitation even though they knew it was happening. It was only after the report that they began to implement social investment plans."

On her visits to parliament and the Foreign Office, Bedoya sought to connect recent British government initiatives on sexual violence in warfare to corporate responsibility. Back home, Colombia's World Cup stars Camilo Vargas, Alexander Mejía and Omar Pérez have signed up for the campaign against sequestration and the abuse of women, as have all the leading domestic teams.

Bedoya lives now with an armed escort. "Here, I've been free to walk the streets," she says. "When I get back, there's the bulletproof car, all the bodyguards. But that's my life, that is what I have chosen."

However, she adds: "The worst that can happen to me has already happened. There are threats against me, and every morning I leave the house knowing that I may not return in the afternoon. But the worst they can do is kill me, and I'd rather die of a bullet in Colombia than of sorrow in exile."

Figure 4.3. *Translation and source text*

4. "Nothing is allowed to get in the way of the arrival of the multinationals," says Bedoya, "but what happens in reality is that the multinationals fund the crime and exploitation. So that any action we demand goes against the investment, which will not happen – so we're back to square one. It's a vicious circle, catch-22."

   Or, to be fair, it was catch-22 until Bedoya recently **published a report** on mining interests. Until then, she says, "of the majority of the mining companies, all of which are foreign, none had any kind of plan to prevent sexual exploitation even though they knew it was happening. It was only after **the report** that they began to implement social investment plans."

All activities reported by and of Bedoya (report, publish a report, pursue a case, document, etc.) are professional activities that are predicated of a journalist. For example, when Bedoya says that "we began to document" through the selection of a category-bound activity, as predicated of the collection she belongs to – i.e., "we" the media workers – she assumes a social and professional role as a relevant identity trait. These textual segments, which in *The Observer*'s story underline Bedoya Lima's identity as a reporter, and most notably her "Speaking in London at the Frontline Club, which focuses on conflict reporting," are omitted in the Italian translation, in a way that is consistent with the reading the Italian headline predisposes the reader to.

In the article, Jineth Bedoya Lima is quoted as saying how she overcame her experience "as a woman and a journalist," which is translated literally into Italian as "come donna e come giornalista." Lists of two terms are ambiguous in that they can be heard as two members of the same device, or as the second category being a specification of the first (Jayyusi 1984, p. 82). It could be argued that the English headline orients the reader toward interpreting journalist as a category selected by a different device than that of the Italian translation. In the Italian text, "giornalista" can be preferentially treated as categorization of Bedoya Lima's identity as a woman, whereas in the English text, gender and professional activities are selected as categories of the device personal identity.

Thus, while both headlines correctly summarize the story, they orient the respective readers toward different interpretations of it, and the patterns of omissions and additions in the texts beyond the headlines can be seen to confirm the analysis. While the two texts are indeed one the translation of the other and thus make reference to the same people and events, they are also two different stories, whose headlines warrant different descriptions, evaluations, and inferences and orient the readers toward different interpretations of the people and events represented. While in English the story can be read as that of a Colombian reporter traveling through England to promote a social project against sexual violence, the story in Italian is preferably interpretable as that of a woman victim of violence who goes through an empowerment process.

4.4.2 *Categorization, Corpora, and Translation*

According to Schegloff (2007a, 2007b), categorization analysis is only applicable to the study of talk-in-interaction in as far as categorization is accomplished by shared agreement and as a result of sequential organization. There is not a preexisting device called family; the device is coproduced by interactants in real time by sanctioning or questioning the categorizations heard and integrating, amending, and reorganizing them in conversation. Schegloff suggests that the application of the analysis of membership categorization outside interactional spoken discourse is "promiscuous" since analytical categories are established "on the investigator's authority rather than on what it can be shown that participants are attending to" (Silverman 1998, p. 133), thus running the risk of lapsing "into purely commonsense observations."

Certainly, news media texts – like newspapers articles – are not dialogic in the sense that "[o]ne cannot instantly produce explanations, reformulations, further arguments, backdowns, 'face-savers', more evidence, or the like, in the face of queries, challenges or disagreements as one can in a two-way conversation" (Jayyusi 1991). In newspaper articles, where categorization is not dialogically negotiated during face-to-face interaction, meaning is indexically created both retrospectively, based on the preceding verbal context, and prospectively, by designing a recipient audience through categorization work.[11] Intelligibility rests on the assumption of shared knowledge, and at the same time, it is determined by audience design, by the creation of a prospective reader. Categorization is not produced by filling the slots of preexisting categorization devices but is locally organized through contextual practices. It is locally occasioned and accomplished by describing people, objects, and events as belonging to some categories (and not others) and organizing these categories into specific devices governed by specific relationships (e.g., SRPs, positioning, duplicative organization). Different types of inferences and implications are conventionally implicated with any given

[11] Digital media have allowed in some cases a more direct and immediate audience interaction, as newspaper readers may append their comments to online newspaper articles and posts on social media. Conway and Vaskivska (2010), for instance, have analyzed readers' responses to the translations from English into Russian of articles about Russia in the *New York Times* website. The categorization of people, actions, and events is often the cause of heated arguments between responders, who dispute the categorizations and possible readings suggested by the author(s) of a story, including those resulting from translation. What is disputed is that certain people or events can be assigned to certain categories, and that specific activities may be perceived as entailed, category-bound attributes.

description, and the selection of one instead of another in a list of sequential categorizations implies implicative fits and deletions of further implications. Descriptions are used to accomplish practical tasks such as "deliver judgments, warrant further inferences, ascribe actions, projects possible events, explain prior events, account for behaviour, etc." (Jayyusi 1984).

Written news stories are asynchronous, delayed conversations, extended monologic turns of discourse. A turn that is marked by "an absolute beginning and an absolute end: its beginning is preceded by the utterances of others, and its end is followed by the responsive utterances of others" (Bakhtin 1986, p. 71). According to Conway (2015b, p. 530), "[n]ews . . . is . . . an utterance, a turn taken in the ongoing conversation that shapes the relationship between the social and subjective worlds. Admittedly, it is a complex turn, one that encompasses conversations of its own (for instance, between reporters and the people they interview)." The sequential structure of the reported contributions to the story (often in translation) of different actors – the reported statements by authorities, witnesses, and other sources – which are organized into cohesive and coherent chains of actions and reactions as the journalist reports and mediates between them – have been described by Leudar and Nekvapil (2004) as "dialogic networks."

Media texts are designed for the "public at large" rather than for a specific recipient (Jayyusi 1991). The concept of "recipient design," originally credited to Garfinkel, was used by Sacks et al. (1974, p. 727) to "refer to a multitude of respects in which the talk by a party in a conversation is constructed or designed in ways which display an orientation and sensitivity to the particular other(s) who are the co-participants." Sacks et al.'s (1974) concept of "recipient design," together with Goffman's concept of participation framework, is at the basis of the notion of audience design, first introduced by Clark and Carlson (1982) and more fully developed by Bell (1984).[12] Bell introduces also the concept of "referees" as an "ideal or absent reference group" (Bell 1984, p. 172) of recipients, with particular reference to the mass media. Referees are unratified eavesdropping and overhearing third-person addressees who, though not physically present in an interaction, possess "such salience for a speaker that they influence speech even in their absence" (Bell 1984, p. 186). Bell (1984, p. 177) argues that, "since a mass medium is defined by its general availability" all mass media language could be, in fact, regarded as primarily "referee designed" (p. 191). Media texts have an impersonal recipient design, as the "properly oriented audience member" (Francis & Hart 1997, p. 149) for

[12] Bell developed the concept in connection with individual stylistic variation defined as intraspeaker stylistic variation that mirrors interspeaker sociolinguistic variables such as age, social class, etc. That is, variation depends on who a particular individual is talking to, since "all style shift is at base a speaker's response to the audience" (Bell 1984, p. 184).

which they are designed is not anyone in particular but the public at large. Media texts are "commonsensically knowable object(s), something for the understanding of which what 'anyone knows' is both adequate and relevant for its proper comprehension" (Francis & Hart 1997, pp. 149–150).

When telling a story, people, objects, and events are assigned to categories and organized into category collections. Categorization is carried out against the backdrop of knowledge expected to be shared by the designed recipients, which – in the case of news media texts – largely corresponds to the public at large. To take Sacks's example of how a categorization device is produced in a story fragment, while "baby" may or may not be constituted as part of the same collection as "mommy" in a particular context, its meaning is understood also against the expectancy of a common, shared understanding of "baby" being typically the first part a SRP of which "mommy" is the second part in the device "family." This commonsense knowledge is part of the meaning of "baby," though it is a meaning that can be possibly contradicted by assigning "mommy" to a different collection or questioning her membership in the "family" collection.

While categories and collections of categories are locally organized, their use rests on some conventional semantic knowledge assumed to be shared by the recipient – which, in the case of media texts, includes primarily the public at large. For instance, in their discussion of the headline "Officer's Suicide at Girlfriend's Grave," Hester and Eglin (1997b) argue that the reader understands that "officer" and "girlfriend" can be seen as part of a standardized relational pair because of the implication that the "officer" is (also) an incumbent of the category "boyfriend." However, this incumbency is allowed because the category "boyfriend" is invoked – i.e., it is assumed to be mutually understood with a reader who knows that "girlfriend" is often found as a member of an SRP of which "boyfriend" is the second part. These categories may be implied without being explicitly stated, in that they can be assumed to be available to the general reader (and to the analyst) as part of common ground knowledge.

Commonsense categorial knowledge can be provided by collocational information. While in principle any word could occur next to any other, in practice words tend to preferably co-occur with specific other words, with which they establish categorial relationships. Whereas only the analysis of the text can reveal how categories are deployed to carry out verbal actions on a specific occasion, the analysis of collocational profiles of words in a large reference corpus can provide a backdrop of commonsense knowledge, and the corpus can be used as a repository of textual information about what the audience at large can be expected to know about possible category-related features associated with recurring patterns of textual behavior.

Computational linguistics and the digitalization of knowledge have made it possible for the analyst to look up enormous quantities of text from existing text collections, organized in corpora of various sizes and design. For instance, the Sketch Engine provides an interface for the interrogation of a large collection of corpora in multiple languages, and free access to the Sketch Engine tools and resources is granted to EU academic institutions until March 2022 under the EU-funded ELEXIS project.[13] The corpus manager and text analysis software includes various functionalities and tools used by lexicographers, among others, to provide usage information for dictionary entries. Corpora and corpus analysis tools such as the Sketch Engine allow the analysis, in large reference corpora, of features of words and their interaction with frequent collocates with which they establish categorial relationships. One of the main features of the software is the Word Sketch, "a one-page summary of the word's grammatical and collocational behavior. The results are organized into categories, called grammatical relations, such as *words that serve as an object of the verb*, *words that serve as a subject of the verb*, *words that modify the word* etc."[14] The data used for the examples that follow all come from the "Timestamped JSI web corpus 2014–2020 English," a corpus containing almost sixty billion words from news articles obtained by crawling a list of RSS feeds.[15] For instance, in a Word Sketch of "baby" using as data such a general reference corpus, we can see that the most common collocates of "baby" in the AND/OR "grammatical relation" (i.e., words that are saliently found in a list with "baby") include "mother," "mom," and "mum," while the most frequent activity predicated of babies is "crying" (followed by "dying," "sleeping," and "surviving").[16]

Categorization in written texts is accomplished by designing recipients who are aware of the category-bound activities and other activity-tied predicates that may be presumed to be commonly expected of such categories when used to refer to people and things in the world. While authors and translators do not necessarily select their categories from commonsense MCDs like "family," "sex," or "stage of life," they can draw on commonsense knowledge of MCDs to generate collections of categories. However, while categorization practices are always locally accomplished (categories can be made to belong to different collections), commonsense knowledge may have predictive value on the basis of collocational regularities, such as those observed in Word Sketches, which

[13] The project has received funding from the European Union's Horizon 2020 research and innovation program under grant agreement No. 731015.

[14] www.sketchengine.eu/guide/word-sketch-collocations-and-word-combinations/ (last accessed on October 16, 2020).

[15] Information on the corpus is available at www.sketchengine.eu/timestamped-english-corpus/ (last accessed on October 16, 2020).

[16] The AND/OR "grammatical relation" is created from extracting a list, ordered by salience, of words from the same word class (e.g., a noun, and adjective or a verb), which are found in the corpus in a list of two or more words joined by a comma, the conjunction AND, or the conjunction OR.

are abstracts of word usage in lists generated from large reference corpora. Thus, for example, categories belonging to the MCD "parties to an offence" as evoked by the category "victim" can be recognized in a list of the words most saliently found in a "possessor" relationship with "victim"(as in, e.g., "victim's body") in the Timestamped JSI 2014–2020 English corpus. This list includes the words "witness," "perpetrator," "survivor," "suspect," "offender," "defendant," "abuser", and "bully."

While automatically generated lists of "grammatical relations" do not necessarily correspond to collections of categories used in any specific text, and alternative MCDs are possible for any word in those lists, frequency lists of lexicogrammatical relations may provide information about commonsense associations of categories. The analysis of such data may provide a general picture of the background knowledge that can be assumed to be available to the general public. While the meaning and function of a word can vary in each text, as the same word can be used to refer to incumbents of categories from different collections, automatic usage summaries such as those offered by a Word Sketch provide useful insights into the shared reference knowledge assumed by media texts.

Sacks (1992b, p. 19) observes that content words are co-selected, each from a range of "more or less equivalent words":

> One gross, recurrent thing that is present for stories is that across its sentences one finds that a lot of the words, particularly those that are "carriers of the story" so to speak, i.e., the nouns, verbs, adjectives, can be said to be co-selected. If we take the various words like "drove, " "wreck, " "on the way home," "car, " "smashed," "small space, " etc. then if we took each place in which the word we were considering occurred, we could get easily enough that the word that occurred there was a word from a similar class where one could replace it by more or less equivalent words, i.e., that would in some way "say the same thing."

Sacks's observation that "categories selected to categorize some member performing a category-bound activity and categories selected to categorize that activity are co-selected" (Hester & Eglin 1997a, p. 5) is echoed in the insistence of corpus linguists such as Sinclair on the co-selection of lexical items, whereby collocational relations create "semantic preferences," which can be adhered to or noticeably disattended. Corpus linguistics and MCA belong to different research traditions and concerns – the former being concerned, for example, with qualitative analysis; the latter with quantitative analysis. However, the British tradition of corpus linguistics, following a line that goes from J. R. Firth to M. A. K. Halliday to John Sinclair (Stubbs 1996), shares with categorization analysis a concern with language use, an emphasis on the observation of natural occurring data, the insistence that meaning is displayed on the surface of language rather than being hidden in deep structures that have to be uncovered by the researcher on the basis of some theoretically pre-specified agenda. The discussion of findings is presented not in terms of rules to be followed, but as description of routines, preferences that people display, regularities of behavior oriented to. By typically collocating within a recurring textual environment, words take on conventional meanings, including "semantic prosodies." A "semantic prosody" (Hunston 2007; Louw 1993; Sinclair 1987; Stewart 2010) is a favorable or unfavorable connotation with which a word is assumed to be "colored" because of its preferential patterns of occurrence. For instance, since people are usually "bent on" negative or in some way unpleasant pursuits, if someone is referred to as "bent on" an activity in a positive context, this may be understood to denote "insincerity in the writer," who can be using the term for ironic effects.

Two general reference corpora in source and target language can provide the means to compare the collocational profiles of categories and category-bound activities used in texts in two languages to refer to the same events. When selecting words for translation, translators, like all writers, posit their categories and deploy their collocations and, in doing so, draw on assumed shared linguistic knowledge. Comparable bilingual corpora – for example, of Italian and English news texts over a period of time[17] – can also be used in the comparison and contrast of newspapers about the same events in different languages, in order to explain how the same people and events may be constituted differently by the language used to describe them, and to evaluate whether the translated stories provide consistent descriptions, evaluations, and inferences about the persons involved as displayed for different audiences.

4.4.3 Case Study 2: The Palestinian Man and the Israeli Bulldozer

In Section 4.4.1, I have discussed the Italian translation of a news story as compared to the English source text as a case of "stable" translation, in which two paired texts could be easily discerned. MCA can, however, also be applied to the study of "unstable" news translation, by comparing fragments from translations that may incorporate different source texts and various degrees of editorial intervention. Translated sources may include translingual quotations from official statements and interviews to witnesses and relevant actors, and quoted or unquoted text from other news outlets. In what follows, I consider a corpus of several news reports in English and Italian of events that happened in the Middle East between Sunday, February 23, and Monday, February 24, 2020, and which were reported in the same two days. I focus, in particular, on two pairs of reports, published respectively in *The Guardian* and in *La Repubblica* on the two consecutive days, discussing how the four articles,

[17] For a discussion of comparable bilingual corpora in translation description and translator training, see Zanettin (1998, 2012, 2013).

one of which is the translation of the other, reported on an "incident" filmed on video, which was what originally made the news (the four articles are reproduced in the Appendix). The aim is to show how "events in the world" are transformed into "stories in the news" (Schenkein 1979), both within and across languages.

News agencies, newspapers, and other sources released their reports at different times during the two days, following three different newsworthy events. Some reports only concerned the first "incident" taking place on Sunday morning; others appeared later in the day after the second event; others still the following day also covering the third event, which happened during the night. While what happened on Sunday afternoon and the following night is substantially uncontroversial (the launch of missiles from Gaza into Israel and then Israeli strikes on Gaza and Syria), the "incident" of the morning and its causal relation to the events that followed is described and explained in different terms by different actors and news outlets, as will be shown in what follows.

Reports about the "incident" include the description of the contents of a video recorded in Khan Younis, in the Gaza Strip, on Sunday morning, and reports of surrounding events that could be used to explain and interpret what the video was showing. The latter are provided by either the journalists themselves or by the parties involved, including local witnesses and institutional representatives – namely spokespersons for the Islamic Jihad, Hamas, the Israeli army, the health ministry in Gaza, and the Israeli defense minister, members of the Israeli parliament, local witnesses, other press sources, etc. – though, of course, not all these sources are found in all reports. Sources are, at times, quoted directly; at other times, written or spoken statements by institutional representatives are reported through indirect discourse. Reports thus vary with respect to how what is seen on video is described and to how contextual events are described and by whom. Differences include the way descriptions by other parties are presented, their extent, and the order of presentation.

In the following discussion, I focus on the "Palestinian man" and the "Israeli bulldozer," the two main actors mentioned in descriptions of the video. I consider the sources of the descriptions provided and whether what is reported is reported speech or a direct quotation, and whether the journalist/translator aligns or not with the words used by the sources to describe people and events.

In the morning of February 23, *The Guardian* issued a short report (*Gua23*) attributed to AFP, under the headline

> Israeli forces kill Palestinian near Gaza border. Male had tried to plant a bomb, says IDF, which extracted his body with a bulldozer.

The report was accompanied by a picture of what may be made out to be two soldiers and a tank behind a fence.[18] The article begins with an unquoted statement attributed to the Israeli army, which describes the "incident" as being about the killing of "a Palestinian suspected of placing a bomb" whose body was "extracted" by a bulldozer. There follow three quoted statements by the army, a description of the video that "emerged in Gaza" after the "incident," and an unquoted statement about two wounded civilians attributed to the Gaza health ministry. Finally, the reporter writes that the Israeli defense minister "pursues a policy" of "retaining the bodies of militants" as "bargaining chips."

One the same day, *La Repubblica* (*Rep23*), under the headline

> Israele, raid contro Jihad islamica in Siria e a Gaza: due morti

("Israel, raid against Islamic Jihad in Syria and Gaza: two deaths") published an unsigned article. The article (which is accompanied by a picture credited to AFP, apparently a still image from the video showing some men in the vicinity of a bulldozer) contains an update on the events taking place after the "incident," within which the text of a report previously released by the Italian news agency ANSA from Tel Aviv is embedded.[19] The ANSA report starts by stating that the Islamic Jihad threatened revenge for the killing of a "militant," who is identified by name and age (Muhammad Ali al-Naaman, 27), and described as a "martyr" in a quoted statement. In the following sentence, the Israeli army is reported saying that "una cellula" ("a cell") had been hit. A description of the video is then followed by a quoted statement in which Hamas accuses Israel of "war crimes." *La Repubblica* concludes with a brief report on the missiles' launch. *Gua23* describes the activities in the video as the bulldozer "approaching" and then "collecting" the body of the dead man, whereas according to *Rep23*, the bulldozer "trascina" ("drags") the body. According to *Gua23*, the video also shows "young, apparently unarmed men" who try to collect the body but run away as "gunfire is heard," while *Rep23* specifies that the men on the Palestinian side of the border protest as the body is dragged by the bulldozer and that the video "ha destato forte scalpore tra i palestinesi" ("has outraged Palestinians").

[18] While it is likely that a report in French of the same event was also published, possibly as either a "source" or a "target" text, this does not seem to be readily available on the Internet, and it was not considered in the present analysis.

[19] The original ANSA report, also republished by various newspapers and media, was headlined "Gaza, ucciso militante. Jihad: vendetta. Indignazione per immagini di un cadavere trascinato da una ruspa" ("Gaza, militant killed. Jihad: Revenge. Outrage for the images of a dead body dragged by a bulldozer") and was accompanied by a picture of a crowd chanting around a coffin at a funeral. Available at www.ansa.it/sito/notizie/mondo/mediooriente/2020/02/23/gaza-ucciso-militante.jihad-vendetta_67eec562-2e7b-4f02-bb63-ff489313864c.html (last accessed on October 16, 2020).

The two newspapers, then, provide two different sets of descriptions for the people and activities involved. In *Gua23*, the dead man is referred to by the journalists (reporter and title writer) as a "Palestinian," a "male," and a "suspect." The event is described almost exclusively in the words quoted from the Israeli army that refer to the "Palestinian" as an "attacker" and a "terrorist." In the description of the content of the video, the bulldozer is said to "approach" and then "collect" the body, an activity that is referred to as "extract" in the statement by the Israeli army, a verb that is also used in the headline and in the first sentence of the article and, therefore, proposed by the reporter/title writer as an objective description of reality. *Rep23*, instead, describes the "Palestinian" as a "miliziano" ("militant"), provides his personal identification, and quotes his description as a "martyr" by the Islamic Jihad. In the video, the Israeli bulldozer is said to "drag" rather than "extract," "approach," and "collect" the body. While neither newspaper overtly endorses the categories used to describe the man ("attacker/terrorist" and "martyr," respectively) by the sources quoted, they do point to different interpretations of the "incident" as a result both of the words used and of omitting to quote alternative descriptions from other sources.

The categories used in *Rep23* are similar to those used, for instance, in a report by the state-run Turkish news agency Anadolu,[20] available on the Reuters website on February 23. The report, which includes a link to the video together with a header and a short text, describes the "Palestinian" as "martyred" and "slain," and describes the video as showing the bulldozer "crushing" and "grabbing" the body. In this report, however, the words used in the description of the man are those of the reporter – i.e., they are not directly or indirectly attributed to a source – and the Israeli army is reported as "alleging" in a statement that the man was planting an explosive device. Local residents are also given as sources, and the "incident" is located in the Gaza Strip. The two actions predicated of the bulldozer, "crush" and "grab," characterize it as a violent attacker. Among the most common modifiers that "crush" and "grab" have in common in the TimeStamped newspaper reference corpus is the adverb "violently." The categorization of the bulldozer as a violent attacker (other verbs that appear in AND/OR lists with "crush" and "grab" are, respectively, "chew" and "grind," and "smash," and "pull") is also consistent with the categorization of the "dead Palestinian" as the victim in a standard relational pair "parties to an offence." In the TimeStamped corpus, "victim" is the second-most common word associated with "body" in AND/OR relation list (after "woman" and before "man"), and the only other word, together with "patient," that does not refer to sex, stage of life, or family

[20] Available at www.aa.com.tr/en/middle-east/palestinian-martyred-by-israeli-fire-near-gaza-fence/1742124 (last accessed on October 16, 2020).

relationship. The noun "slain" collocates with modifiers like "remembered" and "mourned," which are, in fact, on top of the list of the activities associated with slain people, as shown by a Word Sketch of "slain." The "dead Palestinian" is described as "martyred," and the main thing that martyrs do, besides appearing in AND/OR lists with saints and heroes, is "sacrifice" and be "honored," "commemorated," and "venerated." The sources of information quoted are "local residents" and the Israeli army, who concur that the Palestinians were fired at.

The bulldozer "incident" and the following events were widely reported by the media. While it would be impossible to analyze the whole coverage, several descriptions of the video are contained in other sources additionally consulted, including news sites in English (*The New York Times*, *Haaretz*, Al Jazeera) and in Italian (*Nena News* and *Il Corriere della Sera*). These outlets all contain interlingual quotations and information incorporated from both Israeli and Palestinian sources. While all these accounts assume a shared understanding of an assumed objective character of the video, the way the events are reported tells different stories. This is done by categorizing people and other agents and the activities that are predicated of them.

One of the most detailed reports of the "incident" is an article by Yaniv Kubovich and Jack Khoury, published by *Haaretz* on February 23. The report has the headline "Video Shows Israeli Army Bulldozer Dragging Gazan's Body after Border Incident."[21] The article reports the army's description of the Palestinian as a suspect and as a terrorist, and his identification by the Islamic Jihad by personal name, age, and as "a fighter" in their military wing. This is followed by a description of the footage, which is "shared widely" on social media. The bulldozer is said to be "rushing Palestinians" and "holding up" an "apparently lifeless body . . . by his clothing" – actions that can be taken to imply less violence than Anadolu's description of the bulldozer "crushing" and "grabbing" the body of someone who has been "martyred" and "slain." Quoted sources include the army statement (referring to the man as an "attacker/terrorist") and the Israeli defense minister, who "confirms" that the bulldozer was used to "collect" and "bring back" the body of a "terrorist." The verb "collect" is given in quotation marks, thus signaling distance from the use of such a category by the Israeli defense minister in the description of the activity predicated of the bulldozer. However, the report also provides alternate descriptions of the "bulldozer" and the "Palestinian" in quotations by opposing actors. For instance, two Palestinian members of the Knesset are quoted as saying that the video shows the bulldozer "stealing," "abducting," "abusing," and "hoarding" a body, as opposed to "collecting" and "bringing it back."

[21] Available at www.haaretz.com/israel-news/.premium-israeli-army-says-it-shot-two-gazans-attempting-to-set-explosive-charge-on-border-1.8565385 (last accessed on October 16, 2020).

A member of the Islamic Jihad is quoted as describing the actions of the bulldozer as "enemy forces infiltrating the territory" and "savagely insulting" the "fighter." The Palestinian is also referred to as an "unarmed young man" by a Hamas representative, and the article quotes a local NGO saying the action seen in the video might qualify as a war crime. The article includes tweets in Arabic with a link to the video.

On February 23, AP published an article by Josef Federman.[22] After an update on the two events following the "incident," the article reports that "Palestinians were furious over the image of the man's lifeless body dangling off the front of an Israeli bulldozer that had crossed into Gaza to retrieve it." The article reports the Islamic Jihad referring to the Palestinian as a "militant, and the Israeli army as a "man" who "planted a bomb." The video is said to show an "Israeli bulldozer crossing into Gaza and then lifting up his body." A Hamas spokesman is then reported as referring to the actions shown in the video as "abusing a body" and as "an ugly crime," and the army as "removing the body." The article says that the images "generated widespread anger in Gaza, where it was seen as a provocation." The Israeli defense minister is quoted as referring to the man as a "terrorist." The AP source article situates the story in the context of the occupation, closing the story with a paragraph that provides as the general context for the events the Israeli and Egyptian blockade, which "has devastated the economy in Gaza, where unemployment is over 50%."

The descriptions of the man and the bulldozer by Palestinian sources, and of what the video shows, are used in an article by Al Jazeera published in February 24 to categorize the "incident" as part of series of incidents that belong to the collection "necroviolence," in the words of "a legal researcher" for a human rights organization.[23] Necroviolence is described as the Israeli practice of "humiliating," "withholding," and "dehumanizing Palestinian bodies." The "necroviolence" MCD contains incumbents of other categories such as bodies of migrants in America and mass graves. The article also provides the occupation as a context and quotes additional sources who offer a description of the "incident." These include a Hamas spokesman referring to it as "Desecrating the dead body of a young unarmed man," and the two Palestinian Israeli members of Knesset quoted in *Haaretz* the day before referring to it as "an act of vampirism." The description of the video by the journalist says that the bulldozer

[22] Available at https://apnews.com/article/7447f9e4fea10f05abb0d1e8f03409db (last accessed on October 16, 2020). The article currently bears the date November 24, 2020.

[23] Available at www.aljazeera.com/news/2020/02/israel-slammed-necroviolence-bodies-palestinians-200224115508023.html (last accessed on October 16, 2020).

ran over al-Naim's body and tried several times to pick it up with its blade before taking it back to the Israeli side as the body dangled from the edge of the blade

There is a victim, identified by his first name, and the bulldozer can be seen as exercising improper violence, as well as unduly trespassing. The body of the victim is violently martyred, and it is this act of desecration, as well as the "unlawful" provocation, which warrants calls of "war crime." It is "una scena orribile" (a horrible sight) in the evaluative description of a report by *Nena News*[24] published on February 24, filmed on camera and said in so many (translated) words by the sources quoted, that enrages Palestinians, makes the Islamic Jihad threaten revenge, and then act on it.

The same images can, however, be described and interpreted in rather different terms, and what is seen and the words that are used to describe it can be disputed. For instance, on February 23, the Reuters website made also available a still image from the video and some accompanying text from Anadolu.[25] The picture bore the caption

What is said to be an Israeli bulldozer carrying the body of a Palestinian killed at the Israel-Gaza border area, is seen in this still image taken from a video, in Gaza

Note that in the caption the description is prefaced by "what is said to be," in what amounts to a disavowal of the description of what is seen on video. What is disputed is, of course, not that the piece of heavy machinery seen in the video is an "Israeli army bulldozer" (which is perhaps the least disputed shared fact of the story) but that what the video shows can be described in the terms of the text accompanying the picture/headline. What is disputed is that what constitutes the story is the content of the video as described in the terms in which it is described.

The picture and caption were also accompanied by a warning to editors

ATTENTION EDITORS – THIS IMAGE HAS BEEN SUPPLIED BY A THIRD PARTY – SENSITIVE MATERIAL. THIS IMAGE MAY OFFEND OR DISTURB

In several Reuters reports circulated the following day, in fact, the Palestinian is described by Israel as "an Islamic Jihad member who was trying to plant explosives." Reuters does not commit to a description of the video, which "caused uproar in Gaza and calls for retaliation" and uses the expression "what appeared to be a lifeless body dangling from an Israeli military bulldozer."

[24] The Italian *Near East News Agency* (*Nena News*), an independent news agency specializing in Near East news. The report is available at https://nena-news.it/raid-israeliani-tra-gaza-e-siria-tre-membri-del-jihad-islamico-uccisi/ (last accessed on October 16, 2020).

[25] It should be noted that the content was only available to subscribers, and the webpage is not publicly available.

In the articles published on February 23 by *The New York Times* and *Il Corriere della Sera*, written by their foreign correspondents in Jerusalem, David M. Halbfinger and Davide Frattini, respectively, both authors describe what the video shows using quoted and unquoted Israeli sources.[26] *The New York Times* article describes "the incident" as a "macabre tug of war" over the "seizure" of the body of a "Palestinian militant." Whereas the Palestinian was "alleged" to be planting an explosive device by Anadolu, his identity as a "militant" is provided as the main relevant description by *The New York Times*. The bulldozer is referred to as "Israeli heavy machinery," and the journalist affiliates with the Israeli army statement by proposing the categories of "recovering" and "seizing" the body as describing the activities of the Israeli bulldozer more appropriately than "crushing" and "grabbing." Both articles propose Israeli politics as a context for the interpretation of the "incident." The article in *Il Corriere della Sera* is headlined

> Il ministro della Difesa Bennett spiega che il corpo è stato preso per usarlo come scambio: Hamas tiene ancora i resti di due soldati israeliani dal conflitto dell'estate 2014

While the context provided in a smaller upper deck "Gaza, palestinese ucciso al confine. Video choc del bulldozer israeliano che trascina via il cadavere" is that of the "shocking footage" showing the "corpse" of a Palestinian "dragged" by an "Israeli bulldozer," the main headline features the Israeli defense minister who "spiega" ("explains") his rationale for what is seen in the video. His description of what the images represent is a body "taken" as a bargaining chip in exchange for the remains of two Israeli soldiers. The article begins with an almost frame-by-frame description of the video, shot by "qualche palestinese" ("some Palestinian") and for which a Twitter link is provided:

> La ruspa avanza verso il corpo. Cerca di tirarlo su con il braccio meccanico, lo trascina sul terreno, il tessuto del maglione resta infilato in uno dei ganci, il cadavere viene sollevato.

("The bulldozer approaches the body, tries to lift it up with its mechanic arm [i.e., not a "blade" as in the Al Jazeera account], drags it on the ground, the fabric of the sweater gets caught in one of hooks, the corpse is lifted up"). The description of the "incident" is based on the Israeli army's statement, according to which a suspected Palestinian was shot at and taken away with a bulldozer, and on extensive reports of and quotations from the Israeli defense minister, who "respinge le accuse di brutalità" ("rejects accusations of

[26] The articles are respectively available at www.nytimes.com/2020/02/23/world/middleeast/israel-gaza-bulldozer-body-palestinian.html and https://www.corriere.it/esteri/20_febbraio_23/gaza-palestinese-ucciso-confine-video-choc-bulldozer-israeliano-che-trascina-via-cadavere-0406220c-5635-11ea-b447-d9646dbdb12a.shtml (last accessed on October 16, 2020).

brutality"). The Islamic Jihad is quoted as promising revenge "per il nostro martire" ("for our martyr"), a description whose appropriateness is clearly contested by the journalist through the use of scare quotes. The journalist describes what the bulldozer does as "interviene" ("comes into play"), while the "provocation" of the bulldozer's trespassing is not included; nor are the statements by the Hamas representative about the bulldozer "abusing a corpse" and committing an "ugly crime."

By using mostly descriptions from either Palestinian or Israeli sources and both quoting them and using them in their descriptions, these reports provide different descriptions of reality, all presented as objective. The reports published on February 23 by *The Guardian* and *La Repubblica* (*Gua23* and *Rep23*) align with somewhat different sets of descriptions. The AFP report published by *Gua23* follows mostly the descriptions provided by the Israeli army and defense minister, downplaying the violence in the description of the actions of the bulldozer. The ANSA report published within the *Rep23* report provides descriptions and identification of the dead Palestinian by the Islamic Jihad and Hamas, and the violence and outrage in the video are part of its description.

The following day, both *La Repubblica* and *The Guardian* published new reports (*Gua24* and *Rep24*). *The Guardian* published an article by Oliver Holmes in Jerusalem (*Gua24*), while the article in *La Repubblica* is seemingly a translation of the report by AFP published the previous day in *The Guardian*

The headline of *Gua24* provides an updated summary of events with respect to *Gua23*:

Israeli strikes in Syria and Gaza kill two Islamic Jihad fighters. Israel launches fresh strikes after its killing of a fighter on the Gaza border at the weekend prompted rocket fire from Gaza

The report (accompanied by a picture of explosions in the night), begins by stating that "the intense violence erupted" after the "incident," in which an "Islamic Jihad militant" was shot dead "while attempting to plant a bomb."[27] The video is described as showing what "appears to be" an Israeli bulldozer "scooping up" the body and "apparently" firing at Palestinians nearby. However, the journalist also adds that the video could not be "independently verified by the Guardian." The article concludes by saying that the video was shared online and that what happened seems to be in line with the "controversial" Israeli bargaining chip policy. Thus, the author misaligns himself both from a description of the contents of the video (even though this was, and still

[27] This report has been updated and extended since it was first downloaded on the day it was published. The text reproduced in the appendix is that of the report as downloaded at the time.

is, available to viewers) and from the Israeli defense minister, the moral legitimacy of whose description is questioned.

Rather than distancing itself from a description of what is shown in the video and its explanation by the Israeli defense minister, on February 24, *La Repubblica* (*Rep24*) translates the AFP report published in *Gua23* (and other news outlets) the previous day, aligning with and updating Israeli sources' description of events. As opposed to *Rep23* and *Gua24*, *Rep24* provides only a report of the bulldozer "incident" and does not include reports of later events. The news is the circulation of the video, and the report is about explaining what the video is about. The headline, "Israele uccide miliziano e rimuove il corpo con un bulldozer," describes the Palestinian as a "militant" and the bulldozer as "removing" the body. The blurb rephrases the headline and adds that "Sui social gira il video shock dell'azione israeliana" ("the video of the shocking Israeli action is circulating on the social networks"). The new report is jointly attributed to Muthana Al-Najaar (the author of the video) and AFP and is accompanied by the same AFP picture of the previous day, with a caption saying that what is depicted is "un bulldozer israeliano si avvicina al corpo del miliziano per caricarlo" ("an Israeli bulldozer nearing the body of the militant to load it up"). Whereas in *Rep23* it was "trascinato" ("dragged") by the bulldozer, in *Rep24* the body of the Palestinian is also "rimosso," "portato via," "estratto," all given as translations of the English "extract," and "recuperate" ("collected"). The Palestinian is not referred to as a "martyr" as in the quotation from a Hamas spokesman provided in *Rep23*. In *Rep24*, the victim is the victim of a legitimate action, the result of the reaction of Israeli soldiers to an Islamic Jihad militant planting a bomb.

With respect to *Gua23*, *Rep24* contains omissions and additions, and different formulations. The first paragraph, containing a first quoted statement by the Israeli army, is translated more or less literally. The most notable difference is the words used to describe the man and the actions of the bulldozer. In *Gua23*, the army shoots a "Palestinian," whereas the translation in *Rep24* "updates" the description to "un militante della Jihad islamica" ("an Islamic Jihad militant"). Whereas the body of the "aggressore" ("attacker") was "extracted" by a bulldozer in *Gua23*, it is less crudely "portato via" ("taken away") in *Rep24*. The next paragraph in *Gua23*, containing a quotation from the Israeli army in which the man is referred to as a "terrorist," is omitted in the Italian translation, as is the statement by the Gaza health ministry reporting on the wounded civilians. The description of the video in translation, which – the translation adds – was shot by "un fotografo dell'agenzia France Presse" ("an AFP photographer" whose name is given in the article's attribution) is a shorter version of that in *Gua23*. It omits details about the sound of gunfire, the presence of a tank, and the Palestinian men attempting to collect the body being "young" and "apparently unarmed." The footage is said to show the bulldozer "avvicinarsi e costringere i due alla fuga, recuperare il cadavere e tornare verso il territorio israeliano" ("approaching and forcing the two [Palestinians] to flee, collecting the corpse and retreating back towards Israeli territory"). There apparently seems to be nothing outrageous in the description of the body "taken away," even if the translation adds that the video "ha creato molte polemiche sui media arabi" ("generated much controversy in the Arab media").

While, like in the representation of "incident" provided by *Rep23* and *Gua24*, the description of the man as a "miliziano/militant" is considered primarily relevant to the story, his personal identification is given in *Rep24* only after the description of his and the bulldozer's activities provided by the army. The article's story is that the video is about the killing of an attacker from an armed Islamic group planting a bomb, whose body was removed by a bulldozer and not – like, for instance, in the reports by Anadolou and *Al Jazeera* – about the body of a dead man being desecrated. The Palestinian is properly described as a militant in the Islamic Jihad attempting to plant a bomb. However, he could also be properly described as a son and a father, as he is, in fact, described in interviews with his family provided in other articles published during those days. All these descriptions are appropriate, though each selects different moral implications. The descriptions (or the omission of the descriptions) of certain actions and features of the "Palestinian man" and of the "Israeli bulldozer," provided as relevant to the story, define what the story is about. One thing is being the victim of an Israeli bulldozer violently attacking and desecrating a body, and another being the victim of soldiers who thwarted an attack of Islamic Jihad fighters, whose killing is a legitimate war action. It is one thing to "drag a corpse among the protests," something that is described as outrageous and possibly a war crime in *Rep23*, and quite another to take the body away after the legitimate killing of an attacker. Whereas the personal identity of the man is provided by *Rep23* (as well as by *Nena News* and *Al Jazeera*) at the outset as the identity of the body of the victim who is shown in the video, *Rep24* refers to the man as "la vittima" ("the victim") and identifies him by name and age and as a member of the Islamic Jihad's armed wing only after he has been described as a "militant" who was killed while attempting to plant an explosive. The noun "militant" features prominently, together with "civilian," "soldier," and "combatant" in the list of the most common instances of the category "casualty" in the TimeStamped corpus – i.e., the collocates related to the noun "casualty" by a "is-a" relationship (e.g., "the first casualty is the truth," "many casualties were pedestrians"). Arguably, then, "victim" could be seen as not selected here as part of an SRP whose other part is "offender," but as a category of the device "casualties in a conflict."

The translation adds that the Islamic Jihad, which – as opposed to Hamas – is not observing a truce with Israel, "ha riconosciuto che l'uomo voleva mettere esplosivi lungo la barriera" ("has admitted that the man was planting explosives near the barrier"). The choice of the reporting verb can be revealing of a reporter's acceptance or rejection of the description provided by a source. While in *Gua23* all reported speech, both indirectly and in direct quotations, is introduced by the verb "say," in the translation in *Rep24*, the army spokesmen "hanno confermato" ("confirmed") that the body was removed. According to the TimeStamped corpus, "confirm" is something typically done by an authority ("spokesperson," "official") and what is confirmed is typically "death," "news" "incident," "identity." On the other hand, what is "admitted" is typically "defeat," "guilt," and "mistakes." Thus, for instance, *Nena News* orients the reader to categorize the Israeli army statement as a morally questionable admission rather than an official confirmation, writing that the army "ha ammesso" ("admitted") the killing and "si è difeso" ("defended itself") by offering a reason for the shooting. Disaffiliation can also be signaled through the use of scare quotes – i.e., quotations marks around single words or expressions (rather than longer quotations). For instance, both *Haaretz* and *Al Jazeera* signal their distance from the Israeli defense minister's categorization of the bulldozer's actions when they write that he "confirmed the bulldozer had been used to 'collect' the body" (quotes within quotes in the source), while the author of the article in *Il Corriere della Sera* signals through quotes his disaffiliation from the use of the word "martyr." The translated report is concluded by a sentence stating that Israel "spesso tiene" ("often keeps") the corpses of dead militants to use them as bargaining chips, a policy attributed to the Israeli defense minister the previous day in *Gua23*. The matter-of-factness of this final statement can be contrasted with the distancing devices used *The Guardian*'s foreign correspondent in *Gua24*.

In *Rep24*, the relevant identification of the dead man is that of a militant who died in consequence of an attack. In *Rep24*, like in *Gua23* and *Gua24*, the newsworthy event is the video that is circulating widely on the Internet, showing the "seizure" of the body of an "Islamic Jihad fighter" killed by the Israeli army while planting a bomb, to be used as a bargaining chip, which triggered an "escalation of violence" (quoted from a Reuter's report signed by Libby Hogan on February 24). In the articles from Anadolou, *Nena News*, and *Al Jazeera*, but also to some extent in *Rep23*, the video can be seen as showing territorial provocation involving the desecration of the body of a victim, a young Palestinian, in violation of moral values and legal norms. In one story line, the "incident" is part of Israeli politics; in the other, it is part of Palestinian occupation.

Membership categorization analysis provides a set of conceptual tools that can be used for the investigation of how different reports of the same news story – including those that can be traced back to one or more source texts in another language, refer to people, and describe their activities – and the implications that are conventionally attached to them. The way categorization is textually accomplished produces different accounts, which are presented as objective representations of reality. Narratives are constructed by categorizing people and activities, and the analysis of categorization can be usefully supplemented with information derived from large reference corpora. Corpus linguistics tools and resources can offer a methodology for investigating common sense categorizations of people and activities, offering a backdrop of shared knowledge to the analysis of the categorization devices employed.

As argued by Rapley et al. (2003, p. 440), "the deployment of identifications/categorizations can and does, in and of itself, do the work of explanation." When a news text is translated, events, people, and activities may be described in new terms, and a translation may orient the reader to interpret what happened as part of a story that is different from the one narrated by other reports, including in traceable sources. News translation is thus an act of textual transformation, a social action in which categorization is accomplished in a dialogue with other news texts, within and across languages.

Conclusion

Translation plays a fundamental role in the daily production, dissemination, and consumption of information in the news media, as shown by the wide range of inter- and multidisciplinary approaches that are currently brought to bear on the study of translation in the news media, spanning fields such as translation studies, linguistics, journalism, and media studies. I have examined key issues and concepts related to the translation of information in the light of discussions of the concept of translation from historical, theoretical, and descriptive perspectives, as well as of the current social and technological news media environment. News media translation challenges traditional approaches to translation that adopt a dichotomic opposition between source and target. As noted by Kothari (2014, p. 96) "[t]he fundamental paradigm of a 'source' in both language and text also arises from a certitude that boundaries of a language and text are definable and sealed, and that translation as well as original compositions are necessarily in the written tradition." The concept of translation is historically determined and tied to material culture and is being redefined as digital technologies and globalization accompany the transition of news translation from print to screen culture. At a time when linguistic and cultural identities are renegotiated, and national identities are simultaneously dissolved by digital communication and migration flows and reaffirmed by neo-nationalist forces (Eger & Valdez 2015), the practices of news translation blur the boundaries between intralingual and interlingual translation, as digital convergence blends them with those of intersemiotic translation.

Several examples of process-, product-, and culture-oriented analyses of various cultural contexts and language pairs have shown that, although translation practices and work routines may vary considerably across news organizations in different parts of the world, translated news texts also share common traits. For instance, while in global news agencies and local European newspapers, translation and editing are often carried out by the same person (the journalist-translator), in Chinese and South Korean media outlets, the two roles are more distinct. Translation is carried out by trained translators, and final publication is overseen by senior editors. However, remarkably similar textual operations are involved in translation carried out in news outlets all over the world, often performed in the name of "faithfulness." Everywhere, news translation is characterized by textual transformations involving omission, addition, and other forms of rewriting, which have been variously classified as generalization, synthesis, reorganization, reduction, particularization, re-perspectivization, substitution, and so on.

In the last chapter of this book, I have offered first-hand analyses of news texts in English and Italian. In two case studies, I have illustrated how membership categorization analysis can provide insights into the way information is translated across different media and languages. In order to show how journalistic translation practices affect the way the "same" story can be told in different languages, my analysis of the written texts was supplemented with the use of corpus data and methods, thus bringing together qualitative and quantitative methods. Like linguistic approaches such as SFL and appraisal theory, MCA is based on close textual analysis. However, unlike these approaches, it focuses on the mechanisms by which categorization is accomplished rather than the way linguistic categories and features are mapped onto discourse. Analytic concepts such as membership categorization device, standardized relational pair, and category-tied features can be used to describe the methods through which journalists and translators organize and present people and activities, and construct alternative narratives in translated news texts. MCA can also be applied, of course, to spoken and visual interaction and, thus, to the analysis of interpreted and multimedia news translation.

Digital media have given private and public interest groups and citizens the means to produce as well as consume information, and the circulation of news in the digital age is characterized now by alternative modes of translation and groups of translators, besides foreign correspondents and professional news translators. On the one hand, for instance, models of volunteer, crowdsourcing, nonprofessional translation that have emerged in connection with the translation of audiovisual content are also relevant to news translation carried out by activist communities and citizen journalist organizations. On the other, as researchers claim that the quality of news translated by machine translation systems is comparable to that of human translation (e.g., Hassan et al. 2018; Popel et al. 2020), research in news media translation should not only investigate whether, or to what extent, human- and machine-translated news texts differ (in their patterns of omission or addition, for example), but also interrogate the impact of this mode of translation on news production and reception. For example, research could be carried out on the ways in which journalists and news translators integrate MT and other electronic tools in their workflow (Vobič 2013, p. 186) and how machine translation facilities, which have been progressively incorporated by social media providers into their networks, affect news readers.

Research in news media translation is benefiting from multi- and interdisciplinary approaches and from the combination and triangulation of data from different studies, and a growing number of investigations are being published on several news media production and reception contexts. In the current scenario of convergence and integration between traditional information providers – such as newspapers and TV networks – and global social media – including not only those supplied by providers such as Google, Facebook, and Twitter, but also primarily non-English services such as WeChat, Weibo, and VK – research will need to take into account the increasing importance of social media not only as a channel via which to share information but also as a source of (mis)information, and the way this information is communicated in translated texts.

Appendix A

The Observer

Colombian reporter Jineth Bedoya Lima gives voice to abused women
Journalist tortured and raped by paramilitary fighters is now working to raise awareness of sexual violence in warfare

by Ed Vulliamy

14 December 2013

On the first day that Jineth Bedoya Lima arrived for work at the offices of Colombia National Radio in Bogotá, she was assigned to cover a story that would become her life. That day, in December 1996, her task was to report on a riot at what is probably the most dangerous prison in the world, La Modelo, infamous as a focal point for trafficking in drugs and arms between the forces of state, cartels and rival militias.

Less than four years later, on 25 May 2000, Bedoya returned to the jail after the massacre of 42 prisoners by inmates belonging to rightwing paramilitary groups, who were terrifying the country. This time, she was seized at the prison gates, kidnapped, tortured and raped by the paramilitaries' men on the outside.

Three years later she was kidnapped and held again, this time by the leftist militia that the fascists claimed to be fighting – the Fuerzas Armadas Revolucionarias de Colombia, or Farc.

Then, in 2009, Bedoya emerged from this wind tunnel of violence and violation and – with resilience that defies imagination – became the voice of the many thousands of survivors and victims of Colombia's greatest hidden crime: described by a report published this month as the "habitual, extensive and systematic" kidnap and rape of women in the country's internal wars.

Earlier this month, Bedoya toured Britain and Ireland to lobby politicians and rally supporters as a new movement calling itself Now Is Not the Time to Stay Silent bursts defiantly into the open – and to promote the report, compiled by the London-based ABColombia.

She is slight of frame in a way that belies her gale-force energy. Asked why she did not, as most would, crawl away into a cave after these experiences, she says: "How did I overcome my fear, when it looked like my life was over? How did I continue as a woman and a journalist when faced with this black wall? I needed to know what happened. When I leave this world, I need to have known what happened to Jineth Bedoya, to my colleagues and so many other women."

Bedoya was born in 1974 to parents who were – like millions of other Colombians – displaced to Bogotá from the countryside by the long civil war the country calls La Violencia. She grew up in the fallout of that war, as the narco lord Pablo Escobar waged his cartel's battle against state and society. And she began her work as a reporter on the slipstream of that war, after Escobar was killed and his empire fragmented into a labyrinth of paramilitary units and new cartels, while the state armed forces, Marxist guerrillas and gangs calling themselves combos mobilised further murderous forces.

"After that first day, when I had been the only reporter granted access to the jail, I began to work on what I found out there: complicity by the army in many of the massacres carried out by the paramilitaries, and ways in which the military were arming the paramilitaries – some members of the military were even selling weapons to Farc," Bedoya said last week.

She was not, she says, "working then on the violation of women. But I can see now that as well as being furious at what I was writing, they were offended by the fact I was a woman – young, pretty, petite, but sticking my nose into their affairs."

Honing in on the corrupt and vicious duplicities of Colombia's wars, Bedoya moved to the newspaper El Espectador, and secured, in May 2000, an interview with a paramilitary leader, jailed in La Modelo, who went by the name of El Panadero – "the Baker".

"I knew about arms trafficking to the paramilitary prisoners with state complicity," she says, "and he wanted to tell the story of why the massacre in the prison happened. What I did not know then, but do know now, was that gun-running into the jail was happening on the authority of people high up in the military and police command.

"When I got to the prison entrance, a woman asked if I was the journalist. I was about to answer when a man came, put his arm round my waist, a gun to my side, and said he would kill me if I did not start walking." Bedoya was "taken to a warehouse where there were other men. They tied my hands and feet, blindfolded me and put me in a truck. We drove for a long time to a place where they raped me, tortured me and held me kidnapped, prisoner."

After some time, Bedoya was driven to another location when "a phone call came. I understand that it was a warning about the scale of the rescue operation." And she was suddenly dumped, naked, on a roadside – "freed".

Two weeks later, she was back at work – "though I cannot believe it, and cannot think why" – writing now for the prestigious newspaper El Tiempo. Her work reporting on crime did not change, but "I began to contact other women to whom the same had happened, for my own reasons, not for work."

In 2003, Bedoya "was travelling to meet the Farc with a photographer. But we didn't have permission to enter what they regarded as their territory. We were kidnapped, held – this time not raped, but humiliated and beaten. After eight days, they released us."

For six more years, Bedoya continued to work only as a journalist, "and said not a word about what had happened to me". But in 2009 she broke her silence. She did so, she says, because "I had met so many women who had experiences similar to mine, yet the state would not recognise these crimes. No one wanted to look into it, or even talk about it. When I wanted to pursue my own case, and contacted the police hospital for the evidence, it had all been destroyed."

Bedoya's discourse goes beyond Colombia – it addresses the crisis of the misogynisation of warfare. "It happens in all wars now, the abuse of women's bodies as a weapon of war," she says. "But in Colombia, after decades, women had come to regard their bodies as weapons of war as almost normal. It was only when we began to document the abuse of women's bodies as a weapon of war that we understood the scale."

Speaking in London at the Frontline Club, which focuses on conflict reporting, Bedoya said: "There are dramatic cases in rural areas in Colombia where women have been beaten, where their breasts have been cut off, where they've been amputated, where – and this is especially a practice of the paramilitaries – they've been abused and beaten to serve as a warning."

But the crisis transcends war. "Violation against women is not just a result of the conflict," she says. "This is also a business, a commercial opportunity" that accompanies modern Colombia's efforts to secure investment by multinational corporations. "I can tell you that, today," says Bedoya, "a bus will arrive in Medellín, and girls aged 12 to 16 will be taken to camps for miners and their bodies will be sold and they will be abused for four days and then returned to Medellín." Such girls are known as "the pre-paid", she says, "like a phone card".

Reporting from Colombia this year, on the much-trumpeted resurrection of Medellín, I stumbled into a drama workshop run for displaced and violated women, who are encouraged to act out their stories. I spoke to Rosney and Blanca, who had been serially raped and who told me such violation was ubiquitous.

Bedoya said: "In Colombia, the levels of impunity for crimes of sexual violence have reached 98%. Of the 150,000 rapes of women that had been recognised by the paramilitary groups, only 2% have resulted in guilty verdicts."

Apart from being endemic in all societies, this happens partly because "in Colombia today, those in charge of drug trafficking and the exploitation and trafficking of women are like a holding company. Most of them were paramilitaries, who agreed to disarm so they could consolidate their drug and business interests, and now they offer their services to a corporation; they may be the heads of security for a new multinational investment.

"Nothing is allowed to get in the way of the arrival of the multinationals," says Bedoya, "but what happens in reality is that the multinationals fund the crime and exploitation. So that any action we demand goes against the investment, which will not happen – so we're back to square one. It's a vicious circle, catch-22."

Or, to be fair, it was catch-22 until Bedoya recently published a report on mining interests. Until then, she says, "of the majority of the mining companies, all of which are foreign, none had any kind of plan to prevent sexual exploitation even though they knew it was happening. It was only after the report that they began to implement social investment plans."

On her visits to parliament and the Foreign Office, Bedoya sought to connect recent British government initiatives on sexual violence in warfare to corporate responsibility. Back home, Colombia's World Cup stars Camilo Vargas, Alexander Mejía and Omar Pérez have signed up for the campaign against sequestration and the abuse of women, as have all the leading domestic teams.

Bedoya lives now with an armed escort. "Here, I've been free to walk the streets," she says. "When I get back, there's the bulletproof car, all the bodyguards. But that's my life, that is what I have chosen."

However, she adds: "The worst that can happen to me has already happened. There are threats against me, and every morning I leave the house knowing that I may not return in the afternoon. But the worst they can do is kill me, and I'd rather die of a bullet in Colombia than of sorrow in exile."

Internazionale

Jineth Bedoya Lima

Mai più in silenzio

Nel 2000 è stata sequestrata e torturata dai paramilitari colombiani. Tre anni dopo è stata rapita dai guerriglieri delle Farc. Ora ha lanciato una campagna contro la violenza sulle donne

Translation by Giusy Muzzopappa

28 marzo 2014

Quando Jineth Bedoya Lima ha cominciato a lavorare per la radio nazionale colombiana a Bogotá, le è stata affidata una notizia che sarebbe diventata la sua vita. Quel giorno, nel dicembre del 1996, le hanno chiesto di occuparsi di una ribellione a La Modelo, probabilmente la prigione più pericolosa del mondo, uno snodo cruciale per il traffico di droga e armi tra le forze dello stato, i cartelli e le milizie rivali. Meno di quattro anni dopo, il 25 maggio del 2000, Bedoya è tornata in quella prigione dopo il massacro di 42 prigionieri compiuto da altri detenuti che appartenevano a gruppi paramilitari di destra, in quel periodo responsabili di una campagna di terrore in tutto il paese. È stata sequestrata all'ingresso della prigione, torturata e stuprata dagli uomini di un gruppo paramilitare.

Tre anni dopo, Jineth Bedoya Lima è stata rapita e tenuta prigioniera di nuovo, stavolta dai guerriglieri delle Forze armate rivoluzionarie della Colombia (Farc). Poi, nel 2009, Bedoya è riemersa da questo tunnel di violenza e, con una forza che va oltre ogni immaginazione, è diventata la voce di migliaia di donne vittime del più grave crimine nascosto della Colombia, descritto così in un rapporto pubblicato a dicembre: "L'abituale, diffuso e sistematico" rapimento e stupro di donne nel quadro delle guerre interne al paese.

Nel dicembre del 2013 Bedoya è andata nel Regno Unito per fare pressione sui politici e promuovere il suo nuovo movimento chiamato No es hora de callar, non è il momento di tacere.

La sua figura esile nasconde l'energia di un uragano. Quando le chiedono perché, dopo tutto quello che ha passato, non abbia deciso di lasciare tutto, lei risponde: "Come avrei potuto sconfiggere la mia paura in un momento in cui la mia vita sembrava finita? Come avrei potuto andare avanti, come donna e come giornalista, avendo questo muro nero davanti a me? Avevo bisogno di sapere cosa fosse successo a me e a tante altre donne".

Bedoya è nata nel 1974 da genitori che – come milioni di altri colombiani provenienti dalle campagne – sono stati costretti a trasferirsi a Bogotá a causa della lunga guerra civile conosciuta come La Violencia. È cresciuta tra le conseguenze di questa guerra, mentre il narcotrafficante Pablo Escobar portava avanti la sua guerra contro lo stato e la società. Bedoya ha cominciato a lavorare come giornalista dopo che Escobar è stato ucciso e il suo impero si è frammentato in un labirinto di unità paramilitari e nuovi cartelli, mentre le forze armate dello stato, la guerriglia marxista e le gang che si definiscono combos scatenavano ulteriore violenza. A quel tempo, racconta la giornalista, non si occupava "di violenza sulle donne. Ma oggi mi rendo conto del fatto che oltre a essere furiosi per quello che scrivevo, si sentivano offesi dal fatto che una donna ficcasse il naso nei loro affari". Continuando a occuparsi delle guerre colombiane, Bedoya è passata al quotidiano El Espectador, e nel maggio del 2000 è riuscita a intervistare il leader di un gruppo paramilitare, detenuto a La Modelo e noto con il nome di El Panadero, "il panettiere".

Come un business "Sapevo dei traffici di armi gestiti dai detenuti dei gruppi paramilitari con la complicità dello stato", dice. "El Panadero voleva raccontarmi le ragioni del massacro nella prigione. Quello che non sapevo è che quei passaggi di armi nella prigione si verificavano con l'autorizzazione di persone ai massimi vertici delle forze armate e della polizia. Quando sono arrivata all'ingresso della prigione, una donna mi ha chiesto se fossi una giornalista. Stavo per rispondere, quando è arrivato un uomo che mi ha messo un braccio attorno a un fianco, mi ha appoggiato una pistola sull'altro e mi ha detto che mi avrebbe uccisa se non avessi iniziato a camminare".

Bedoya è stata "condotta in un magazzino dove c'erano altri uomini. Mi hanno legato mani e piedi, mi hanno bendata e mi hanno messa in un camion. Abbiamo viaggiato per molto tempo fino a raggiungere un luogo dove mi hanno violentata, torturata e tenuta prigioniera". Dopo un po' di tempo Bedoya è stata condotta in un altro posto dove "è arrivata una telefonata. Penso si trattasse di un avvertimento sulla portata delle operazioni di salvataggio". È stata subito scaricata, nuda, al bordo di una strada. Era "libera". Due settimane dopo era di nuovo al lavoro, stavolta per il quotidiano El Tiempo. Continuava a occuparsi di crimini ma, aggiunge, "mi sono anche messa in contatto con altre donne che avevano avuto esperienze simili".

Nel 2003 Bedoya si stava recando a un incontro con le Farc in compagnia di un fotografo: "Ma non avevamo il permesso di entrare in quello che i guerriglieri consideravano il loro territorio. Siamo stati rapiti e tenuti prigionieri. Stavolta non mi hanno stuprata, ma mi hanno umiliata e picchiata. Dopo otto giorni ci hanno liberati". Per altri sei anni Bedoya ha continuato a lavorare solo come giornalista, "e non ho detto una parola su quello che mi era successo". Ma nel 2009 ha rotto il silenzio. Lo ha fatto, racconta, perché "avevo incontrato tante donne che avevano avuto esperienze simili alle mie, senza che lo stato ammettesse l'esistenza di questi crimini. Nessuno voleva occuparsene, nemmeno parlarne".

Bedoya spiega che la violenza sulle donne non è solo una conseguenza del conflitto. È anche un affare, un'opportunità commerciale che va di pari passo con gli sforzi compiuti dalla Colombia per garantirsi gli investimenti delle multinazionali. "Oggi succede che un autobus arrivi a Medellin pieno di ragazze tra i 12 e i 16 anni. Vengono portate nei campi dell'estrazione mineraria, poi i loro corpi sono venduti e vengono violentate per quattro giorni prima di tornare a Medellin". Queste ragazze sono chiamate "prepagate", dice Bedoya, "come se fossero delle schede telefoniche".

Continua la giornalista: "In Colombia il 98 per cento dei crimini sessuali resta impunito". Questo accade in parte perché "oggi in Colombia quelli che si occupano di traffico di droga e di sfruttamento e traffico di donne si muovono come una holding. Molti sono ex paramilitari che hanno accettato di deporre le armi per consolidare i loro interessi nel traffico di droga, e ora offrono i loro servizi alle multinazionali; a volte sono assunti come responsabili della sicurezza per le aziende che investono nel paese".

Durante le sue visite nel Regno Unito, Bedoya ha cercato di mettere in relazione le iniziative del governo britannico sulla violenza sessuale nei contesti di guerra e la responsabilità sociale d'impresa. In Colombia alcune star della nazionale di calcio hanno aderito alla campagna contro il sequestro e la violenza sulle donne.

Bedoya oggi vive con una scorta armata. "Qui sono libera di camminare per strada", dice. "Quando torno a casa ho una macchina blindata e molte guardie del corpo. Ma è la mia vita, è quello che ho scelto". Tuttavia, aggiunge, "il peggio che poteva succedermi mi è già successo. Ricevo minacce, e ogni giorno esco sapendo che potrei non tornare a casa. Ma il massimo che possono fare è uccidermi, e preferirei morire per un proiettile in Colombia che per il dolore in esilio".

Gua23

The Guardian, 23 February 2020

Agence France-Presse

Sun 23 Feb 2020 11.28 GMT Last modified on Mon 24 Feb 2020 00.45 GMT

Israeli forces kill Palestinian near Gaza border

Male had tried to plant a bomb, says IDF, which extracted his body with a bulldozer

Israeli forces shot dead a Palestinian suspected of placing a bomb near the Gaza border, before extracting his body with a bulldozer, the Israeli army has said.

"Following the successful thwarting of the attack near the Gaza Strip fence earlier this morning, an IDF [Israel Defence Forces] bulldozer extracted the body of one of the attackers," a military spokeswoman said.

Earlier on Sunday, the army had said it "spotted two terrorists approaching the security fence in the southern Gaza Strip and placing an explosive device adjacent to it".

"The troops opened fire towards them. A hit was identified," a military statement said.

After the incident, a video from Gaza emerged showing a bulldozer approaching the body as young, apparently unarmed men, were trying to collect it. The sound of gunfire is heard and the men run away as the bulldozer collects the body. A tank can be seen nearby.

The Gaza health ministry said two civilians were wounded by Israeli gunfire at the scene.

The Israeli defence minister, Naftali Bennett, has pursued a policy of retaining the bodies of militants from Gaza as bargaining chips to pressurise Hamas, the Islamist group that controls the Palestinian enclave, which has been holding the bodies of two Israeli soldiers since 2014.

www.theguardian.com/world/2020/feb/23/israeli-forces-kill-palestinian-near-gaza-border (last accessed on October 16, 2020).

Rep23

La Repubblica, 23 febbraio 2020

Israele, raid contro jihad islamica in Siria e a Gaza: due morti/La conferma delle Forze armate dopo un fitto lancio di razzi dalla Striscia a seguito dell'uccisione di un miliziano palestinese

Israele ha confermato di aver effettuato raid aerei contro obiettivi della Jihad islamica in Siria e a Gaza, in risposta al lancio di 21 razzi dalla Striscia verso Israele. Lo hanno detto le forze armate, citate dai media israeliani. In serata, l'agenzia siriana Sana aveva riferito di "attacchi nemici" nei pressi di Damasco, contro i quali si sono attivate le difese aeree siriane. Due combattenti sono stati uccisi a Damasco.

Nel corso della giornata, la jihad islamica aveva minacciato vendetta nei confronti di Israele dopo la uccisione di un suo miliziano – Muhammad Ali al-Naaman (27 anni) – da parte di soldati israeliani avvenuta al confine di Gaza presso Khan Yunes: "Manteniamo il dito sul grilletto per vendicare il sangue dei nostri martiri – aveva affermato la Jihad islamica – così come abbiamo già vendicato in passato sparando verso Tel Aviv".

Secondo il portavoce militare una cellula della Jihad islamica ha deposto ieri mattina un ordigno a ridosso dei recinti di confine ed è stata colpita dal fuoco dei militari. Immagini apparse sul web mostrano una ruspa militare israeliana mentre, al termine dell' incidente, trascina il cadavere di un miliziano fra le proteste dei compagni che si trovano sul versante palestinese del confine. Quelle immagini hanno destato forte indignazione fra i palestinesi. Hamas ha accusato Israele di aver compiuto "un crimine di guerra".

Qualche ora dopo le sirene di allarme antimissili israeliane hanno risuonato in molte zone attorno alla Striscia di Gaza, in particolare nella cittadina costiera di Ashkelon. Il sistema di difesa israeliano Iron Dome è stato attivato. Una salva di 21 razzi, come detto, è stata lanciata da Gaza verso le aree israeliane attorno alla Striscia. Come numero di razzi, questo di oggi è il più alto da molto tempo.

www.repubblica.it/esteri/2020/02/23/news/israele_raid_contro_jihad_islamica_in_siria_e_a_gaza-249413434/ (last accessed on October 16, 2020).

Gua24

The Guardian, 24 February 2020

Oliver Holmes in Jerusalem

Published on Mon 24 Feb 2020 06.52 GMT

Israeli strikes in Syria and Gaza kill two Islamic Jihad fighters

Israel launches fresh strikes after its killing of a fighter on the Gaza border at the weekend prompted rocket fire from Gaza

The intense violence erupted after an Islamic Jihad militant was shot dead while attempting to plant a bomb at the fence that separates Gaza and Israel, according to the Israeli military.

Tensions exploded after a graphic video was later shared on social media showing what appeared to be an Israeli army bulldozer scooping up the body, and apparently firing on Palestinians nearby who rushed to try to retrieve the body.

The Guardian has been unable to verify the video, but it was widely decried online. It also appeared in line with a controversial new policy announced last year by Israel's far-right defence minister, Naftali Bennett. He said he intended to hoard the bodies of militants from Gaza to use as bargaining chips with Palestinian militants in body-swap deals.

www.theguardian.com/world/2020/feb/24/israeli-strikes-in-syria-and-gaza-kill-two-islamic-jihad-fighters (last accessed on October 16, 2020).

Rep24

La Repubblica, 24 febbraio 2020

Israele uccide miliziano e rimuove il corpo con un bulldozer

Un palestinese di un gruppo islamista è stato ucciso al confine con la Striscia di Gaza e il suo corpo rimosso da un bulldozer. Sui social gira il video shock dell'azione israeliana

GAZA – Le forze israeliane hanno ucciso ieri un militante della Jihad islamica sospettato di aver posizionato un esplosivo nei pressi della barriera che divide Gaza da Israele. Il corpo dell'uomo è stato portato via con un bulldozer, come hanno confermato i portavoce militari: «Dopo aver sventato con successo l'attacco vicino al recinto della Striscia di Gaza questa mattina, un bulldozer dell'IDF (esercito israeliano) ha estratto il corpo di uno degli aggressori», hanno detto.

La scena è stata ripresa da un fotografo dell'agenzia France Presse e ha creato molte polemiche sui media arabi: la sequenza mostra infatti due palestinesi che cercano di avvicinarsi al cadavere, presumibilmente per portarlo via, poi il bulldozer avvicinarsi e costringere i due alla fuga, recuperare il cadavere e tornare verso il territorio israeliano.

La vittima è stata identificata come Mohammed al Naem, 27 anni, membro delle Brigate Al Quds, braccio armato della Jihad islamica, gruppo islamista presente a Gaza che, al contrario di Hamas, che governa la Striscia, non è in stato di tregua con Israele. La Jihad islamica ha riconosciuto che l'uomo voleva mettere esplosivi lungo la barriera. Spesso Israele tiene i corpi dei miliziani uccisi per usarli come merce di scambio con i gruppi palestinesi.

www.repubblica.it/esteri/2020/02/24/news/israele_uccide_miliziano_e_rimuove_il_corpo_con_un_bulldozer-249427535/ (last accessed on October 16, 2020).

References

Abend-David, D. (ed.). (2014). *Media and Translation: An Interdisciplinary Approach*, New York, London, New Delhi & Sydney: Bloomsbury.

Abudayeh, H., & Dubbati, B. (2020). Politeness strategies in translating Donald Trump's offensive language into Arabic. *Perspectives: Studies in Translation Theory and Practice*, **28**(3), 424–439.

Al-Hejin, B. (2012). Linking critical discourse analysis with translation studies: An example from BBC News. *Journal of Language and Politics*, **11**(3), 311–335.

Al-Mohannadi, S. (2008). Translation and ideology. *Social Semiotics*, **18**(4), 529–542.

Alvarez-Benito, G., & Inigo-Mora, I. (2015). Discourse analysis. In G. Mazzoleni, ed., *The International Encyclopedia of Political Communication*, Hoboken, NJ: John Wiley & Sons.

Anderson, B. (1991). *Imagined Communities*, London & New York: Verso.

(2016). *A Life beyond Boundaries*, London & New York: Verso.

Angelelli, C. (ed.). (2014). *The Sociological Turn in Translation and Interpreting Studies*, Amsterdam & Philadelphia: John Benjamins.

Apter, E. (2006). *The Translation Zone: A New Comparative Literature*, Princeton & Oxford: Princeton University Press.

Aragrande, G. (2015). Migrants in translation: A corpus-based approach to the representation of migrants by four news broadcasting channels. In I. Ranzato & S. Zanotti, eds., *Linguistic and Cultural Representation in Audiovisual Translation*, London & New York: Routledge.

(2016). Investigating multilingual audio-visual and written news: Theoretical and methodological convergence. *GENTES*, **3**(3), 1–13.

(2018). Empowering the Italo-Australian community through news translation: A case study on *Il Globo* community newspaper. *Cultus: The Intercultural Journal of Mediation and Communication*, **10**(2), 76–92.

Arblaster, P., Belo, A., Espejo, C., et al. (2016). The lexicons of early modern news. In J. Raymond & N. Moxham, eds., *News Networks in Early Modern Europe*, Leiden & Boston: Brill, pp. 64–101.

Archetti, C. (2012). Which future for foreign correspondence? London foreign correspondents in the age of global media. *Journalism Studies*, **13**(5–6), 847–856.

Armstrong, G. (2015). Coding continental: Information design in sixteenth-century English vernacular language manuals and translations. *Renaissance Studies*, **29**(1), 78–102.

Atkinson, J. M., & Heritage, J. (eds.). (1984). *Structures of Social Action: Studies in Conversation Analysis*, Cambridge: Cambridge University Press.

Azodi, J. (2016). *Ideology, Power & News Translation: Investigating the Impact of Ideology & Power on Translation of News Stories*, Saarbrucken: Lambert.

Bachmann-Medick, D. (2009). Introduction: The translational turn. *Translation Studies*, **2**(1), 2–16.

Bachmann-Medick, D. (2016). *Cultural Turns: New Orientations in the Study of Culture* (A. Blauhut, trans.), Berlin & Boston: De Gruyter.

Baker, M. (1993). Corpus linguistics and translation studies: Implications and applications. In M. Baker, J. Francis, & E. Tognini-Bonelli, eds., *Text and Technology: In Honour of John Sinclair*, Amsterdam & Philadelphia: John Benjamins, pp. 233–252.

(1997). Non-cognitive constraints and interpreter strategies in political interviews. In K. Simms, ed., *Translating Sensitive Texts: Linguistic Aspects*, Amsterdam & Atlanta: Rodopi, pp. 11–130.

(2006). *Translation and Conflict: A Narrative Account*, London & New York: Routledge.

(2009). Resisting state terror: Theorizing communities of activist translators and interpreters. In E. Bielsa & C. W. Hughes, eds., *Globalization, Political Violence and Translation*, Basingbroke & New York: Palgrave Macmillan, pp. 222–242.

(2013). Translation as an alternative space for political action. *Social Movement Studies*, **12**(1), 23–47.

(2018). Narrative analysis. In K. Malmkjær, ed., *The Routledge Handbook of Translation Studies and Linguistics*, Abingdon & New York: Routledge, pp. 179–193.

Baker, M., & Maier, C. (2011). Ethics in interpreter & translator training: Critical perspectives. *Interpreter and Translator Trainer*, **5**(1), 1–14.

Bakhtin, M. M. (1986). *Speech Genres and Other Late Essays*, Austin: University of Texas Press.

Ballard, M. (2007). *De Cicéron à Benjamin, Traducteurs, traductions, réflexions*, Villeneuve d'Ascq: Presses Universitaires du Septentrion [Septentrion University Press].

Bani, S. (2006). An analysis of press translation process. In K. Conway & S. Bassnett, eds., *Proceedings of the Conference Held at the University of Warwick 23 June 2006*, Warwick: The Centre for Translation and Comparative Cultural Studies, University of Warwick, pp. 36–46.

Baraldi, C., & Gavioli, L. (eds.). (2012). *Coordinating Participation in Dialogue Interpreting*, Amsterdam & Philadelphia: John Benjamins.

(2014). Are close renditions the golden standard? Some thoughts on translating accurately in healthcare interpreter-mediated interaction. *Interpreter and Translator Trainer*, **8**(3), 336–353.

Barker, S. K. (2013). "Newes lately come": European news books in English translation. In S. K. Barker & B. M. Hosington, eds., *Renaissance Cultural Crossroads: Translation, Print and Culture in Britain, 1473–1640*, Leiden & Boston: Brill, pp. 227–244.

Barkho, L. (2008). The BBC's discursive strategy and practices vis-à-vis the Palestinian–Israeli conflict. *Journalism Studies*, **9**(2), 278–294.

Barnard, C. (2000). The Tokaimura nuclear accident in Japanese *Newsweek*: Translation or censorship? *Japanese Studies*, **20**(3), 281–294.

Barratt, A. (1984). Works of religious instruction. In A. S. G. Edwards, ed., *Middle English Prose*, New Brunswick, NJ: Rutgers University Press, pp. 413–432.

Barthélémy, M. (2003). Temporal perspectives in the practical-textual handling of a European public problem. *Social Science Information*, **42**(3), 403–430.

Bassnett, S. (1998). The translation turn in cultural studies. In S. Bassnett & A. Lefevere, eds., *Constructing Cultures: Essays on Literary Translation*, Clevedon, Philadelphia, Toronto, Sydney & Johannesburg: Multilingual Matters, pp. 123–140.

(2005a). Bringing the news back home: Strategies of acculturation and foreignisation. *Language and Intercultural Communication*, **5**(2), 120–130.

(2005b). Guest editorial. *Language and Intercultural Communication*, **5**(2), 105–107.

(2006). Introduction. In K. Conway & S. Bassnett, eds., *Translation in Global News*, Warwick: The Centre for Translation and Comparative Cultural Studies, University of Warwick, pp. 5–8.

Bassnett, S., & France, P. (2006). Translation, politics and the law. In P. France & K. Hayes, eds., *The Oxford History of Literary Translation in English*, vol. 4: 1790–1900, Oxford: Oxford University Press, pp. 48–58.

Bassnett, S., & Lefevere, A. (1990a). Introduction: Proust's grandmother and the Thousand and One Nights: The "cultural turn" in translation studies. In S. Bassnett & A. Lefevere, eds., *Translation, History and Culture*, London & New York: Pinter Publishers, pp. 1–13.

(eds.). (1990b). *Translation, History and Culture*, London & New York: Pinter Publishers.

Bassnett-McGuire, S. (1980). *Translation Studies*, London: Methuen.

Bates, E. S. (1911). *Touring in 1600: A Study in the Development of Travel as a Means of Education*, Boston: Houghton Mifflin.

Baule, G. (2016). Lo sguardo traduttore. Design e traduzione per il campo editoriale. In G. Baule & E. Caratti, eds., *Design è traduzione. Il paradigma traduttivo per la cultura del progetto*, Milano: Franco Angeli, pp. 39–70.

Bauman, R., & Briggs, C. L. (1990). *Poetics and Performance as Critical Perspectives on Language and Social Life*, **19**(1990), 59–88.

Bauman, Z. (2000). *Liquid Modernity*, Cambridge: Polity Press.

Baumann, G., Gillespie, M., & Sreberny, A. (2011a). Transcultural journalism: Translations, transmissions and transformations. *Journalism*, **12**(2), 235–238.

(2011b). Transcultural journalism and the politics of translation: Interrogating the BBC World Service. *Journalism*, **12**(2), 135–142.

Bazzi, S. (2009). *Arab News and Conflict. Discourse Approaches to Politics, Society and Culture*, Amsterdam & Philadelphia: John Benjamins.

(2014). Foreign metaphors and Arabic translation: An empirical study in journalistic translation practice. *Journal of Language and Politics*, **13**(1), 120–151.

(2015). Ideology and Arabic translations of news texts. *Translation and Translanguaging in Multilingual Contexts*, **1**(2), 135–161.

(2019). How can CDA unravel power relations in media representations of conflict in the Middle East? *Pragmatics and Society*, **10**(4), 584–612.

BBC Monitoring. (2019). What is BBC Monitoring? Retrieved January 9, 2019, from https://monitoring.bbc.co.uk/about.

Beeby Lonsdale, A. (2009). Directionality. In *Routledge Encyclopedia of Translation Studies,* 2nd ed., London & New York: Routledge, pp. 84–88.

Bell, A. (1984). Language style as audience design. *Language in Society*, **13**, 145–204.
(1991). *The Language of News Media*, Oxford: Blackwell.
Bellos, D. (2011). *Is That a Fish in Your Ear? Translation and the Meaning of Everything*, New York: Faber & Faber.
Berman, A. (1984). *L'épreuve de l'étranger: Culture et traduction dans l'Allemagne romantique: Herder, Goethe, Schlegel, Novalis, Humboldt, Schleiermacher, Hölderlin*, Paris: Gallimard.
Bermann, S. (2005). Introduction. In S. Bermann & M. Wood, eds., *Nation, Language, and Translation*, Princeton, NJ: Princeton University Press, pp. 1–10.
Bezhan, F. (2014). Tarjomān or interpreter, the first satirical newspaper and the emergence of modern satire in Afghanistan. *Media History*, **20**(3), 302–321.
Bhabha, H. K. (1994). *The Location of Culture*, London & New York: Routledge.
Bialik, K., & Matsa, K. E. (2017). Key trends in social and digital news media. Retrieved from www.pewresearch.org/fact-tank/2017/10/04/key-trends-in-social-and-digital-news-media.
Bidder, B. (2013). Putin's weapon in the war of images. Spiegel Online. Retrieved from www.spiegel.de/international/business/putin-fights-war-of-images-and-propaganda-with-russia-today-channel-a-916162.html.
Bielsa, E. (2007). Translation in global news. *Target*, **19**(1), 135–155.
(2014). Cosmopolitanism as translation. *Cultural Sociology*, **8**(4), 392–406.
(2020). News translation. In M. Baker & G. Saldanha, eds., *Routledge Encyclopedia of Translation Studies*, 3rd ed., London & New York: Routledge, pp. 365–370.
Bielsa, E., & Bassnett, S. (2009). *Translation in Global News*, London & New York: Routledge.
Bishara, A. A. (2013). *Back Stories: U.S. News Production and Palestinian Politics*, Stanford, CA: Stanford University Press.
Blackledge, A. (2006). *Discourse and Power in a Multilingual World*, Amsterdam & Philadelphia: John Benjamins.
Bloomfield, C., & Robert-Foley, L. (2017). Tweetranslating Trump: Outranspo's "bad translations" of Trump's tweets. *Contemporary French and Francophone Studies*, **21**(5), 469–476.
Bolden, G. B. (2000). Toward understanding practices of medical interpreting: interpreters' involvement in history taking. *Discourse Studies*, **2**(4), 387–419.
Bolter, J. D., & Grusin, R. (1999). *Remediation: Understanding New Media*, Cambridge, MA: MIT Press.
Bourdon, J. (2016). Strange strangers: The Jerusalem correspondents in the network of nations. *Journalism: Theory, Practice & Criticism*, **17**(6), 760–775.
Bovet, A. (2012). Configuring a television debate: Categorisation, questions and answers. In W. Housley & R. Fitzgerald, eds., *Media, Policy and Interaction*, Farnham & Burlington: Ashgate, pp. 27–48.
Brienza, C. (2016). *Manga in America: Transnational Book Publishing and the Domestication of Japanese Comics*, London: Bloomsbury.
Brownlees, N. (2005). Spoken discourse in early English newspapers. *Media History*, **11**(1), 69–85.
(2009). "Alwayes in te Orbe of honest Mirth, and next to Truth" Proto-infotainment in The Welch Mercury. In A. H. Jucker, ed., *Early Modern English News Discourse*, Amsterdam & Philadelphia: John Benjamins, pp. 57–72.

(2019). "A true and faithfull relation [...] translated out of Dutch": The role and translation of Dutch news in early seventeenth-century England. *inTRAlinea*, **21** (Special Issue: *Transit and Translation in Early Modern Europe*), 1–8.
Brownlie, S. (2007). Situating discourse on translation and conflict. *Social Semiotics*, **17**(2), 135–150.
Bruner, J. (1991). The narrative construction of reality. *Critical Inquiry*, **18**(1), 1–21.
Bugnot, M.-A. (2012). Traduction des discours sur l'islam dans la presse de France et d'Espagne. *Meta: Journal des traducteurs*, **57**, 977.
Bulic, K. (2011). The aesthetic alchemy of sounding impartial: Why Serbs still listen to "the BBC conspiracy." *Journalism*, **12**(2), 183–197.
Bulut, A. (2012). Translating political metaphors: Conflict potential of zenci [Negro] in Turkish-English. *Meta: Journal des traducteurs*, **57**(4), 909.
Burkette, A. (2016). Response by Burkette to "Translation and the materialities of communication". *Translation Studies*, **9**(3), 318–322.
Caimotto, M. C. (2010). Translating foreign articles with local implications: A case study. In C. Schäffner & S. Bassnett, eds., *Political Discourse, Media and Translation*, Newcastle upon Tyne: Cambridge Scholars Publishing, pp. 76–93.
(2016). Images of turmoil: Italy portrayed in Britain and re-mirrored in Italy. In L. van Doorslaer, P. Flynn, & J. Leerssen, eds., *Interconnecting Translation Studies and Imagology*, Amsterdam & Philadelphia: John Benjamins, pp. 239–256.
Caimotto, M. C., & Gaspari, F. (2018). Corpus-based study of news translation: Challenges and possibilities. *Across Languages and Cultures*, **19**(2), 205–220.
Callon, M. (1986). Some elements of a sociology of translation: Domestication of the scallops and the fishermen of Saint-Brieuc Bay. In J. Law, ed., *Power, Action and Belief: A New Sociology of Knowledge?*, London: Routledge, pp. 196–223.
Callon, M., & Latour, B. (1981). Unscrewing the big Leviathan: How actors macro-structure reality and how sociologists help them to do so. In K. Knorr-Cetina & A. V. Cicourel, eds., *Advances in Social Theory and Methodology: Towards an Integration of Micro- and Macro-Sociologies*, Boston: Routledge, pp. 277–303.
Caniglia, E. (2009). *La notizia*, Roma & Bari: Laterza.
Catford, J. C. (1965). *A Linguistic Theory of Translation: An Essay in Applied Linguistics*, Oxford: Oxford University Press.
Chang, N.-F. (2011). The development of translation studies into a discipline in China. In R. Sela-Sheffy & G. Toury, eds., *Culture Contacts and the Making of Cultures: Papers in Homage to Itamar Even-Zohar,* Tel Aviv: Unit of Culture Research, Tel Aviv University.
Cheesman, T., & Nohl, A.-M. (2011). Many voices, one BBC World Service? The 2008 US elections, gatekeeping and trans-editing. *Journalism: Theory, Practice & Criticism*, **12**(2), 217–233.
Chen, Y. (2009). Quotation as a key to the investigation of ideological manipulation in news trans-editing in the Taiwanese press. *TTR: Traduction, Terminologie, Rédaction*, **22**(2), 203–238.
(2011a). The ideological construction of solidarity in translated newspaper commentaries: Context models and inter-subjective positioning. *Discourse & Society*, **22**(6), 693–722.
(2011b). The translator's subjectivity and its constraints in news transediting: A perspective of reception aesthetics. *Meta: Journal des traducteurs*, **56**(1), 119–144.

Chesterman, A. (2001). Proposal for a Hieronymic oath. *The Translator*, **7**, 139–154.
(2006). Interpreting the meaning of translation. In M. Suominen, A. Arppe, A. Airola, et al., eds., *A Man of Measure. Festschrift in Honour of Fred Karlsson on His 60th Birthday,* Turku: Linguistic Association of Finland, pp. 3–11.
Chomsky, N. (1965). *Aspects of the Theory of Syntax*, Cambridge, MA: MIT Press.
Clapham, E. (1957). Printing. In C. Singer, E. J. Holmyard, A. R. Hall, & T. J. Williams, eds., *A History of Technology: From the Renaissance to the Industrial Revolution c.1500–c.1750, vol. III*, Oxford: Claredon Press, pp. 377–416.
Clark, H. H., & Carlson, T. B. (1982). Hearers and speech acts. *Language*, **58**(2), 332–373.
Clausen, L. (2004). Localizing the global: "Domestication" processes in international news production. *Media, Culture & Society*, **26**(1), 25–44.
Clayman, S. E., & Heritage, J. (2002). *The News Interview. Journalists and Public Figures on the Air*, Cambridge: Cambridge University Press.
Coldiron, A. E. B. (2016). Response. *Translation Studies*, **9**(1), 96–102.
Collet, T. (2009). Civilization and civilized in post-9/11 US presidential speeches. *Discourse & Society*, **20**(4), 455–475.
Colucci, C. (2011). Modalisation and pragmatics in simultaneous TV interpreting: A case study: American presidential debates. *The Interpreters' Newsletter*, **16**, 61–80.
Connolly, D., & Bacopoulou-Halls, A. (2009). Greek tradition. In *Routledge Encyclopedia of Translation Studies*, 2nd ed., London & New York: Routledge, pp. 418–426.
Constantinou, M. (2017). Mediating terror through narratives: A corpus-based approach to media translation. *Lodz Papers in Pragmatics*, **12**(1), 53–76.
Constanza Guzman, M. (2019). Introduction. *Translation and Interpreting Studies*, **14**(2), 169–173.
Conway, K. (2006). A cultural studies approach to translation in the news: The case of Canada and Quebec. In K. Conway & S. Bassnett, eds., *Proceedings of the Conference Held at the University of Warwick 23 June 2006*, Warwick: The Centre for Translation and Comparative Cultural Studies, University of Warwick, pp. 29–43.
(2010a). News translation and cultural resistance. *Journal of International and Intercultural Communication*, **3**(3), 187–205.
(2010b). Paradoxes of translation in television news. *Media, Culture & Society*, **32**(6), 979–996.
(2011). *Everyone Says No: Public Service Broadcasting and the Failure of Translation*, Montreal: McGill-Queen's University Press.
(2012). A conceptual and empirical approach to cultural translation. *Translation Studies*, **5**(3), 264–279.
(2014). Vagaries of news translation on Canadian broadcasting corporation television: Traces of history. *Meta: Journal des traducteurs*, **59**(3), 620–635.
(2015b). What is the role of culture in news translation? A materialist approach. *Perspectives: Studies in Translatology*, **23**(4), 521–535.
(ed.). (2015a). Culture and news translation. *Perspectives: Studies in Translatology*, **23**(4, Special Issue).
Conway, K., & Bassnett, S. (eds.). (2006). *Translation in Global News*, Warwick: The Centre for Translation and Comparative Cultural Studies, University of Warwick.

Conway, K., & Vaskivska, T. (2010). Consuming news translation: *The New York Times* online and the "Kremlin Rules" experiment. *Across Languages and Cultures*, **11**(2), 233–253.

Cornia, A., Ghersetti, M., Mancini, P., & Odén, T. (2016). The partisans, the technocrats and the watchdogs. *Journalism Studies*, **17**(8), 1030–1050.

Cornish, A. (2011). *Vernacular Translation in Dante's Italy: Illiterate Literature; Cambridge Studies in Medieval Literature*, Cambridge: Cambridge University Press.

Cortés Zaborras, C., & Hernández Guerrero, M. J. (eds.). (2005). *La traducción periodística*, Cuenca: Universidad de Castilla-La Mancha.

Creech, B. (2015). Disciplines of truth: The "Arab Spring," American journalistic practice, and the production of public knowledge. *Journalism: Theory, Practice & Criticism*, **16**(8), 1010–1026.

Cronin, M. (2003). *Translation and Globalization*, Abingdon & New York: Routledge.

(2006). *Translation and Identity*, London & New York: Routledge.

(2010). The translation crowd. *Revista Tradumatica*, **08**(December), 1–7.

(2013). *Translation in the Digital Age*, London & New York: Routledge.

Crystal, D. (2003). *English as a Global Language*, Cambridge: Cambridge University Press.

Cunico, S., & Munday, J. (2007). Encounters and clashes: Introduction to translation and ideology. *The Translator*, **13**(2), 141–149.

Cunningham, D., & Browning, B. (2004). The emergence of worthy targets: Official frames and deviance narratives within the FBI. *Sociological Forum*, **19**(3), 347–369.

Dal Fovo, E. (2012). Question/answer topical coherence in television interpreting. A corpus-based pilot study of American presidential debates. In C. J. Kellett Bidoli, ed., *Interpreting across Genres: Multiple Research Perspectives*, Trieste: EUT, pp. 54–77.

Darwish, A., & Orero, P. (2014). Rhetorical dissonance of unsynchronized voices: Issues of voice-over in news broadcasts. *Babel*, **60**(2), 129–144.

David Francis, & Hart, C. (1997). Narrative intelligibility and membership categorization in a television commercial. In S. Hester & P. Eglin, eds., *Culture in Action: Studies in Membership Categorization Analysis*, Lanham, MD & London: International Institute for Ethnomethodology and Conversation Analysis & University Press of America, pp. 123–152.

Davidson, B. (2002). A model for the construction of conversational common ground in interpreted discourse. *Journal of Pragmatics*, **34**(9), 1273–1300.

Davier, L. (2014). The paradoxical invisibility of translation in the highly multilingual context of news agencies. *Global Media and Communication*, **10**(1), 53–72.

(2015). "Cultural translation" in news agencies? A plea to broaden the definition of translation. *Perspectives: Studies in Translatology*, **23**(4), 536–551.

(2019). Technological convergence threatening translation and the cultural other: The professional vision of francophone journalists in Canada. In L. Davier & K. Conway, eds., *Journalism and Translation in the Era of Convergence*, Amsterdam & Philadelphia: John Benjamins, pp. 177–207.

Davier, L., & Conway, K. (2019a). Introduction: Journalism and translation in the era of convergence. In L. Davier & K. Conway, eds., *Journalism and Translation in the Era of Convergence*, Amsterdam & Philadelphia: John Benjamins, pp. 1–11.

(eds.). (2019b). *Journalism and Translation in the Era of Convergence*, Amsterdam & Philadelphia: John Benjamins.
Davier, L., & van Doorslaer, L. (2018). Translation without a source text: Methodological issues in news translation. *Across Languages and Cultures*, **19**(2), 241–257.
Davier, L., Schäffner, C., & van Doorslaer, L. (2018). The methodological remainder in news translation research: Outlining the background. *Across Languages and Cultures*, **19**(2), 155–164.
de Vreese, C. H. (2005). News framing: Theory and typology. *Information Design Journal + Document Design*, **13**(1), 51–62.
Delisle, J., & Woodsworth, J. (2012). *Translators through History*, Amsterdam & Philadelphia: John Benjamins.
Demers, G. (1994). Actualité internationale: Les titres de presse en anglais et en français. *Meta: Journal des traducteurs*, **39**(3), 520–529.
Derrida, J. (1992). From Des Tours de Babel. In R. Schulte & J. Biguenet, eds., *Theories of Translation. An Anthology of Essays from Dryden to Derrida*, Chicago & London: The University of Chicago Press, pp. 218–227.
Desjardins, R. (2017). *Translation and Social Media. In Theory, in Training and in Professional Practice*, London: Palgrave Macmillan.
Dickens, A. G. (1968). *Reformation and Society in Sixteenth Century Europe*, New York.
Dooley, B. (2001). Introduction. In B. Dooley & S. A. Baron, eds., *The Politics of Information in Early Modern Europe*, New York & London: Routledge, pp. 1–16.
Dooley, B., & Baron, S. A. (eds.). (2001). *The Politics of Information in Early Modern Europe*. New York & London: Routledge.
Dosquet, E. (2016). "We have been informed that the French are carrying desolation everywhere": The desolation of the Palatinate as a European news event. In J. Raymond & N. Moxham, eds., *News Networks in Early Modern Europe*, Leiden & Boston: Brill, pp. 541–674.
Dragovic-Drouet. (2007). The practice of translation and interpreting during the conflicts in the former Yugoslavia (1991–1999). In M. Salama-Carr, ed., *Translating and Interpreting Conflict*, Amsterdam & New York: Rodopi, pp. 29–41.
Drew, P., & Heritage, J. (eds.). (1993). *Talk at Work: Interaction in Institutional Settings*, Cambridge: Cambridge University Press.
Eco, U. (2001). *Experiences in Translation*, Toronto, Buffalo & London: University of Toronto Press.
(2003). *Dire quasi la stessa cosa. Esperienze di traduzione*, Milano: Bompiani.
Eger, M. A., & Valdez, S. (2015). Neo-nationalism in Western Europe. *European Sociological Review*, **31**(1), 115–130.
Eglin, P., & Hester, S. (1999). Moral order and the Montreal Massacre: A story of membership categorization analysis. In P. L. Jalbert, ed., *Media Studies: Ethnomethodological Approaches*, Lanham, MD & Oxford: International Institute for Ethnomethodology and Conversation Analysis & University Press of America, pp. 195–230.
(2003). *The Montreal Massacre: A Story of Membership Categorization Analysis*, Waterloo, Ontario: Wilfrid Laurier University Press.

Ehrensberger-Dow, M., & Perrin, D. (2009). Capturing translation processes to access metalinguistic awareness. *Across Languages and Cultures*, **10**(2), 275–288.

(2013). Applying a newswriting research approach to translation. *Target*, **25**(1), 77–92.

Eisenstein, E. L. (2005). *The Printing Revolution in Early Modern Europe*, Cambridge: Cambridge University Press.

Emmerich, M. (2014). Translating Japanese into Japanese: Bibliographic translation from woodblock to moveable type. In S. Bermann, ed., *A Companion to Translation Studies*, Chichester: Wiley Blackwell, pp. 599–611.

Entman, R. M. (1993). Framing: Toward clarification of a fractured paradigm. *Journal of Communication*, **43**(4), 51–58.

Espejo, C. (2011). European communication networks in the early modern age: A new framework of interpretation for the birth of journalism. *Media History*, **17**(2), 189–202.

(2016). The invention of the gazette: Design standardization in Spanish newspapers, 1600–1650. *Media History*, **22**(3–4), 296–316.

Ettinghausen, H. (2001). Politics and the press in Spain. In B. Dooley & S. Baron, eds., *The Politics of Information in Early Modern Europe*, London & New York: Routledge, pp. 199–215.

(2016). International relations: Spanish, Italian, French, English and German printed single event newsletters prior to Renaudot's *Gazette*. In J. Raymond & N. Moxham, eds., *News Networks in Early Modern Europe*, Leiden & Boston: Brill, pp. 261–279.

Fairclough, N. (1995). *Media discourse*, London: Edward Arnold.

Fairclough, N., & Wodak, R. (1997). Critical discourse analysis. In T. A. Van Dijk, ed., *Discourse Studies: A Multidisciplinary Introduction. vol. 2: Discourse as Social Interaction*, London: Sage, pp. 258–284.

Fattah, A. A. (2020). Ideological and evaluative shifts in media translation/trans-editing. In S. F. Hanna, H. El-Farahaty, & A.-W. Khalifa, eds., *The Routledge Handbook of Arabic Translation*, London & New York: Routledge, pp. 115–144.

Federici, F. (2010). Translations in Italian media: The Calipari case and legitimised texts. In C. Schäffner & S. Bassnett, eds., *Political Discourse, Media and Translation*, Newcastle upon Tyne: Cambridge Scholars Publishing, pp. 116–141.

(2011). The Calipari case: Political machinations and journalistic manipulations. *Journal of Siberian Federal University: Humanities & Social Sciences*, **10**(2011 4), 1394–1409.

Federici, F. M. (ed.). (2016). *Mediating Emergencies and Conflicts. Frontline Translating and Interpreting*, London: Palgrave Macmillan.

Filmer, D. (2014). Journalators? An ethnographic study of British journalists who translate. *Cultus: The Intercultural Journal of Mediation and Communication*, **7**, 135–157.

(2016). Images of Italy? The words Berlusconi never (officially) said. In L. van Doorslaer, P. Flynn, & J. Leerssen, eds., *Interconnecting Translation Studies and Imagology*, Amsterdam & Philadelphia: John Benjamins, pp. 257–276.

(2018). Anti-gay, sexist, racist: Backwards Italy in British news narratives. *Modern Languages Open*, **2018**(1), 1–21.

(2019). Voicing diversity? Negotiating Italian identity through voice-over translation in BBC broadcasting. *Perspectives: Studies in Translation Theory and Practice*, **27**(2), 299–315.

Fisher, W. R. (1984). Narration as a human communication paradigm: The case of public moral argument. *Communication Monographs*, **51**(1), 1–22.

(1985). The narrative paradigm: In the beginning. *Journal of Communication*, **35**(4), 74–89.

(1987). *Human Communication as Narration: Toward a Philosophy of Reason, Value and Action*, Colombia: University of South Carolina Press.

Fitzgerald, R. (2012). Membership categorization analysis: Wild and promiscuous or simply the joy of Sacks? *Discourse Studies*, **14**(3), 305–311.

Fitzgerald, R., & Housley, W. (2002). Identity, categorization and sequential organization: The sequential and categorial flow of identity in a radio phone-in. *Discourse and Society*, **13**(5), 579–602.

Flew, T. (2016). Entertainment media, cultural power, and post-globalization: The case of China's international media expansion and the discourse of soft power. *Global Media and China*, **1**(4), 278–294.

Floros, G. (2012). News translation and translation ethics in the Cypriot context. *Meta: Journal des traducteurs*, **57**(4), 924–942.

Folena, G. (1991). *Volgarizzare e tradurre*, Torino: Einaudi.

Footitt, H. (2012). Incorporating languages into histories of war: A research journey. *Translation Studies*, **5**(2), 217–231.

Footitt, H., & Kelly, M. (2012). *Languages at War: Policies and Practices of Language Contacts in Conflict*, Basingbroke & New York: Palgrave Macmillan.

Footitt, H., & Tobia, S. (2013). *WarTalk. Foreign Languages and the British War Effort in Europe, 1940–47*, Basingbroke & New York: Palgrave Macmillan.

Fortea Gil, C., & Santana Lopez, B. (2012). Ensanchando los límites: una aproximación desde la didáctica a la traducción literaria. Enlarging the limits: a didactic approach to literary translation. *Revista Teoría de La Educación: Educación y Cultura En La Sociedad de La Información*, **13**(1), 90–110.

Foucault, M. (1989). *The Archeology of Knowledge*, London: Routledge.

Fowler, R. (1991). *Language in the News: Discourse and Ideology in the Press*, London & New York: Routledge.

Franco Aixelá, J. (2013). Who's who and what's what in Translation Studies: A preliminary approach. In C. Way, S. Vandepitte, R. Maylaerts, & M. Barlomiejczyk, eds., *Tracks and Treks in Translation Studies*, Amsterdam & Philadelphia: John Benjamins, pp. 7–28.

Franjié, L. (2009). Quand la traduction devient communication orientée: Le cas du Courrier international pendant la guerre du Liban de 2006. In M. Guidère, ed., *Traduction et communication orientée*, Paris: Le Manuscrit, pp. 61–86.

Fujii, A. (1988). News translation in Japan. *Meta: Journal des traducteurs*, **33**(1), 32–37.

Gagnon, C. (2012). La visibilité de la traduction au Canada en journalisme politique: Mythe ou réalité? *Meta: Journal des traducteurs*, **57**, 943.

Gagnon, C., Boulanger, P.-P., & Kalantari, E. (2018). How to approach translation in a financial news corpus? *Across Languages and Cultures*, **19**(2), 221–240.

Gambier, Y. (2003). Introduction: Screen transadaptation; Perception and reception. *The Translator*, **9**(2), 171–190.

(2009). Challenges in research on audiovisual translation. In A. Pym & A. Perekrestenko, eds., *Translation Research Project 2*, Tarragona: Intercultural Studies Group Universitat Rovira i Virgili, pp. 17–25.

Gamson, W. A., & Modigliani, A. (1987). The changing culture of affirmative action. In R. G. Braungart & M. M. Braungart, eds., *Research in Political Sociology*, vol. 3, Greenwich, CT: JAI Press, pp. 137–177.

Garfinkel, H. (1967). *Studies in Ethnomethodology*, Englewood Cliffs, NJ: Prentice Hall, p. 288.

Gasca Jiménez, L., Álvarez, M. E., & Fernández, S. (2019). Language and translation practices of Spanish-language newspapers published in the U.S. borderlands between 1808 and 1930. *Translation and Interpreting Studies*, **14**(2), 218–242.

Gaspari, F. (2013). A phraseological comparison of international news agency reports published online: Lexical bundles in the English-language output of ANSA, Adnkronos, Reuters and UPI. *Studies in Variation, Contacts and Change in English*, **13**, 1–16.

(2015). Exploring Expo Milano 2015: A cross-linguistic comparison of food-related phraseology in translation using a comparallel corpus approach. *The Translator*, **21**(3), 327–349.

Gavioli, L. (2012). Minimal responses in interpreter-mediated medical talk. In C. Baraldi & L. Gavioli, eds., *Coordinating Participation in Dialogue Interpreting*, Amsterdam & Philadelphia: John Benjamins, pp. 201–228.

(2015a). Negotiating territories of knowledge: On interpreting talk in guided tours. *The Interpreters' Newsletter*, **20**, 73–86.

(2015b). On the distribution of responsibilities in treating critical issues in interpreter-mediated medical consultations: The case of "le spieghi(amo)." *Journal of Pragmatics*, **76**, 169–180.

Gellner, E. (1983). *Nations and Nationalism*, Ithaca, NY: Cornell University Press.

Gendron, P., Conway, K., & Davier, L. (2019). News translation on the Canadian Broadcasting Corporation's English and French websites. In L. Davier & K. Conway, eds., *Journalism and Translation in the Era of Convergence*, Amsterdam & Philadelphia: John Benjamins, pp. 63–81.

Gentzler, E. (n.d.). Translation without borders. *Translation. A Transdisciplinary Journal*. Retrieved from http://translation.fusp.it/articles/translation-without-borders.

Gibbs, G. C. (1987). Huguenot contributions to England's intellectual life and England's intellectual commerce with Europe, c. 1680–1720. In I. Scouloudi, ed., *Huguenots in Britain and Their French Background, 1550–1800*, Basingbroke & London: Macmillan, pp. 20–41.

Goffman, E. (1974). *Frame Analysis: An Essay on the Organization of Experience*, Boston: Northeastern University Press.

(1981). *Forms of Talk*, Philadelphia: University of Pennsylvania Press.

Goggin, G., Martin, F., & Dwyer, T. (2015). Locative news. *Journalism Studies*, **16**(1), 41–59.

Goodwin, C. (2000). Practices of seeing: Visual analysis; An ethnomethodological approach. In T. van Leeuwen & C. Jewitt, eds., *Handbook of Visual Analysis*, London: Sage, pp. 157–182.

Gotsbachner, E. (2009). Asserting interpretive frames of political events: Panel discussions on television news. In W. Housley & R. Fitzgerald, eds., *Media, Policy and Interaction*, Farnham & Burlington, VT: Ashgate, pp. 49–72.

Gu, C. (2018). Forging a glorious past via the "present perfect": A corpus-based CDA analysis of China's past accomplishments discourse mediat(is)ed at China's interpreted political press conferences. *Discourse, Context & Media*, **24**, 137–149.

(2019). (Re)manufacturing consent in English: A corpus-based critical discourse analysis of government interpreters' mediation of China's discourse on PEOPLE at televised political press conferences. *Target*, **31**(3), 465–499.
Gu, C., & Tipton, R. (2020). (Re-)voicing Beijing's discourse through self-referentiality: A corpus-based CDA analysis of government interpreters' discursive mediation at China's political press conferences (1998–2017). *Perspectives: Studies in Translation Theory and Practice*, **28**(3), 406–423.
Guangjun, W., & Huanyao, Z. (2015). Translating political ideology: A case study of the Chinese translations of the English news headlines concerning South China Sea disputes on the website of www.ftchinese.com. *Babel*, **61**(3), 394–410.
Gurevitch, M., Levy, M., & Roeh, I. (1991). The global newsroom: Convergences and diversities in the globalisation of television news. In P. Dahlgren & C. Sparks, eds., *Communications and Citizenship: Journalism and the Public Sphere in the New Media Age*, London: Routledge, pp. 195–216.
H⊘yer, S. (2003). Newspapers without journalists. *Journalism Studies*, **4**(4), 451–463.
Haapanen, L., & Perrin, D. (2019). Translingual quoting in journalism: Behind the scenes of Swiss television newsrooms. In L. Davier & K. Conway, eds., *Journalism and Translation in the Era of Convergence*, Amsterdam & Philadelphia: John Benjamins, pp. 15–42.
Haddadian-Moghaddam, E., & Meylaerts, R. (2014). Translation policy in the media. *Translation Spaces*, **3**(2014), 71–98.
Halliday, M. A. K. (1978). *Language as Social Semiotic: The Social Interpretation of Language and Meaning*, London: Edward Arnold.
(1985). *Introduction to Functional Grammar*, London: Edward Arnold.
Halliday, M. A. K., & Hasan, R. (1976). *Cohesion in English*, London: Pearson.
Halliday, M. A. K., & Matthiessen, C. M. I. M. (2014). *Halliday's Introduction to Functional Grammar, 4th ed. Revised by Christian M.I.M. Matthiessen*, London & New York: Routledge.
Hallin, D. C., & Mancini, P. (2004). *Comparing Media Systems: Three Models of Media and Politics*, Cambridge: Cambridge University Press.
Halverson, S. (1999a). Conceptual work and the "translation" concept. *Target*, **11**(1), 1–31.
(1999b). Image schemas, metaphoric processes, and the "translate" concept. *Metaphor and Symbol*, **14**(3), 199–219.
Hamill, P. (1998). *News Is a Verb: Journalism at the End of the Twentieth Century*, New York: Ballantine.
Hamilton, J. M., & Jenner, E. (2004). Redefining foreign correspondence. *Journalism*, **5**(3), 301–321.
Hammersley, M. (2003). Conversation analysis and discourse analysis: Methods or paradigms? *Discourse & Society*, **14**(6), 751–781.
(2018). *The Radicalism of Ethnomethodology: An Assessment of Sources and Principles*, Manchester: Manchester University Press.
Han, B.-C. (2017). *Shanzai: The Copy Is the Original*, Boston and London: The MIT Press.
Hanusch, F. (2008). Valuing those close to us: A comparison of German and Australian quality newspapers' reporting of death in foreign news. *Journalism Studies*, **9**(3), 341–356.

Harding, S.-A. (2011). Translation and the circulation of competing narratives from the wars in Chechnya: A case study from the 2004 Beslan hostage disaster. *Meta: Journal des traducteurs*, **56**(1), 42–62.
(2012a). *Beslan. Six Stories of the Siege*, Manchester & New York: Manchester University Press.
(2012b). Translating eyewitness accounts. *Journal of Language and Politics*, **11**(2), 229–249.
Hartley, J., Montgomery, L., & Siling Li, H. (2017). A new model for understanding global media and China: "Knowledge clubs" and "knowledge commons." *Global Media and China*, **2**(1), 8–27.
Hassan, H., Aue, A., Chen, C., et al. (2018). Achieving human parity on automatic Chinese to English news translation. Retrieved from http://arxiv.org/abs/1803.05567.
Hatim, B., & Mason, I. (1990). *Discourse and the Translator*, New York & London: Longman.
(2004). *Translation: An Advanced Resource Book*, Abingdon & New York: Routledge.
Heilbron, J. (1999). Towards a sociology of translation: Book translations as a cultural world-system. *European Journal of Social Theory*, **2**(4), 429–444.
Helle-Valle, J., & Slettemeas, D. (2008). ICTs, domestication and language-games: A Wittgensteinian approach to media uses. *New Media & Society*, **10**(1), 45–66.
Hemmungs Wirtén, E. (1998). *Global Infatuation: Explorations in Transnational Publishing and Texts; The Case of Harlequin Enterprise and Sweden*, Uppsala University.
(2004). *No Trespassing: Authorship, Intellectual Property Rights, and the Boundaries of Globalization*, Toronto, Buffalo & London: University of Toronto Press.
Henningham, J. P. (1979). Kyodo gate-keepers: A study of Japanese news flow. *International Communication Gazette*, **25**, 23–30.
Heritage, J. (1984). *Garfinkel and Ethnomethodology*, Cambridge: Polity Press.
(1993). Ethnomethodology. In E. F. Borgatta & R. J. V. Montgomery, eds., *Encyclopedia of Sociology*, vol. 2, New York: Macmillan, pp. 856–861.
Herman, D. (2009). *Basic Elements of Narrative*, Singapore: Wiley-Blackwell.
Herman, E. S., & Chomsky, N. (1988). *Manufacturing Consent: The Political Economy of the Mass Media*, New York: Pantheon Books.
Hermans, T. (1985). *The Manipulation of Literature: Studies in Literary Translation*, London & Sydney: Croom Helm.
(2009). Translation, ethics, politics. In P. Kuhiwczak & K. Littau, eds., *The Routledge Companion to Translation Studies*, Clevedon, Buffalo & Toronto: Routledge, pp. 93–105.
Hernández Guerrero, M. J. (2009). *Traducción y periodismo*, Bern: Peter Lang.
(2010). Translated interviews in printed media: A case study of the Spanish daily *El Mundo. Across Languages and Cultures*, **11**(2), 217–232.
(2011). Presencia y utilización de la traducción en la prensa española. *Meta: Journal des traducteurs*, **56**(1), 101–118.
(2012). La traducción al servicio de una línea editorial: La primavera árabe en el diario *El País. Meta: Journal des traducteurs*, **57**(4), 960.

(2013). Translation in *The Huffington Post*. *Hermeneus*, **17**, 111–136.

(2016). Traducción y opinión pública global: El caso de Project Syndicate. In M. R. Martín Ruano & Á. Vidal Claramonte, eds., *Traducción, medios de comunicación, opinión pública*, Grenada: Comares, p. 322.

(2017). Translation in new independent online media: The case of Mediapart. *Perspectives: Studies in Translation Theory and Practice*, **25**(2), 294–307.

(2019). La traducción en las nuevas formas de periodismo. *MonTI*, (5, Special Issue), 73–94.

(2020). The translation of tweets in Spanish digital newspapers. *Perspectives: Studies in Translation Theory and Practice*, **28**(3), 376–392.

Hernández Hernández, T. P. (2017). Translation, a hybrid form of capital: The translators of *Le Monde diplomatique en español* (1979–1988). *Perspectives: Studies in Translation Theory and Practice*, **25**(3), 509–520.

Hester, S. (2002). Bringing it all back home: Selecting topic, category and location in TV news programmes. In S. Hester & W. Housley, eds., *Language Interaction and National Identity*, Aldershot: Ashgate, pp. 16–37.

Hester, S., & Eglin, P. (1997a). Membership categorization analysis: An introduction. In S. Hester & P. Eglin, eds., *Culture in Action: Studies in Membership Categorization Analysis*, Lanham, MD & London: International Institute for Ethnomethodology and Conversation Analysis & University Press of America, pp. 1–23.

(1997b). The reflexive constitution of category, predicate and context in two settings. In S. Hester & P. Eglin, eds., *Culture in Action: Studies in Membership Categorization Analysis*, Lanham, MD & London: International Institute for Ethnomethodology and Conversation Analysis & University Press of America, pp. 25–48.

Hijjo, N. F. M., & Kaur, S. (2017a). Recontextualizing terror: ISIS narratives in the English Media. *International Journal of Euro-Mediterranean Studies*, **10**(2), 49–77.

(2017b). The paratextual analysis of English translations of Arabic media narratives on Daesh. *3L: Language, Linguistics, Literature*, **23**(3), 21–36.

Hijjo, N. F. M., Kaur, S., & Kadhim, K. A. (2019). Reframing the Arabic narratives on Daesh in the English media: The ideological impact. *Open Linguistics*, **5**(1), 81–93.

Hoey, M. (1991). *Patterns of Lexis in Text*, Oxford: Oxford University Press.

(2005). *Lexical Priming: A New Theory of Words and Language*, London & New York: Routledge.

Hojmohammadi, A. (2005). Translation evaluation in a news agency. *Perspectives: Studies in Translatology*, **13**(3), 215–224.

Holland, R. (2006). Language(s) in the global news: Translation, audience design and discourse (mis)representation. *Target*, **18**(2), 229–259.

(2013). News translation. In C. Milan & F. Bartina, eds., *The Routledge Handbook of Translation Studies*, Abingdon & New York: Routledge, pp. 332–346.

Holz-Mänttäri, J. (1984). *Translatorisches Handeln. Theorie und Methode*, Helsinki: Suomalainen Tiedeakatemia.

Hong, J. (2019). News translators' para-textual visibility in South Korea. *Babel*, **65**(1), 26–50.

(2021). Translation of attribution and news credibility. *Journalism*, **22**(3), 787–803.

Hosseini, F. (2016). BBC versus Euro news: Discourse and ideology in news translation. *Russian Linguistic Bulletin*, **3**(7), 128–132.

House, J. (2003). English as a lingua franca: A threat to multilingualism? *Journal of Sociolinguistics*, **7**(4), 556–578.

(2013). English as a lingua franca and translation. *Interpreter and Translator Trainer*, **7**(2), 279–298.

(2015). *Translation Quality Assessment: Past and Present*, Abingdon & New York: Routledge.

Housley, W., & Fitzgerald, R. (2009). Membership categorization, culture and norms in action. *Discourse & Society*, **20**(3), 345–362.

(2015). Introduction to membership categorization analysis. In R. Fitzgerald & W. Housley, eds., *Advances in Membership Categorization Analysis*, London, Thousand Oaks, New Delhi & Singapore: Sage, pp. 1–21.

Hu, W., & Wang, X. (2019). Balancing university teaching and media industry needs: A case study of teaching finance and economics news translation. *International Journal of Higher Education*, **8**(3), 247–256.

Hunston, S. (2007). Semantic prosody revisited. *International Journal of Corpus Linguistics*, **12**(2), 249–268.

Hursti, K. (2001). An insider's view on transformation and transfer in international news communication: An English-Finnish perspective. *The Electronic Journal of the Department of English at the University of Helsinki*, **1**(1), 1–5.

Hutchby, I. (2006). *Media Talk. Conversation Analysis and the Study of Broadcasting. Language in Society*, Maidenhead & New York: Open University Press.

Hutt, A. (1973). *The Changing Newspaper: Typographic Trends in Britain and America 1622–1972*, London: Gordon Fraser.

Inghilleri, M. (2005). The sociology of Bourdieu and the construction of the "object" in translation and interpreting studies. *The Translator*, **11**(2), 125–145.

(2009). Translators in war zones: Ethics under fire in Iraq. In E. Bielsa & C. W. Hughes, eds., *Globalization, Political Violence and Translation*, Basingbroke & New York: Palgrave Macmillan, pp. 207–221.

(2017). *Translation and Migration*, London & New York: Routledge.

Inghilleri, M., & Maier, C. (2009). Ethics. In *Routledge Encyclopedia of Translation Studies*, 2nd ed., London & New York: Routledge, pp. 100–103.

Iser, W. (1978). *The Act of Reading: A Theory of Aesthetic Response*, Baltimore: Johns Hopkins University Press.

Italiano, F. (2012). Translating geographies: The Navigatio Sancti Brendani and its Venetian translation. *Translation Studies*, **5**(1), 1–16.

Jaber, M., & Baumann, G. (2011). The BBC World Service in the Middle East: Claims to impartiality, or a politics of translation? *Journalism*, **12**(2), 171–182.

Jakobson, R. (1959). On linguistic aspects of translation. In R. A. Brower, ed., *On Translation*, Cambridge, MA: Harvard University Press, pp. 232–239.

Jalbert, P. L. (1984). "News speak" about the Lebanon War. *Journal of Palestine Studies*, **14**(1), 16–35.

(1992). Charting the logical geography of the concept of "cease-fire." *Human Studies*, **15**(2–3), 265–290.

(1994). Structures of the "unsaid." *Theory, Culture & Society*, **11**, 127–160.

(1999). Preface. In P. L. Jalbert, ed., *Media Studies: Ethnomethodological Approaches*, Lanham, MD & Oxford: International Institute for Ethnomethodology and Conversation Analysis & University Press of America, pp. xv–xvii.

Jauss, H. R. (1982). *Toward an Aesthetic of Reception: The Journal of Aesthetics and Art Criticism* (T. Bahti, trans.), Minneapolis: University of Minnesota Press.

Jaworski, A., Fitzgerald, R., & Morris, D. (2003). Certainty and speculation in news reporting of the future: The execution of Timothy McVeigh. *Discourse Studies*, **5** (1), 33–48.

Jayyusi, L. (1984). *Categorization and the Moral Order*, London & New York: Routledge.

(1991). The equivocal text and the objective world: An ethnomethodological analysis of a news report. *Continuum*, **5**(1), 166–190.

Jefferson, G. (1973). A case of precision timing in ordinary conversation: Overlapped tag-positioned address terms in closing sequences. *Semiotica*, **9**(1), 47–96.

(1974). Error correction as an interactional resource. *Language in Society*, **2**, 181–199.

(1978). Sequential aspects of story-telling in conversation. In J. Schenkein, ed., *Studies in the Organization of Conversational Interaction*, New York: Academic Press, pp. 219–248.

(1987). On exposed and embedded correction in conversation. In G. Button & J. R. E. Lee, eds., *Talk and Social Organization*, Clevedon & Philadelphia: Multilingual Matters, pp. 86–100.

(1996). A case of transcriptional stereotyping. *Journal of Pragmatics*, **26**, 159–170.

Jenkins, H. (2006). *Convergence Culture: Where Old and New Media Collide*, New York & London: New York University Press.

Jenkins, J. (2007). *English as a Lingua Franca: Attitude and Identity*, Oxford: Oxford University Press.

Ji, M., Hareide, L., Defeng, L., & Oakes, M. (2017). Introduction to *Corpus Methodologies Explained: An Empirical Approach to Translation Studies*. In M. Ji, M. Oakes, L. Defeng, & L. Hareide, eds., *Corpus Methodologies Explained: An Empirical Approach to Translation Studies*, London & New York: Routledge, pp. 6–19.

Jiménez-Crespo, M. Á. (2012). Translation under pressure and the web: A parallel corpus- study of Obama's inaugural speech in the online media. *Translation and Interpreting*, **4**(1), 56–76.

(2017). Translation crowdsourcing: Research trends and perspectives. In A. Cordingley & C. Frigau Manning, eds., *Collaborative Translation. From the Renaissance to the Digital Age*, London & New York: Bloomsbury, pp. 192–211.

Kadhim, K. A., Habeeb, L. S., Sapar, A. A., Hussin, Z., & Abdullah, M. M. R. T. L. (2013). An evaluation of online machine translation of Arabic into English news headlines: Implications on students' learning purposes. *Turkish Online Journal of Educational Technology*, **12**(2), 39–50.

Kaindl, K. (2014). Going fictional! Translators and interpreters in literature and film: An introduction. In K. Kaindl & K. Spitzl, eds., *Transfiction: Research into the Realities of Translation Fiction*, Amsterdam & Philadelphia: John Benjamins, pp. 1–26.

Kalanzade, G.-A., Morovati, A., & Bakhtiarvand, M. (2013). Translation quality assessment of news translation in ISNA news agency. *The International Journal of Language Learning and Applied Linguistics*, **2**(2), 94–104.

Kamyanets, A. (2017). Translating irony in media texts: A relevance theory perspective. *Across Languages and Cultures*, **18**(2), 261–278.

(2020). Evaluation in translation: A case study of Ukrainian opinion articles. *Perspectives: Studies in Translation Theory and Practice*, **28**(3), 393–405.

Kang, J.-H. (2007). Contextualisation of news discourse: A case study of translation of news discourse on North Korea. *The Translator*, **13**(2), 219–42.

(2010). Positioning and fact construction in translation: Intertextual and translational chains in *Newsweek Korea*. In M. Baker, M. Olohan, & C. P. María, eds., *Text and Context: Essays on Translation and Interpreting in Honour of Ian Mason*, Manchester: St Jerome, pp. 157–187.

(2012). Translating mad cow disease: A case study of subtitling for a television news magazine. *Meta: Journal des traducteurs*, **57**(2), 439.

(2014). Institutions translated: Discourse, identity and power in institutional mediation. *Perspectives: Studies in Translatology*, **22**(4), 469–478.

Károly, K. (2012). News discourse in translation: Topical structure and news content in the analytical news article. *Meta: Journal des traducteurs*, **57**, 884.

(2017a). *Aspects of Cohesion and Coherence in Translation: The Case of Hungarian-English News Translation*, Amsterdam & Philadelphia: John Benjamins.

(2017b). Logical relations in translation: The case of Hungarian–English news translation. *Perspectives: Studies in Translation Theory and Practice*, **25**(2), 273–293.

Károly, K., Ábrányi, H., Deák, S., Laszkács, Á., Mészáros, A., & Seresi, M. (2013). Cohesion and news translation. *Acta Linguistica Hungarica*, **60**(4), 365–407.

Katan, D., & Straniero Sergio, F. (2001). Look who's talking: The ethics of entertainment and talkshow interpreting. *The Translator*, **7**(2), 213–237.

(2003). Submerged ideologies in media interpreting. In M. Calzada Pérez, ed., *Apropos of Ideology*, Manchester: St Jerome, pp. 131–144.

Ke, G., Cuilin, S., & Wei, W. (2004). Globalizing the local. *Media Asia*, **31**(1), 51–60.

Kelly-Holmes, H. (2012). Multilingualism and the media. In M. Martin-Jones, A. Blackledge, & A. Creese, eds., *The Routledge Handbook of Multilingualism*, Abingdon & New York: Routledge, pp. 333–346.

Khanjan, A., Amouzadeh, M., Eslami Rasekh, A., & Tavangar, M. (2014). Ideological aspects of translating news headlines from English to Persian. *Meta*, **58**(1), 87–102.

Kim, K. H. (2014). Examining US news media discourses about North Korea: A corpus-based critical discourse analysis. *Discourse and Society*, **25**(2), 221–244.

(2017). Newsweek discourses on China and their Korean translations: A corpus-based approach. *Discourse, Context and Media*, **15**, 34–44.

Kittel, H., & Poltermann, A. (2009). German tradition. In M. Baker & G. Saldanha, eds., *Routledge Encyclopedia of Translation Studies*, 2nd ed., London & New York: Routledge, pp. 411–418.

Kontos, P., & Sidiropoulou, M. (2012a). Political routines in press translation. *Meta: Journal des traducteurs*, **57**, 1013.

(2012b). Socio-political narratives in translated English-Greek news headlines. *Intercultural Pragmatics*, **9**(2), 195–224.

Kothari, R. (2014). Response. *Translation Studies*, **7**(1), 96–99.

Kovalyova, N. (2010). Media practices in reporting political crises. In U. Okulska & P. Cap, eds., *Perspectives in Politics and Discourse*, Amsterdam & Philadelphia: John Benjamins, pp. 279–297.

Kuo, S.-H., & Nakamura, M. (2005). Translation or transformation? A case study of language and ideology in the Taiwanese press. *Discourse & Society*, **16**(3), 393–417.

Kurz, I. (1987). Conference interpreting: Myth and reality. In M. Kummer, ed., *Proceedings of the 28th Annual Conference of the American Translators Association, Albuquerque, New Mexico, October 8–11, 1987*, Medford, NJ: Learned Information, pp. 315–320.

(1997). Getting the message across: Simultaneous interpreting for the media. In M. Snell-Hornby, Z. Jettmarová, & K. Kaindl, eds., *Translation as Intercultural Communication*, Amsterdam & Philadelphia: John Benjamins, pp. 195–205.

(2002). Physiological stress responses during media and conference interpreting. In G. Garzone & M. Viezzi, eds., *Interpreting in the 21st Century: Challenges and Opportunities*, Amsterdam & Philadelphia: John Benjamins, pp. 195–202.

Larwill, P. H. (1934). *La théorie de la traduction au début de la Renaissance*, Munich: Wolf.

Latour, B. (1987). *Science in Action*, Cambridge, MA: Harvard University Press.

(2005). *Reassembling the Social: An Introduction to Actor-Network-Theory*, Oxford: Oxford University Press.

(2012). The Berlin key or how to do words with things. In P. Graves-Brown, ed., *Matter, Materiality and Modern Culture*, London: Routledge, pp. 10–21.

Laurenti, F. (2015). *Tradurre. Storie, teorie, pratiche dall'antichità al XIX secolo*, Roma: Armando Editore.

Lautamatti, L. (1990). Coherence in spoken and written discourse. In U. Connor & A. M. Johns, eds., *Coherence in Writing: Research and Pedagogical Perspectives*, Alexandria, VA: TESOL, pp. 29–40.

Laviosa, S. (2004). Corpus-based translation studies: Where does it come from? Where is it going? *TradTerm*, **10**, 29–57.

Laviosa, S., Pagano, A., Kempannen, H., & Ji, M. (2017). A corpus analysis of translation of environmental news on BBC China. In *Textual and Contextual Analysis in Empirical Translation Studies*, Singapore: Springer, pp. 129–157.

Lee, C. (2006). Differences in news translation between broadcasting and newspapers: A case study of Korean-English translation. *Meta: Journal des traducteurs*, **51**(2), 317.

Lee, J. (1984). Innocent victims and evil-doers. *Women's Studies International Forum*, **7**(1), 69–73.

Leech, P. (2020). *Cosmopolitanism, Dissent and Translation: Translating Radicals in Eighteenth-Century Britain and France*, Bologna: Bononia University Press.

Lefevere, A. (1977). *Translating Literature: The German Tradition*, Assen: Van Gorcum.

(1992). *Translation, Rewriting, and the Manipulation of Literary Fame*, London & New York: Routledge.

Lepper, G. (2000). *Categories in Text and Talk: A Practical Introduction to Categorization Analysis*, London, Thousand Oaks & New Delhi: Sage.

Leudar, I., & Nekvapil, J. (2004). Media dialogical networks and political argumentation. *Journal of Language and Politics*, **3**(2), 247–266.

Leudar, I., Marsland, V., & Nekvapil, J. (2004). On membership categorization: "us," "them" and "doing violence" in political discourse. *Discourse & Society*, **15**(2–3), 243–266.

Leung, M. W.-K. (2006). The ideological turn in translation studies. In J. Ferreira Duarte, A. Assis Rosa, & T. Seruya, eds., *Translation Studies at the Interface of Disciplines*, Amsterdam & Philadelphia: John Benjamins, pp. 129–145.

Li, J. (2009). Intertextuality and national identity: Discourse of national conflicts in daily newspapers in the United States and China. *Discourse and Society*, **20**(1), 85–121.

(2020). Political TV documentary subtitling in China: A critical discourse analysis perspective. *Perspectives: Studies in Translation Theory and Practice*, **28**(4), 554–574.

Li, J., & Li, S. (2015). New trends of Chinese political translation in the age of globalisation. *Perspectives: Studies in Translatology*, **23**(3), 424–439.

Liao, S., & Pan, L. (2018). Interpreter mediation at political press conferences. *Interpreting. International Journal of Research and Practice in Interpreting*, **20** (2), 188–203.

Lim, L. (2017). Going global and local control: Reflections on research directions on media policy in East Asia. *Global Media and China*, **2**(1), 43–56.

Littau, K. (2011). First steps towards a media history of translation. *Translation Studies*, **4**(3), 261–281.

(2016a). Translation's histories and digital futures. *International Journal of Communication*, **10**, 907–928.

(2016b). Translation and the materialities of communication. *Translation Studies*, **9** (1), 82–96.

Liu, N. X. (2017). Same perspective, different effect: Framing the economy through financial news translation. *Perspectives: Studies in Translation Theory and Practice*, **25**(3), 452–463.

(2019). *News Framing through English-Chinese Translation: A Comparative Study of Chinese and English Media Discourse*, Abingdon & New York: Routledge.

Lobe, A. (2018). Wir steuern auf ein digitales Dark Age zu. *Neue Zürcher Zeitung*. Retrieved from www.nzz.ch/feuilleton/wir-steuern-auf-ein-digitales-dark-age-zu-ld.1375956.

Lomal, L. (2016). Promoting the Catholic cause on the Italian peninsula: Printed Avvisi on the Dutch revolt and the French wars of religion, 1562–1600. In J. Raymond & N. Moxham, eds., *News Networks in Early Modern Europe*, Leiden & Boston: Brill, pp. 675–694.

Lorenzo-Dus, N. (2009). *Television Discourse: Analysing Language in the Media*, Basingbroke: Palgrave Macmillan.

Loupaki, E. (2010). Investigating translators' strategies in rendering ideological conflict: The case of news translation. In C. Schäffner & S. Bassnett, eds., *Political Discourse, Media and Translation*, Newcastle upon Tyne: Cambridge Scholars Publishing, pp. 55–75.

Louw, B. (1993). Irony in the text or insincerity in the writer? — The diagnostic potential of semantic prosodies. In M. Baker, G. Francis, & E. Tognini-Bonelli, eds., *Text and Technology: In Honour of John Sinclair*, Amsterdam & Philadelphia: John Benjamins, pp. 157–176.

Luo, Y. (2015). News translation as a site of framing Chinese identity: The case of *Yeeyan Sport*. *Ethnicities*, **15**(6), 829–847.
Lynch, M. (2019). Garfinkel, Sacks and formal structures: Collaborative origins, divergences and the history of ethnomethodology and conversation analysis. *Human Studies*, **42**(2), 183–198.
Maitland, S. (2015). Culture in translation: The case of British *Pathé News*. *Perspectives: Studies in Translatology*, **23**(4), 570–585.
Manfredi, M. (2018). Investigating ideology in news features translated for two Italian media. *Across Languages and Cultures*, **19**(2), 185–203.
Mann, W. C., & Thompson, S. A. (1986). Relational propositions in discourse. *Discourse Processes*, **9**(1), 57–90.
Marantz, A. (2020). Big swinging brains and fashy trolls: How the world fell into a clickbait death spiral. *The Guardian*. Retrieved from www.theguardian.com/technology/2020/feb/07/big-swinging-brains-fashy-trolls-clickbait-death-spiral-internet-media.
Marra, M. (2015). Language and culture in sociolinguistics. In F. Sharifian, ed., *The Routledge Handbook of Language and Culture*, Abingdon & New York: Routledge, pp. 373–385.
Martin, J. R., & White, P. R. R. (2005). *The Language of Evaluation: Appraisal in English*, Basingbroke: Palgrave Macmillan.
Mason, I. (2012). Gaze, positioning and identity in interpreter-mediated dialogues. In C. Baraldi & L. Gavioli, eds., *Coordinating Participation in Dialogue Interpreting*, Amsterdam & Philadelphia: John Benjamins, pp. 177–200.
Matsushita, K. (2019a). Globalization of the emerging media newsroom: Implications for translation and international news flow in the case of BuzzFeed Japan. In L. Davier & K. Conway, eds., *Journalism and Translation in the Era of Convergence*, Amsterdam & Philadelphia: John Benjamins, pp. 135–153.
(2019b). *When News Travels East: Translation Practices by Japanese Newspapers*, Leuven: Leuven University Press.
Matsushita, K., & Schäffner, C. (2018). Multilingual collaboration for news translation analysis: Possibilities and limitations. *Across Languages and Cultures*, **19**(2), 165–184.
Maynard, D. W., & Clayman, S. E. (2003). Ethnomethodology and conversation analysis. In L. T. Raynolds & N. J. Herman-Kinney, eds., *Handbook of Symbolic Interactionism*, Walnut Creek, CA: Altamira Press, pp. 173–202.
Maynard, D. W., & Peräkylä, A. (2003). Language and social interaction. In *Handbook of Social Psychology*, New York: Kluwer-Plenum, pp. 233–258.
McElduff, S. (2009). Living at the level of the word Cicero's rejection of the interpreter as translator. *Translation Studies*, **2**(2), 133–146.
(2015). Speaking as Greeks, speaking over Greeks: Orality and its problems in Roman translation. *Translation Studies*, 8(2), 128–140.
McLaughlin, M. (2013). News translation as a source of syntactic borrowing in Italian. *The Italianist*, **33**(3), 443–463.
McLaughlin, M. L. (2011). *Syntactic Borrowing in Contemporary French: A Linguistic Analysis of News Translation*, Oxford: Legenda.
McLuhan, M. (1962). *The Gutenberg Galaxy: The Making of Typographic Man*, Toronto: University of Toronto Press.

Merkle, D. (2008). Translation constraints and the "sociological turn" in literary translation studies. In A. Pym, M. Schlesinger, & D. Simeoni, eds., *Beyond Descriptive Translation Studies: Investigations in Homage to Gideon Toury*, Amsterdam & Philadelphia: John Benjamins, pp. 175–186.

Meschonnic, H. (1973). *Pour la poétique II: Épistémologie de l'écriture. Poétique de la traduction*, Paris: Gallimard.

Metzger, M. (1999). *Sign Language Interpreting: Deconstructing the Myth of Neutrality*, Washington, D.C.: Gallaudet University Press.

Morini, M. (2008). Outlining a new linguistic theory of translation. *Target*, **20**(1), 29–51.

Morris, M. (2006). *Identity Anecdotes: Translation and Media Culture*, Thousand Oaks, CA: Sage.

Mortier, R. (1982). *L'Originalité: Une nouvelle catégorie esthétique au siècle des lumières*, Geneva: Droz.

Mossop, B. (1990). Translating institutions and "idiomatic" translation. *Meta: Journal des traducteurs*, **35**(2), 342–355.

Mounin, G. (1955). *Les Belles infidels: Essai sur la traduction*, Paris: Cahiers du Sud.

(1963). *Les problèmes théoriques de la traduction*, Paris: Gallimard.

(1965). *Teoria e storia della traduzione*, Torino: Einaudi.

Munday, J. (2007). Translation and ideology: A textual approach. *The Translator*, **13**(2), 195–217.

(2018). A model of appraisal: Spanish interpretations of President Trump's inaugural address 2017. *Perspectives: Studies in Translation Theory and Practice*, **26**(2), 180–195.

Nakane, I. (2007). Problems in communicating the suspect's rights in interpreted police interviews. *Applied Linguistics*, **28**(1), 87–112.

(2011). The role of silence in interpreted police interviews. *Journal of Pragmatics*, **43**(9), 2317–2330.

(2014). *Interpreter-Mediated Police Interviews: A Discourse-Pragmatic Approach*, Basingbroke & New York: Palgrave Macmillan.

Navarro, A. E., & Hart, C. P. (2019). Translating from/for the margins of empire: *The Gaceta de Guatemala* (1797–1807) and the enlightened elites. *Target*, **31**(2), 207–227.

Nida, E. (1964). *Toward a Science of Translating*, Leiden: Brill.

Nord, C. (1997). *Translating as a Purposeful Activity: Functionalist Approaches Explained*, Manchester: St Jerome.

(2005). *Text Analysis in Translation: Theory, Methodology, and Didactic Application*, 2nd ed., Amsterdam: Rodopi.

Nossek, H. (2004). Our news and their news: The role of national identity in the coverage of foreign news. *Journalism*, **5**(3), 343–368.

Nye, Jr., J. S. (1990). *Bound to Lead: The Changing Nature of American Power*, New York: Basic Books.

(2004). *Soft Power: The Means to Success in World Politics*, New York: Public Affairs.

O'Hagan, M. (2009). Evolution of user-generated translation: Fansubs, translation hacking and crowdsourcing. *The Journal of Internationalisation and Localisation*, **1**, 94–121.

(2011). Community translation: Translation as a social activity and its possible consequences in the advent of Web 2.0 and beyond. *Linguistica Antverpiensia New Series: Themes in Translation Studies*, **10**, 11–23.

(2016). Response by O'Hagan to "Translation and the materialities of communication". *Translation Studies*, **9**(3), 322–326.

O'Hagan, M., & Mangiron, C. (2013). *Game Localization*, Amsterdam & Philadelphia: John Benjamins.

Och, F. (2012). Breaking down the language barrier: Six years in. *Google Official Blog*. Retrieved from http://googleblog.blogspot.it/2012/04/breaking-down-language-barriersix-years.html.

Olausson, U. (2011). Explaining global media: A discourse approach. In P. Pachura, ed., *The Systemic Dimension of Globalization*, Rijeka, Croatia: Intech Open Access Publisher. pp. 135–148.

(2014). The diversified nature of "domesticated" news discourse. *Journalism Studies*, **15**(6), 711–725.

Ondelli, S., & Nadalutti, P. (2018). Distanza intertestuale e lingua fonte: Analisi di un corpus giornalistico. In G. Palumbo, ed., *Testi, corpora, confronti interlinguistici: Approcci qualitativi e quantitativi*, Trieste: EUT, pp. 43–64.

Ondelli, S., & Viale, M. (2010). L'assetto dell'italiano delle traduzioni in un corpus giornalistico: Aspetti qualitativi e quantitativi. *Rivista internazionale di tecnica della traduzione [International Journal of Translation]*, **12**, 1–62.

Orengo, A. (2005). Localising news: Translation and the "global-national" dichotomy. *Language and Intercultural Communication*, **5**(2), 168–187.

Oxford English Dictionary. (n.d.). "newspaper, n.". Retrieved from www.oed.com/view/Entry/126631?rskey=WrKXUm&result=1&isAdvanced=false.

Pagano, A. S. (2000). Sources for translation theory: Fiction in Latin America. *ATA Chronicle*, **29**(3), 38–44.

Palmer, J. (2007). Interpreters and translators on the front line: Interpreting and translation for Western media in Iraq. In M. Salama-Carr, ed., *Translating and Interpreting Conflict*, Amsterdam & New York: Rodopi, p. 302.

(2009). News gathering and dissemination. In M. Baker & G. Saldanha, eds., *Routledge Encyclopedia of Translation Studies*, 2nd ed., London & New York: Routledge, pp. 186–189.

Palmer, J., & Fontan, V. (2007). "Our ears and our eyes": Journalists and fixers in Iraq. *Journalism*, **8**(1), 5–24.

Palmer, L. (2019). *The Fixers: Local News Workers' Perspectives on International Reporting*, Oxford: Oxford University Press.

Pan, L. (2014a). Investigating institutional practice in news translation: An empirical study of a Chinese agency translating discourse on China. *Perspectives: Studies in Translatology*, **22**(4), 547–565.

(2014b). Mediation in news translation: A critical analytical framework. In D. Abend-David, ed., *Media and Translation: An Interdisciplinary Approach*, New York, London, New Delhi & Sydney: Bloomsbury, pp. 247–266.

(2015). Ideological positioning in news translation: A case study of evaluative resources in reports on China. *Target*, **27**(2), 215–237.

(2017a). Translation and the intersection of texts, contexts and politics: Historical and socio-cultural perspectives. In M. Albakry, ed., *Translation and the Intersection of Texts, Contexts and Politics: Historical and Socio-Cultural Perspectives*, Basingbroke & New York: Palgrave Macmillan, pp. 201–222.

Pan, Y. (2017b). Raising trainee translators' critical language awareness in news translation. *Asia Pacific Translation and Intercultural Studies*, **4**(2), 160–190.

Pariser, E. (2011). *The Filter Bubble: What the Internet Is Hiding from You*, New York: The Penguin Press.

Park, M. J. (2016). Semiotic analysis of photojournalism captions: A comparison of Korean–English and Korean–Japanese translations. *Perspectives: Studies in Translatology*, **24**(3), 498–518.

Pasquandrea, S. (2011). Managing multiple actions through multimodality: Doctors' involvement in interpreter-mediated interactions. *Language in Society*, **40**(4), 455–481.

Paulussen, S., & Harder, R. A. (2014). Social media references in newspapers: Facebook, Twitter and YouTube as sources in newspaper journalism. *Journalism Practice*, **8**(5), 542–551.

Pedersen, D. (2014). Exploring the concept of transcreation-transcreation as "more than translation"? *Cultus: The Intercultural Journal of Mediation and Communication*, **7**, 57–71.

Peräkylä, A. (2008). Analysing talk and text. In N. K. Denzin & Y. S. Lincoln, eds., *The SAGE Handbook of Qualitative Research*, Thousand Oaks, CA: Sage, pp. 869–886.

Pérez-González, L. (2010). "Ad-hocracies" of translation: Activism in the blogosphere; A genealogical study. In M. Baker, M. Olohan, & C. P. María, eds., *Text and Context: Essays on Translation and Interpreting in Honour of Ian Mason*, Manchester: St Jerome, pp. 259–287.

(2012a). Amateur subtitling as immaterial labour in digital media culture: An emerging paradigm of civic engagement. *Convergence: The International Journal of Research into New Media Technologies*, **19**(2), 157–175.

(2012b). Co-creational subtitling in the digital media: Transformative and authorial practices. *International Journal of Cultural Studies*, **16**(1), 3–21.

(2012c). Translation, interpreting and the genealogy of conflict. *Journal of Language and Politics*, **11**(2), 169–184.

(2014a). *Audiovisual Translation: Theories, Methods and Issues*, London: Routledge.

(2014b). Translation and new(s) media: Participatory subtitling practices in networked mediascapes. In J. House, ed., *Translation: A Multidisciplinary Approach*, Basingbroke: Palgrave Macmillan.

Perrin, D. (2013). *The Linguistics of Newswriting*, Amsterdam & Philadelphia: John Benjamins.

Perrin, D., & Ehrensberger-Dow, M. (2018). Translation in journalism: Local practices in multilingual newsflows. In P. Chew Ghim Lian, C. Chua, K. Taylor-Leech, & C. Williams, eds., *Un(intended) Language Planning in a Globalising World: Multiple Levels of Players at Work*, Warsaw & Berlin: De Gruyter, pp. 163–182.

Perrin, D., Ehrensberger-Dow, M., & Zampa, M. (2017). Translation in the newsroom: Losing voices in multilingual newsflows. *Journal of Applied Journalism & Media Studies*, **6**(3), 463–483.

Pettegree, A. (2014). *The Invention of the News: How the World Came to Know about Itself*, New Haven, CT & London: Yale University Press.

Pettersson, B. (1999). The postcolonial turn in literary translation studies: Theoretical frameworks reviewed. *Æ. Canadian Aesthetics Journal/Revue Canadienne d'esthétique*, **4**. Retrieved from www.uqtr.ca/AE/vol_4/petter.htm.

Ping, Y. (2019). News translation in the representations of Hong Kong: A critical narrative analysis of the Legislative Council oath-taking controversy. *Asia Pacific Translation and Intercultural Studies*, **5**(3), 231–249.

Pöchhacker, F. (2006). "Going social?" On pathways and paradigms in interpreting studies. In A. Pym, M. Schlesinger, & Z. Jettmarová, eds., *Sociocultural Aspects of Translating and Interpreting*, Amsterdam & Philadelphia: John Benjamins, pp. 215–232.

(2010). Media interpreting. In Y. Gambier & L. van Doorslaer, eds., *Handbook of Translation Studies*, vol. 4, Amsterdam & Philadelphia: John Benjamins, pp. 224–226.

(2013). The position of interpreting studies. In C. Millan & F. Bartina, eds., *The Routledge Handbook of Translation Studies*, Abingdon & New York: Routledge, pp. 60–72.

(ed.). (2015). *Routledge Encyclopedia of Interpreting Studies*, Abingdon & New York: Routledge.

Poldsaar, R. (2010). Foucault framing Foucault: The role of paratexts in the English translation of the order of things. *Neohelicon*, **37**(1), 263–273.

Polezzi, L. (2012). Translation and migration. *Translation Studies*, **5**(3), 345–356.

Pomerantz, A. (1984). Agreeing and disagreeing with assessments: Some features of preferred/dispreferred turn shapes. In J. M. Atkinson & J. Heritage, eds., *Structures of Social Action: Studies in Conversation Analysis*, Cambridge: Cambridge University Press, pp. 57–101.

Popel, M., Tomkova, M., Tomek, J., et al. (2020). Transforming machine translation: A deep learning system reaches news translation quality comparable to human professionals. *Nature Communications*, **11**(1), 1–15.

Pormouzeh, A. (2014). Translation as renarration: Critical analysis of Iran's cultural and political news in English western media and press from 2000 to 2012. *Mediterranean Journal of Social Sciences*, **5**(9), 608–619.

Price, M. E., Haas, S., & Margolin, D. (2008). New technologies and international broadcasting: Reflections on adaptations and transformations. *The Annals of the American Academy of Political and Social Science*, **616**, 150–172.

Pym, A. (2000). *Negotiating the Frontier: Translators and Intercultures in Hispanic History*, Manchester: St Jerome.

(2001). Introduction. *The Translator*, **7**(2), 129–138.

(2004). *The Moving Text: Localization, Translation, and Distribution*, Amsterdam & Philadelphia: John Benjamins.

(2014). *Exploring Translation Theories*, 2nd ed., London & New York: Routledge.

(2015). Translating as risk management. *Journal of Pragmatics*, **85**, 67–80.

Pym, A., & Matsushita, K. (2018). Risk mitigation in translator decisions. *Across Languages and Cultures*, **19**(1), 1–18.

Qin, B., & Zhang, M. (2018). Reframing translated news for target readers: A narrative account of news translation in Snowden's discourses. *Perspectives: Studies in Translation Theory and Practice*, **26**(2), 261–276.

Rapley, M., McCarthy, D., & McHoul, A. (2003). Mentality or morality? Membership categorization, multiple meanings and mass murder. *British Journal of Social Psychology*, **42**, 427–444.

Rawnsley, G. D. (2015). To know us is to love us: Public diplomacy and international broadcasting in contemporary Russia and China. *Politics*, **35**(3–4), 273–286.

Reiss, K., & Vermeer, H. J. (1984). *Grundlegung einer allgemeinen Translationstheorie*, Tübingen: Niemeyer.

Rener, F. M. (1989). *Interpretatio: Language and Translation from Cicero to Tytler*, Amsterdam & New York: Rodopi.

Renzi, L. (1997). Gianfranco Folena: Un italiano in Europa. In H. Stammerjohann & H. Radatz, eds., *Italiano: Lingua di cultura europea: atti del Simposio intemazionale in memoria di Gianfranco Folena. Weimar, 11–13 aprile 1996*, Tübingen: Narr.

Reuters. (2008). *Handbook of Journalism*, Reuters. Retrieved from http://handbook .reuters.com/index.php?title=Main_Page.

Ries, P. (2001). The politics of information in seventeenth-century Scandinavia. In B. Dooley & S. Baron, eds., *The Politics of Information in Early Modern Europe*, New York & London: Routledge, pp. 237–272.

Robinson, D. (1997). *Western Translation Theory from Herodotus to Nietzsche*, Manchester: St Jerome.

(2016a). *Semiotranslating Pierce*, Tartu: Tartu University Press.

(2016b). Towards an intercivilizational turn: Naoki Sakai's cofigurative regimes of translation and the problem of Eurocentrism. *Translation Studies*, **9**(1), 51–66.

Roca-Cuberes, C., & Ventura, R. (2016). When the "other" runs in front of the bull: A membership categorization analysis of a television news story. *Text and Talk*, **36** (5), 565–588.

Romagnuolo, A. (2009). Political discourse in translation: A corpus-based perspective on presidential inaugurals. *Translation and Interpreting Studies*, **4**(1), 1–30.

Rothman, N. E. (2015). Dragomans. In *Routledge Encyclopedia of Interpreting Studies*, London & New York: Routledge, pp. 119–124.

Roumanos, R., & Noblet, A. (2019). Framing terrorism in the U.S., French, and Arabic editions of HuffPost. In L. Davier & K. Conway, eds., *Journalism and Translation in the Era of Convergence*, Amsterdam & Philadelphia: John Benjamins, pp. 107–132.

Roy, C. B. (2000). *Interpreting as a Discourse Process*, Oxford: Oxford University Press.

Sabbadini, R. (1916). Maccheroni e tradurre (per la Crusca). *Rendiconti: Reale Istituto Lombardo Di Scienze e Lettere, Serie II*, **49**, 221–224.

Sacks, H. (1963). Sociological description. *Berkeley Journal of Sociology*, **8**, 1–16.

(1972a). An initial investigation of the usability of conversational data for doing sociology. In D. Sudnow, ed., *Studies in Social Interaction*, New York: Free Press, pp. 30–74.

(1972b). On the analyzability of stories by children. In J. H. Gumperz & D. Hymes, eds., *Directions in Sociolinguistics*, New York: Holt, Rinehart and Winston, pp. 325–345.

(1974). An analysis in the course of a joke's telling in conversation. In R. Bauman & J. F. Sherzer, eds., *Explorations in the Ethnography of Speaking*, Cambridge: Cambridge University Press, pp. 337–353.

(1992a). *Lectures on Conversation, vol. I.* (G. Jefferson, ed.), Oxford: Blackwell.

(1992b). *Lectures on Conversation, vol. II.* (G. Jefferson, ed.), Oxford: Blackwell.

Sacks, H., Schegloff, E. A., & Jefferson, G. (1974). A simplest systematics for the organization of turn taking for conversation. *Language*, **50**(4), 696–735.

Sakai, N. (1997). *Translation and Subjectivity: On "Japan" and Cultural Nationalism*, Minneapolis: University of Minnesota Press.

(2009). How do we count a language? Translation and discontinuity. *Translation Studies*, **2**(1), 71–88.

Sanatifar, M. S. (2015). Lost in political translation: (Mis)translation of an intertextual reference and its political consequences: The case of Iran. *Jostrans: The Journal of Specialised Translation*, **24**, 1–9.

Sanatifar, M. S., & Jalalian Daghigh, A. (2018). Translation as re-narration: A case of Iran's nuclear program as circulated in the Western and Iranian media. *Asia Pacific Translation and Intercultural Studies*, **5**(1), 3–20.

Sandrelli, A. (2015). "And maybe you can translate also what I say": Interpreters in football press conferences. *The Interpreters' Newsletter*, **20**, 87–105.

(2017). Simultaneous dialogue interpreting: Coordinating interaction in interpreter-mediated football press conferences. *Journal of Pragmatics*, **107**, 178–194.

Sapiro, G. (2012). Editorial Policy and Translation. In Y. Gambier & L. van Doorslaer, eds., *Handbook of Translation Studies, vol. 3,* Amsterdam & Philadelphia: John Benjamins, pp. 32–38.

Scammell, C. (2018). *Translation Strategies in Global News: What Sarkozy Said in the Suburbs*, Cham: Palgrave Macmillan.

Schäffner, C. (2005). Bringing a German voice to English-speaking readers: *Spiegel International. Language and Intercultural Communication*, **5**(2), 154–167.

(2008). "The Prime Minister said…": Voices in translated political texts. *Synaps*, **22**, 3–25.

(2010). Political communication: Mediated by translation. In U. Okulska & P. Cap, eds., *Perspectives in Politics and Discourse*, Amsterdam & Philadelphia: John Benjamins, pp. 255–278.

(2012a). Rethinking transediting. *Meta: Journal des traducteurs*, **57**, 866–833.

(2012b). Unknown agents in translated political discourse. *Target*, **24**(1), 103–125.

(2015). Speaker positioning in interpreter-mediated press conferences. *Target*, **27**(3), 422–439.

(2018). Language, interpreting, and translation in the news media. In K. Malmkjær, ed., *The Routledge Handbook of Translation Studies and Linguistics*, Abingdon and New York: Routledge, pp. 327–341.

Schäffner, C., & Bassnett, S. (2010). Introduction: Politics, media and translation; Exploring synergies. In C. Schäffner & S. Bassnett, eds., *Political Discourse, Media and Translation*, Newcastle upon Tyne: Cambridge Scholars Publishing, pp. 1–29.

Schäffner, C., Tcaciuc, L. S., & Tesseur, W. (2014). Translation practices in political institutions: A comparison of national, supranational, and non-governmental organisations. *Perspectives: Studies in Translatology*, **22**(4), 493–510.

Schäler, R. (2009). Localization. In M. Baker & G. Saldanha, eds., *Routledge Encyclopedia of Translation Studies, 2nd ed.,* London & New York: Routledge, pp. 157–161.

Schegloff, E. A. (1972). Notes on a conversational practice: Formulating place. In D. Sudnow, ed., *Studies in Social Interaction*, New York: Free Press, pp. 75–119.

(1979). The relevance of repair to syntax-for-conversation. In T. Givón, ed., *Syntax and Semantics 12: Discourse and Syntax*, New York: Academic Press, pp. 261–288.

(1980). Preliminaries to preliminaries: "Can I ask you a question?" *Sociological Enquiry*, **50**(3–4), 104–152.

(1984). On questions and ambiguities in conversation. In J. M. Atkinson & J. Heritage, eds., *Structures of Social Action: Studies in Conversation Analysis*, Cambridge: Cambridge University Press, pp. 28–51.

(1988). From interview to confrontation: Observations of the Bush/Rather encounter. *Research on Language & Social Interaction*, **22**(1–4), 215–240.

Schegloff, E. a. (2007a). A tutorial on membership categorization. *Journal of Pragmatics*, **39**(3), 462–482.

(2007b). Categories in action: Person-reference and membership categorization. *Discourse Studies*, **9**(4), 433–461.

Schegloff, E. A., & Sacks, H. (1973). Opening up closings. *Semiotica*, **8**(4), 289–327.

Schegloff, E. A., Jefferson, G., & Sacks, H. (1977). The preference for self-correction in the organization of repair in conversation. *Language*, **53**(2), 361–382.

Schenkein, J. (ed.). (1978). *Studies in the Organization of Conversational Interaction*, New York: Academic Press.

(1979). The radio raiders story. In G. Psathas, ed., *Everyday Language: Studies in Ethnomethodology*, New York: Irvington, pp. 187–202.

Schleiermacher, F. (1997). On the different methods of translating. In D. Robinson, ed., *Western Translation Theory from Herodotus to Nietzsche*, Manchester: St Jerome, pp. 225–238.

Schrijver, I., Van Vaerenbergh, L., Leijten, M., & Van Waes, L. (2016). The impact of writing training on transediting in translation, analyzed from a product and process perspective. *Perspectives: Studies in Translatology*, **24**(2), 218–234.

Shahi, M., & Talebinejad, M. R. (2017). The ideological role of selective translation in reconfiguration of news frames. *FORUM: Revue Internationale d'interprétation et de Traduction [International Journal of Interpretation and Translation,]* **15**(1), 85–105.

Sharifian, F. (2011). *Cultural Conceptualisations and Language*, Amsterdam & Philadelphia: John Benjamins.

Sharrock, W. (1989). Ethnomethodology. *The British Journal of Sociology*, **40**(4), 657–677.

Shi, X. (2014). English-Chinese news headlines translation from a Skopostheorie perspective. *Theory and Practice in Language Studies*, **4**(9), 1881–1885.

Shoemaker, P. J., & Riccio, J. R. (2015). Gatekeeping. In G. Mazzoleni, ed., *The International Encyclopedia of Political Communication*, Hoboken, NJ: John Wiley & Sons, pp. 322–334.

Siddig Abdalla, M. (2018). *The Influence of Translation on the Arabic Language: English Idioms in Arabic Satellite TV Stations*, Newcastle upon Tyne: Cambridge Scholars Publishing.

Sidiropoulou, M. (1995a). Causal Shifts in News Reporting: English vs. Greek Press. *Perspectives: Studies in Translatology*, **3**(1), 83–98.

(1995b). Headlining in Translation: English vs. Greek Press. *Target*, **7**(2), 285–304.

(1998). Quantities in Translation: English vs. Greek Press. *Target*, **10**(2), 319–333.

Silverman, D. (1998). *Harvey Sacks: Social Science and Conversation Analysis*, Oxford: Oxford University Press.

(2012). Beyond armed camps: A response to Stokoe. *Discourse Studies*, **14**(3), 329–336.

Simeček, Z. (1972). The First Brussels, Antwerp and Amsterdam Newspapers: Additional Information. *Revue Belge de Philologie et d'histoire*, **50**(4), 1098–1115.

Simon, S. (2007). "A single brushstroke": Writing through translation; Anne Carson. In P. St-Pierre & P. C. Kar, eds., *Translation: Reflections, Refractions, Transformations*, Amsterdam & Philadelphia: John Benjamins, pp. 107–116.

Sinclair, J. M. (1987). *Looking Up*, London & Glasgow: Collins.

Skorokhod, O. (2016). Analysis of representation of the war in Afghanistan as a US War in Russian and Western news media: Systemic-functional linguistics model. In F. M. Federici, ed., *Mediating Emergencies and Conflicts: Frontline Translating and Interpreting*, London: Palgrave Macmillan, pp. 159–178.

Snell-Hornby, M. (2006). *The Turns of Translation Studies*, Amsterdam & Philadelphia: John Benjamins.

(2009). What's in a turn? On fits, starts and writhings in recent translation studies. *Translation Studies*, **2**(1), 41–51.

(2010). The turns of translation studies. In Y. Gambier & L. van Doorslaer, eds., *Handbook of Translation Studies*, vol. 1, Amsterdam & Philadelphia: John Benjamins, pp. 366–370.

(ed.). (1986). *Übersetzungswissenschaft: Eine Neuorientierung*, Tübingen: Francke.

Somers, M. R. (1994). The narrative constitution of identity: A relational and network approach. *Theory and Society*, **23**(5), 605–649.

Song, Y. (2017). Impact of power and ideology on news translation in Korea: A quantitative analysis of foreign news gatekeeping. *Perspectives: Studies in Translation Theory and Practice*, **25**(4), 658–672.

Sonzogni, M. (2011). *Re-covered Rose: A Case Study in Book Cover Design as Intersemiotic Translation*, Amsterdam & Philadelphia: John Benjamins.

Sparks, C., Wang, H., Huang, Y., Zhao, Y., Lü, N., & Wang, D. (2016). The impact of digital media on newspapers: Comparing responses in China and the United States. *Global Media and China*, **1**(3), 186–207.

Sperber, D., & Wilson, D. (1995). *Relevance: Communication and Cognition*, 2nd ed., Oxford: Blackwell.

Spiessens, A. (2019). Deep memory during the Crimean crisis. *Target*, **31**(3), 398–419.

Spiessens, A., & van Poucke, P. (2016). Translating news discourse on the Crimean crisis: Patterns of reframing on the Russian website InoSMI. *The Translator*, **22** (3), 319–339.

St. André, J. (2010). Translation and metaphor: Setting the terms. In J. St. André, ed., *Thinking through Translation with Metaphors*, Manchester: St Jerome, pp. 1–16.

Stanyer, J. (2009). Web 2.0 and the transformation of news and journalism. In A. Chadwick & P. N. Howard, eds., *The Routledge Handbook of Internet Politics*, New York & London: Routledge, pp. 501–513.

Stetson, J. (1999). Victim, offender and witness in the emplotment of news stories. In P. L. Jalbert, ed., *Media Studies: Ethnomethodological Approaches*, Lanham, MD & Oxford: International Institute for Ethnomethodology and Conversation Analysis & University Press of America, pp. 77–110.

Stetting, K. (1989). Transediting: A new term for coping with the grey area between editing and translating. In G. Caie, K. Haastrup, A. L. Jakobsen, et al., eds.,

Proceedings from the Fourth Nordic Conference for English Studies, Copenhagen: University of Copenhagen, Department of English, pp. 371–382.

Stewart, D. (2008). Vocational translation training into a foreign language. *inTRAlinea*, **10**. Retrieved from www.intralinea.org/archive/article/1646.

(2010). *Semantic Prosody: A Critical Evaluation*, London & New York: Routledge.

Stokoe, E. H. (2012). Categorial systematics. *Discourse Studies*, **14**(3), 345–354.

Straniero Sergio, F. (1999). The interpreter on the (talk) show. *The Translator*, **5**(2), 303–326.

(2003). Norms and quality in media interpreting: The case of formula one press-conferences. *The Interpreters' Newsletter*, **12**, 135–174.

(2007). *Talkshow Interpreting: La mediazione linguistica nella conversazione spettacolo*, Trieste: EUT.

(2011). Language mediation in news making: From simultaneous interpreting to other (hybrid) transfer modes. *The Interpreters' Newsletter*, **16**, 175–197.

(2012a). Repetition in dialogue interpreting. In C. J. Kellett Bidoli, ed., *Interpreting across Genres: Multiple Research Perspectives*, Trieste: EUT, pp. 27–53.

(2012b). "You are not too funny": Challenging the role of the interpreter on Italian talkshows. In C. Baraldi & L. Gavioli, eds., *Coordinating Participation in Dialogue Interpreting*, Amsterdam & Philadelphia: John Benjamins, pp. 71–98.

(2013). *Media Interpreting*. In C. A. Chapelle, ed., *The Encyclopedia of Applied linguistics*, Blackwell Publishing.

Straniero Sergio, F., & Falbo, C. (2012). Studying interpreting through corpora: An introduction. In F. Straniero Sergio & C. Falbo, eds., *Breaking Ground in Corpus-Based Interpreting Studies,* Bern: Peter Lang, pp. 9–52.

Stubbs, M. (1996). *Text and Corpus Analysis: Computer-Assisted Studies of Language and Culture*, Oxford: Blackwell.

Talebinejad, M. R., & Shahi, M. (2017). The labyrinth of ethics in journalistic translated discourse. *Babel*, **63**(1), 89–108.

Talens, M. (2010). The languages of Tlaxcala: A short history of a long walk. In J. Boéri & C. Maier, eds., *Compromiso social y traducción/Interpretación – Translation/Interpreting and Social Activism*, Granada, Spain: ECOS, pp. 19–24.

Taviano, S. (2010). *Translating English as a Lingua Franca*, Milano: Mondadori.

(2013). English as a lingua franca and translation: Implications for translator and interpreter education. *Interpreter and Translator Trainer*, **7**(2), 155–167.

Tesseur, W. (2014). Institutional multilingualism in NGOs: Amnesty International's strategic understanding of multilingualism. *Meta: Journal des traducteurs*, **61**(3), 1–18.

(2017). The translation challenges of INGOs: Professional and non-professional translation at Amnesty International. *Translation Spaces*, **6**(2), 209–229.

Thiranagama, S. (2011). Ethnic entanglements: The BBC Tamil and Sinhala services amidst the civil war in Sri Lanka. *Journalism: Theory, Practice & Criticism*, **12**(2), 153–169.

Thornborrow, J., & Fitzgerald, R. (2004). Storying the news through category, action, and reason. *The Communication Review*, **7**(4), 345–352.

(2013). "Grab a pen and paper": Interaction v. interactivity in a political radio phone-in. *Journal of Language and Politics*, **12**(1), 1–28.

Tian, D., & Chao, C. C. (2012). Testing news trustworthiness in an online public sphere: A case study of *The Economist*'s news report covering the riots in Xinjiang, China. *Chinese Journal of Communication*, **5**(4), 455–474.

Torop, P. (2002). Translation as translating as culture. *Sign Systems Studies*, **30**(2), 593–605.

Toury, G. (1986). Translation. In T. Sebeok, ed., *Encyclopedic Dictionary of Semiotics*, vol. 2, Berlin: Mouton de Gruyter, pp. 1107–1124.

(1995). *Descriptive Translation Studies and Beyond*, Amsterdam & Philadelphia: John Benjamins.

(2012). *Descriptive Translation Studies and Beyond*, Revised Edition, Amsterdam & Philadelphia: John Benjamins.

Traverso, V. (2012). Ad-hoc interpreting in multilingual work meetings: Who translates for whom? In C. Baraldi & L. Gavioli, eds., *Coordinating Participation in Dialogue Interpreting*, Amsterdam & Philadelphia: John Benjamins, pp. 149–176.

Trivedi, H., & Bassnett, S. (eds.). (1999). *Post-colonial Translation. Theory and Practice*, London & New York: Routledge.

Troqe, R., & Marchan, F. (2017). News translation: Text analysis, fieldwork, survey. In S. Hansen-Schirra, O. Czulo, & S. Hofmann, eds., *Empirical Modelling of Translation and Interpreting*, Berlin: Language Science Press, pp. 277–310.

Tsai, C. (2005). Inside the television newsroom: An insider's view of international news translation in Taiwan. *Language and Intercultural Communication*, **5**(2), 145–153.

(2006). Translation through interpreting: A television newsroom model. In K. Conway & S. Bassnett, eds., *Proceedings of the Conference Held at the University of Warwick 23 June 2006*, Warwick: The Centre for Translation and Comparative Cultural Studies, University of Warwick, pp. 59–71.

(2010). News translator as reporter. In C. Schäffner & S. Bassnett, eds., *Political Discourse, Media and Translation*, Newcastle upon Tyne: Cambridge Scholars Publishing, pp. 178–197.

(2012). Television news translation in the era of market-driven journalism. *Meta: Journal des traducteurs*, **57**(4), 1060–1080.

(2015). Reframing humor in TV news translation. *Perspectives: Studies in Translatology*, **23**(4), 615–633.

Tymoczko, M. (2007). *Enlarging Translation, Empowering Translators*, Manchester: St Jerome.

Tymoczko, M., & Gentzler, E. (2002). Introduction. In M. Tymoczko & E. Gentzler, eds., *Translation and Power*, Amherst & Boston: University of Massachusetts Press, pp. xi–xxvii.

Tyulenev, S. (2014). *Translation and Society: An Introduction*, Abingdon & New York: Routledge.

(2018). *Translation in the Public Sphere*, Cham: Palgrave Macmillan.

Ustad Figenschou, T. (2012). The South is talking back: With a white face and a British accent; Editorial dilemmas in Al Jazeera English. *Journalism*, **13**(3), 354–370.

Valdeón, R. A. (2005a). The CNNenEspañol news. *Perspectives: Studies in Translatology*, **13**(4), 255–267.

(2005b). The "translated" Spanish service of the BBC. *Across Languages and Cultures*, **6**(2), 195–220.

(2007a). Political and sexist bias in news translation: Two case studies. *TRANS. Revista de Traductologia*, **11**, 231–243.

(2007b). Translating news from the inner circle: Imposing regularity across languages. *Quaderns. Revista de Traduccion*, **14**, 155–167.

(2008). Anomalous news translation: Selective appropriation of themes and texts in the Internet. *Babel*, **54**(4), 299–326.

(2009). Discursive constructions of terrorism in Spain: Anglophone and Spanish media representations of Eta. *International Journal of Applied Linguistics*, **19**(1), 66–83.

(2011). Embedding anglocentric perceptions of the world: The Falklands-Malvinas binomial in the news. *Meta: Journal des traducteurs*, **56**(1), 63–80.

(2012a). From the Dutch corantos to convergence journalism: The role of translation in news production. *Meta: Journal des traducteurs*, **57**(4), 850–865.

(2012b). Information, communication, translation. In Y. Gambier & L. van Doorslaer, eds., *Handbook of Translation Studies, vol. 3*, Amsterdam & Philadelphia: John Benjamins, pp. 66–72.

(2014). From adaptation to appropriation: Framing the world through news translation. *Linguaculture*, **1**, 51–62.

(2015a). (Un)stable sources, translation and news production. *Target*, **27**(3), 440–453.

(2015b). Fifteen years of journalistic translation research and more. *Perspectives: Studies in Translatology*, **23**(4), 634–662.

(2016a). The construction of national images through news translation: Self-framing in *El País English Edition*. In L. van Doorslaer, P. Flynn, & J. Leerssen, eds., *Interconnecting Translation Studies and Imagology*, Amsterdam & Philadelphia: John Benjamins, pp. 219–238.

(2016b). Translating stable sources in times of economic recession. *Babel*, **62**(1), 1–20.

(2018a). On the use of the term "translation" in journalism studies. *Journalism: Theory, Practice & Criticism*, **19**(2), 252–269.

(2018b). Translation and culture in mainstream media and journalism. In S.-A. Harding & O. Carbonell i Cortés, eds., *The Routledge Handbook of Translation and Culture*, New York & London: Routledge, pp. 558–573.

(2019). Ad hoc corpora and journalistic translation research: BBC News and BBC Mundo's coverage of Margaret Thatcher's death and funeral. *Across Languages and Cultures*, **20**(1), 79–95.

(2020). Journalistic translation research goes global: Theoretical and methodological considerations five years on. *Perspectives: Studies in Translation Theory and Practice*, **28**(3), 325–338.

(ed.). (2010a). *Translating Information*, Oviedo: Ediciones de la Universidad de Oviedo.

(ed.). (2010b). Translating information in the post-industrial society. *Across Languages and Cultures*, **11**(2, Special Issue).

(ed.). (2012c). Journalisme et traduction [Journalism and Translation]. *Meta: Journal des traducteurs*, **57**(4, Special Issue).

van Dijk, T. A. (1988). *News as Discourse*, Hove & London: Lawrence Erlbaum Associates.

van Doorslaer, L. (2009). How language and (non-)translation impact on media newsrooms: The case of newspapers in Belgium. *Perspectives: Studies in Translatology*, **17**(2), 83–92.

(2010a). Journalism and translation. In Y. Gambier & L. van Doorslaer, eds., *Handbook of Translation Studies*, vol. 1, Amsterdam & Philadelphia: John Benjamins, pp. 180–184.

(2010b). The Belgian conflict frame: The role of media and translation in Belgian political ideologies. In C. Schäffner & S. Bassnett, eds., *Political Discourse, Media and Translation*, Newcastle upon Tyne: Cambridge Scholars Publishing, pp. 198–210.

(2010c). The double extension of translation in the journalistic field. *Across Languages and Cultures*, **11**(2), 175–188.

(2012). Translating, narrating and constructing images in journalism with a test case on representation in Flemish TV news. *Meta: Journal des traducteurs*, **57**(4), 1046–1059.

(2013). Impact of translation theory. In Y. Gambier & L. van Doorslaer, eds., *Handbook of Translation Studies*, vol. 4, Amsterdam & Philadelphia: John Benjamins, pp. 77–84.

(2021). Imagology. In F. Zanettin & C. Rundle, eds., *The Routledge Handbook of Translation and Methodology*, New York & London: Routledge.

van Leeuwen, T. (2006). Translation, adaptation, globalization: *The Vietnam News*. *Journalism*, **7**(2), 217–237.

Van Leuven, S., & Berglez, P. (2016). Global journalism between dream and reality. *Journalism Studies*, **17**(6), 667–683.

Van Poucke, P., & Belikova, A. (2016). Foreignization in news translation: Metaphors in Russian translation on the news translation website InoSMI. *Meta: Journal des traducteurs*, **61**(2), 346–368.

van Rooyen, M. (2013). Structure and agency in news translation: An application of Anthony Giddens' structuration theory. *Southern African Linguistics and Applied Language Studies*, **31**(4), 495–506.

(2018). Investigating translation flows: Community radio news in South Africa. *Across Languages and Cultures*, **19**(2), 259–278.

(2019). Tracing convergence in the translation of community radio news. In L. Davier & K. Conway, eds., *Journalism and Translation in the Era of Convergence*, Amsterdam & Philadelphia: John Benjamins, pp. 155–176.

van Rooyen, M., & Naudé, J. A. (2009). A model for the translation of news agency texts (Sapa) for radio (OFM) news. *Communicatio*, **35**(2), 251–275.

Vargas-Urpi, M. (2015). Dialogue interpreting in multi-party encounters: Two examples from educational settings. *The Interpreters' Newsletter*, **20**, 107–121.

Venuti, L. (1995). *The Translator's Invisibility*, London & New York: Routledge.

(2000). 1980s. In L. Venuti, ed., *The Translation Studies Reader*, London & New York: Routledge, pp. 213–220.

Vermeer, H. J. (1978). Ein Rahmen für eine allgemeine Translationstheorie. *Lebende Sprachen*, **23**, 99–102.

(2000). Skopos and commission in translational action. In L. Venuti, ed., *The Translation Studies Reader*, London & New York: Routledge, pp. 221–232.

Viaggio, S. (2001). Simultaneous interpreting for television and other media: Translation doubly constrained. In Y. Gambier & H. Gottlieb, eds., *(Multi)media Translation*, Amsterdam & Philadelphia: John Benjamins, pp. 23–34.

Vieira, E. R. P. (1995). (In)visibilidades na tradução: Troca de olhares teóricos e ficcionais. *Com Textos*, **6**, 50–68.

Viennot, B. (2017). De la difficulté de traduire Donald Trump. *Contemporary French and Francophone Studies*, **21**(5), 598–605.

(2019). *La lingua di Trump*, Torino: Einaudi.

Vinay, J.-P., & Darbelnet, J. (1995). *Comparative Stylistics of French and English*, Amsterdam & Philadelphia: John Benjamins.

Vobič, I. (2013). From one-man band to integrated newsroom. *Journalism Studies*, **16** (2), 175–190.

vom Lehn, D. (2014). *Harold Garfinkel. The Creation and Development of Ethnomethodology*, London & New York: Routledge.

Vuorinen, E. (1997). News translation as gatekeeping. In M. Snell-Hornby, Z. Jettmarová, & K. Kaindl, eds., *Translation as Intercultural Communication: Selected Papers from the EST Congress, Prague 1995*, Amsterdam & Philadelphia: John Benjamins, pp. 161–171.

Wadensjö, C. (1998). *Interpreting as Interaction*, London: Longman.

(2001). Interpreting in crisis: The interpreter's position in therapeutic encounters. In I. Mason, ed., *Triadic Exchanges: Studies in Dialogue Interpreting*, Manchester: St Jerome, pp. 71–85.

(2008a). In and off the show: Co-constructing "invisibility" in an interpreter-mediated talk-show interview. *Meta: Journal des traducteurs*, **53**(1), 184–203.

(2008b). The shaping of Gorbachev: On framing in an interpreter-mediated talk-show interview. *Text and Talk*, **28**(1), 119–146.

(2010). Expanded and minimal answers to yes/no questions in interpreter-mediated trials. In M. Baker, M. Calzada Pérez, & M. Olohan, eds., *Text and Context. Essays on Translation and Interpreting in Honour of Ian Mason*, Manchester: St Jerome, pp. 9–26.

Wang, B., & Feng, D. (2018). A corpus-based study of stance-taking as seen from critical points in interpreted political discourse. *Perspectives: Studies in Translation Theory and Practice*, **26**(2), 246–260.

Watson, R. (2009). *Analysing Practical and Professional Texts: A Naturalistic Approach*, Farnham & Burlington, VT: Ashgate.

Weaver, W. (1955). Translation. In W. N. Locke & D. Booth, eds., *Machine Translation of Languages: Fourteen Essays*, Cambridge, MA & New York: MIT and Wiley, pp. 15–23.

Weber, J. (2006). Strassburg, 1605: The origins of the newspaper in Europe. *German History*, **24**(3), 387–412.

Wehrmeyer, E. (2015). Comprehension of television news signed language interpreters: A South African perspective. *Interpreting*, **17**(2), 195–225.

Welbers, K., & Opgenhaffen, M. (2019). News through a social media filter: Different perspectives on immigration in news on website and social media formats. In L. Davier & K. Conway, eds., *Journalism and Translation in the Era of Convergence*, Amsterdam & Philadelphia: John Benjamins, pp. 85–105.

White, D. M. (1950). The "gate keeper": A case study in the selection of news. *Journalism Quarterly*, **27**(4), 383–390.

Wilke, J., & Rosenberger, B. (1994). Importing foreign news: A case study of the German service of the Associated Press. *Journalism Quarterly*, **71**(2), 421–432.

Winthrop-Young, G., & Wutz, M. (1999). Translators' introduction: Friedrich Kittler and media discourse analysis. In Kettler, F. A. *Gramophone, Film, Typewriter*, Stanford, CA: Stanford University Press, pp. xi–xxxiii.

Wodak, R. (2011). Critical linguistics and critical discourse analysis. In J. Zienkowski, J.-O. Östman, & J. Verschueren, eds., *Discursive Pragmatics*, Amsterdam & Philadelphia: John Benjamins, pp. 50–70.

Wolf, M. (2007). Introduction: The emergence of a sociology of translation. In M. Wolf & A. Fukari, eds., *Constructing a Sociology of Translation*, Amsterdam & Philadelphia: John Benjamins, pp. 1–36.

Woolf, D. (2001). News, history and the construction of the present in Early Modern England. In B. Dooley & S. A. Baron, eds., *The Politics of Information in Early Modern Europe*, New York & London: Routledge, pp. 80–118.

Wu, X. (2018). Framing, reframing and the transformation of stance in news translation: A case study of the translation of news on the China–Japan dispute. *Language and Intercultural Communication*, **18**(2), 257–274.

Xia, L. (2019). *A Discourse Analysis of News Translation in China*, Abingdon & New York: Routledge.

Xiao, X., Chen, X., & Palmer, J. L. (2015). Chinese deaf viewers' comprehension of sign language interpreting on television: An experimental study. *Interpreting*, **17**(1), 91–117.

Xin, X. (2018). Popularizing party journalism in China in the age of social media: The case of Xinhua News Agency. *Global Media and China*, **3**(1), 3–17.

Zanettin, F. (1998). Bilingual comparable corpora and the training of translators. *Meta: Journal des traducteurs*, **43**(4), 616–630.

(2001). *IperGrimus. Ipertesto traduttivo, inTRAlinea Monographs*. Retrieved from www.intralinea.org/monographs/zanettin.

(2008). The translation of comics as localization: On three Italian translations of La piste des Navajos. In F. Zanettin, ed., *Comics in Translation*, Manchester: St Jerome, pp. 200–219.

(2012). *Translation-Driven Corpora: Corpus Resources for Descriptive and Applied Translation Studies*, Manchester & Kinderhook, NY: St Jerome.

(2013). Corpus methods for descriptive translation studies. *Procedia: Social and Behavioral Sciences*, **95**, 20–32.

(2014). Visual adaptation in translated comics. *inTRAlinea*, **16**. Retrieved from www.intralinea.org/archive/article/2019.

(2016a). Giornalista o donna? Traduzione giornalistica e categorizzazione di appartenenza. In F. Gatta, ed., *Parlare insieme: Studi per Daniela Zorzi*, Bologna: Bononia University Press, pp. 363–382.

(2016b). "The deadliest error": Translation, international relations and the news media. *The Translator*, **22**(3), 303–18.

Zanettin, F., Saldanha, G., & Harding, S.-A. (2015). Sketching landscapes in translation studies: A bibliographic study. *Perspectives: Studies in Translatology*, **23**(2), 161–182.

Zhang, M. (2013). Stance and mediation in transediting news headlines as paratexts. *Perspectives: Studies in Translatology*, **21**(3), 396–411.

Zhang, M., & Munday, J. (2018). Innovation in discourse analytic approaches to translation studies. *Perspectives: Studies in Translation Theory and Practice*, **26**(2), 159–165.

Zhang, T. (2007). Protestant missionary publishing and the birth of Chinese elite journalism. *Journalism Studies*, **8**(6), 879–897.

Zhang, X. (2011). China's international broadcasting: A case study of CCTV International. In J. Wang, ed., *Soft Power in China. Public Diplomacy through Communication*, New York: Palgrave Macmillan, pp. 57–72.

Zheng, L., & Ren, W. (2018). Interpreting as an influencing factor on news reports: A study of interpreted Chinese political discourse recontextualized in English news. *Perspectives: Studies in Translation Theory and Practice*, **26**(5), 691–707.

Zoli, G. (2012, May 17). Fedeli alla linea. *Internazionale*. Retrieved from www.internazionale.it/opinione/giulia-zoli/2012/05/17/fedeli-alla-linea.

Zorzi, D. (2012). Mediating assessments in healthcare settings. In C. Baraldi & L. Gavioli, eds., *Coordinating Participation in Dialogue Interpreting*, Amsterdam & Philadelphia: John Benjamins, pp. 229–250.

Subject and Name Index

Lightning Source UK Ltd.
Milton Keynes UK
UKHW022015061121
393523UK00007B/87

9 781108 456401